The Red Hat Society™

The Red Hat Society™

Fun and Friendship After Fifty

Sue Ellen Cooper

Illustrations by Andrea Reekstin

WARNER BOOKS

NEW YORK   BOSTON

Grateful acknowledgment is made to reprint from the following:
"Warning" by Jenny Joseph. © Jenny Joseph, *Selected Poems* (Bloodaxe 1992).
"Red Hat Society" by Mike Harline. Used by permission.

Warner Books

Time Warner Book Group
1271 Avenue of the Americas, New York, NY 10020

Printed in the United States of America

ISBN 0-7394-4370-4

Book design and text composition by HRoberts Design
Cover photo by Wanelle Fitch

To all the wonderful women who have

answered the Red Hat Society's call

to come out and play.

Acknowledgment

Sincere thanks to my editor, Amy Einhorn, for her patience and her expertise in helping me create semi-order out of total chaos.

Contents

Author's Note

Women make up more than 50 percent of the population, and regardless of our current age, each of us is growing older every day. Each one of us travels her own path, yet all of us inevitably share so much in the areas of life experiences, personal relationships, and societal roles.

This book is about the Red Hat Society, a unique "disorganization" of women who are gathering together in small clusters, large crowds, and even massive throngs in order to share one another's lives and to make our own fun. All of us are making a conscious choice about what kind of older women we are on our way to becoming, embracing life and one another in equal measure.

If you are already a member of the Red Hat Society, this book is for you. If you are not yet a member, this book is for you, too. The rest of us are holding out our red-gloved hands in invitation and welcome.

Prologue

Warning

When I am an old woman, I shall wear purple,
With a red hat which doesn't go, and doesn't suit
      me,
And I shall spend my pension on brandy and summer
      gloves
And satin sandals, and say we've no money for butter.
I shall sit down on the pavement when I'm tired
And gobble up samples in shops and press alarm
      bells
And run my stick along the
      public railings
And make up for the
      sobriety of my
      youth.
I shall go out in my
      slippers in the
      rain
And pick flowers in
      other people's
      gardens
And learn to spit.
You can wear terrible shirts and grow more fat
And eat three pounds of sausages at a go
Or only bread and pickle for a week
And hoard pens and pencils and beermats and
      things in boxes.
But now we must have clothes that keep us dry
And pay our rent and not swear in the street

And set a good example for the children.
We will have friends to dinner and read the papers.
But maybe I ought to practice a little now?
So people who know me are not too shocked and
    surprised
When suddenly I am old and start to wear purple.
                                        —Jenny Joseph

I remember clearly the first time I encountered this poem. I was in a funky little used-book store/gift shop called The Blue Wolf, which used to be situated in an alley off the main drag in my town. There was a T-shirt pinned up on the wall, and the poem was printed on its front. As I stood there and read, I smiled and called my shopping companion's attention to it. I felt an immediate kinship with the poem's narrator. At that time, I was probably in my late thirties and not yet concerned about getting old. But the artist in me was drawn to the colors mentioned and the mood of gaiety and abandon that emanated from the poem. I will always feel indebted to Jenny Joseph for planting the concept in my mind that, though I would eventually have to grow old, the kind of old person I would become would be a matter of my own choosing. The poem had registered in my mind, and given me a smile. Little did I know how important this poem would become in my life!

The Red Hat Society

1

Birth of a Notion

People ask how I feel about getting old. I tell them I have the same question. I'm learning as I go.

—Paul Simon

One evening, in the fall of 1997, my husband and I, both Californians, were visiting old friends who had moved to Tucson, Arizona. On this Friday night, in the "artsy" part of town, the shops were open, brightly lighted, and the street was full of strolling window-shoppers and diners. Among the shops was a thrift shop, the type of place that has always attracted me. You never know what treasure you might find in such a store, you know—so much more exciting than "ordinary" shops. What does it say about me, that I would rather hunt for the prize than have it presented to me on a platter? Probably that I possess that notorious feminine gene for shopping.

There it was. Such a beautiful, brilliant color! Such a jaunty, devil-may-care attitude! Such a serendipitous find!

But . . .

I didn't need it.
I had nowhere to wear it.
There was no good reason to buy it. This requirement that
    everything one does must be done for a "good reason"
    was ingrained in me from my childhood. One must have
    a good reason for everything one does, don't you know?
I might look silly in it. (I guess there are worse things than
    looking silly.)
People might think I was weird when they saw me in it.
It would be an unnecessary expenditure. Surely that eight
    dollars could be put to better use. Waste not, want not!
It would have to be squashed in my suitcase to get it home.
Women don't wear hats anymore. I would be out of style.

Obviously, I thought, I should turn around, walk out of this thrift
shop, and put that hat out of my mind. One must not indulge in
flights of fancy. Who knows where that could lead? I might get
totally out of control, and then, who *knows* what I might do?
On the other hand . . .

I was feeling lighthearted.
The little girl inside of me, who had barely managed to sur-
    vive, isolated in the closet, so to speak, for years, was beg-
    ging me to buy it. (Usually, I managed to drown out her
    pleas.)
It might be justifiable to give myself just this one teensy-
    weensy treat.
It probably wouldn't matter to anyone else one way or
    another. Generally speaking, people are concerned pri-
    marily with themselves. It was unlikely they would be
    interested in my finances or apparel.
I could wear it "just for tonight." If it turned out to be a terri-
    ble mistake, I could always quietly dispose of the hat.

I found myself standing in front of the cash register, digging into my wallet. Before I knew it, that bright red fedora was perched on my head, dipping daringly below one eyebrow. As far as I know, I caused no one a moment's pause. The sky did not fall. The only real result was that I experienced some moments of genuine pleasure and managed to surprise myself a bit. (Maybe I am a little less dull than I thought.)

Fast-forward to a couple of months later. . . .

My dear friend Linda Murphy was turning fifty-five, and I wanted to give her an imaginative gift. She isn't the sort of person who particularly cares for trinkets. And I do enjoy a challenge. I began to contemplate what sort of gift I could give her. Fifty-five, while not the beginning of a new decade, *is* rather a milestone birthday. How could I best communicate the occasion? I wondered.

Linda had made a couple of small jokes about getting old, and that had reminded me of the Jenny Joseph poem, and its refreshing, liberating attitude toward aging. And *that* reminded me of my red fedora, languishing in my closet. Now, I certainly do not consider fifty-five "old," but I knew that there were many in our society who probably did. I knew that Linda and I did not consider ourselves anywhere near old, but then, the poem refers to practicing for the day when one does become old. I decided it would be appropriate for us to begin practicing, as a joke between us. I would locate a copy of the poem and frame it. I would buy her a vintage red hat and present her with both items. She could hang the poem on her wall and suspend the hat on a hook next to it, creating a vignette that might make her smile, especially if it was in her bedroom, where she would see it every day when she got up. I didn't want to give her the hat that I already had, but, rather, to find one especially for her. It wasn't hard to find a cute red bowler at a local antique shop. Though similar to my original one, it seemed a bit more decorous, and a bit more Linda.

The gift was a hit! Our mutual friends enjoyed it, too. So the following December, when another friend, Carol Sibley, was turning fifty, I couldn't resist giving her a similar gift. This time, my search had yielded a real treasure, a vintage red hat embellished with a bunch of shiny artificial cherries and a mysterious black veil! It gave Carol a smile, and entertained the other party guests, as well.

After that, I quickly discovered that this had now become the gift that was expected of me, at least within our circle of longtime friends. I began to look for red hats whenever I was in antique or thrift shops, and I found several. One of them even had a red brim with a purple crown! I put that aside for my youngest friend, Marsha Harline, in anticipation of her fiftieth birthday. I had decided that reaching the age of fifty should be treated as a positive, momentous milestone, instead of the beginning of the end. The thrill of the hunt reinforced my efforts. Very soon, there were several of us with red hats.

It occurred to me that there might be some kind of magic in the words of that poem. Perhaps we should all find something purple to wear and go out in public in our purple and red, I thought. I made a few calls and convinced the others to participate in an outing. Purple wasn't a popular color in 1998, so this necessitated visits to resale shops to find castoffs from an earlier era, when purple had been more desirable.

In April 1998, we went to a tearoom within the Spring Field Banquet Center, located a few blocks from my house. I persuaded my husband to stop by with a camera to record this event. We thought we looked quite fetching in our regalia, sitting around the tea table. He thought we looked hilarious! He laughed so hard that he had trouble steadying the camera long enough to snap the shutter. For some reason, he thought we made quite a sight. Interestingly, there was not another soul in the tearoom that day, so we couldn't elicit any attention from anyone other than our waitress, who didn't raise an eyebrow.

Well, ladies, something magical happened that afternoon. Whether it was the outfits, the aura of playing dress-up, or just our own amusement at our perceived daring, I don't know. What I do know is that we had more fun together than we had had in years. Within a few minutes, we knew that we wanted to do this again. Someone (we can't remember who) told me that I was a queen for thinking this whole thing up. I quickly seized upon that notion, embracing the idea wholeheartedly, and declared myself "Queen Mother." What woman hasn't always wanted to be a queen? Well, if I was going to have a title, everyone else should get to have one. Linda was proclaimed "Vice Mother" (we weren't sure what vice she would be the mother of, but we were sure the title would prove to be appropriate in some way), and Cheryl "Hysterian," as she said she would keep a scrapbook for us. We dubbed ourselves the "Red Hat Society" right then and there.

By the time of our next outing, we had added several more fun-loving friends to our little nucleus, including an "Antiparliamentarian" (to make sure that we didn't make any rules) and a "Sergeant in Gloves," who would enforce ladylike behavior, if we could ever determine exactly what that might be.

Linda told a friend of hers, Nancy Manning, who lived in Florida, about our group. Nancy immediately gathered several of her close friends and formed another Red Hat conclave. We thought it was very cool to have a sister chapter all the way across the country. Little did we know what would follow a bit later on.

Linda also mentioned our group to the daughter of an old friend, Eileen Cannon Paulin, who was the editor of *Romantic Homes* magazine. This led to our being featured in the July 2000 issue. They also featured our sister group in Homosassa, Florida—the Steel Magnolias. We were all thrilled to see ourselves in a four-page spread entitled "Growing Old Playfully." Immediately, I began to receive E-mails from *Romantic Homes* readers, saying, "I loved reading about your group! How can my friends and I play, too?" I answered each one of these like-minded women, explaining how easy it would be for them to pattern new groups after ours.

Before I could answer anyone, however, I had to learn to use my husband's computer—at least enough to send and receive E-mail. Technophobe that I am, I considered this a daunting requirement. I have spent my whole life in fear of anything that comes with an instruction manual. With my apologies to Dr. Seuss for using *Green Eggs and Ham* as my inspiration, here is a summary of my attitude at that time:

The Monster on the Desk

I will not learn to use that thing.
I won't admit that it is king.
I will not force myself to learn
And from my pen and paper turn.
I do not like computers, sir!
I do not like them, I aver!
I will not use them on a table.
I'm telling you, I am not able!
I will not deign to press those keys,
Not even if you pay me fees!
I do not want to use that thing,
Not even for a diamond ring!
I'd really rather have a spinal.
And this decision must be final!

Well, I was wrong. I had to learn a few computer fundamentals, and this machine was not the demon I had imagined it to be. In fact, it was a miracle of sorts. The problem now was that my husband and I were a one-computer couple, and I began to use it a lot, essentially crowding him out of his business-related activities. So we bought a computer for me (bright red, of course) and a garage-sale school desk to put it on.

The following December, the *Orange County Register*, our local newspaper, featured the founding chapter of the Red Hat Society on the front page of its "Accent" section. While this was exciting in itself, what was *really* exciting was the pickup of the article by the major wire services! Now the trickle of E-mails turned into a torrent!

Publicity, which we had never sought, continued to propel the Red Hat Society forward at a speed that seemed to accelerate almost daily. In June 2001, a few hundred of us red-hatted Southern Californians took the train to San Juan Capistrano for a day of shopping, lunching, and getting to know one another. Florence Henderson, Mrs. Brady herself, was sent, along with a camera crew, from the

Today show to cover the event. Over the course of several hours, we taught her how to be a Red Hatter, both in dress and attitude. The segment was aired in September of 2001, and it stimulated our growth even more than we had thought possible.

I am often asked if I was surprised by the incredible growth of our group. Perhaps *bewildered* would be a better word for my initial emotion. I couldn't help but think of the scene in *Forrest Gump* when Forrest begins running for no particular reason. A few people start to jog along behind him, and then a few more—and then a *huge* crowd! I felt as puzzled as Forrest did. Where were we all going? Were all these women counting on me to lead them somewhere? If so, where was I taking them?

With all this attention, I rented a tiny office outside of my home, as I was pushing my husband right out of his study with my boxes and files. July 2001 found me and my first employee, Carol Reekstin (immediately nicknamed "Lady Lavender"), working several hours per day answering E-mails, mailing charters, et cetera. It wasn't long before we had two more part-time helpers—my sister Jane Farrington (aka "PrinSis"), and Susan Meyer ("Duchess of Violet"). We expanded our office space and equipment. The challenge by then was just to keep up with the Red Hat Society as it grew; and that remains our challenge today!

In April 2002, we staged our first national convention, gathering over four hundred Red Hatters from all over the country in Chicago for three days of carefully orchestrated mayhem. We called our event Paint the Town Red, and we sure did! We had speakers, a city tour, a banquet, a talent show, and a pajama breakfast. And we had something we had never expected—one of the best times of our collective life! Attendees vowed not only to return the next year but to bring their friends with them, so they wouldn't miss out, a second time, on an incredibly special experience.

The following spring, in May 2003, a large number of those women did come to our second national convention, in Nashville, Tennessee, and they *did* bring their friends. This time, we were two thousand strong. Because Nashville is known as "Music City," we chose the name Hats Off to Harmony for this convention. We had about five times as much fun as the year before, probably because there were five times as many Red Hatters there to show us how.

The Red Hat Society is spreading like a wildfire through dry grass! Not only have multiple chapters sprung up in every state; it has gained significant ground in Canada, and has begun appearing in such countries as Australia, New Zealand, and Belgium, to name just a few. Now that it has become something of an international phenomenon, virtually every reporter I have spoken to has asked me to explain its appeal. What are the reasons for the size and speed of the response? Why does it appeal to such diverse groups of women, people from every conceivable walk of life? When I began to search for the answers to these questions, I discovered, to my surprise, myriad reasons for this response. And, as usual, I found the answers only in retrospect. As I have said, I had not set out to form anything beyond a small group of friends. How in the world had that first simple tea party touched off such a movement?

It seems to me, our primary appeal is our determination to find the joy in life, to grasp the fun there is to be had at this age—fifty and beyond. We have been wives, mothers, and, often, career women. We are now in a different place in our lives. Our children are mostly gone from our homes. We may (or may not) be retired from the workforce. We have survived the busiest, most hectic years and have a little more discretionary time. I don't know about you, but when my children were young, I found the effort of making time for myself akin to trying to stir a hole in a pan of syrup. Each of us knows that she probably has less life left than she has already experienced. Time is even more precious than before. None of us wants to squander any of it. But we have an evolved idea of what "squandering" time means. We are more likely to see real value in some of the things that we might previously have seen as somewhat frivolous—such as joy, play, perhaps a little bit of self-indulgence. A woman has time to ask herself questions: What do I want to do with the rest of my life? Whom do I want to spend that time with? It's kind of like having a limited amount of money to spend in a department store. Whereas we might

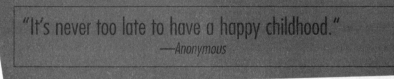

> "It's never too late to have a happy childhood."
> —*Anonymous*

once have spent *all* of our money on staples, we are now a little more likely to be found in the toy department—buying toys for ourselves!

Women who are discovering this form of liberation are finding that there is even more fun to be found in play when that play is shared with other women. Obviously, we can get together with friends anytime. But how about friends wearing red hats and purple clothing? That adds a new element. As I have said, the red and purple, and the clubbiness that it represents to all of us, seems to inject something magical into any get-together. People stare. People wave. We feel a little bit like celebrities, and we get a little high on that!

We middle-aged women have gotten used to going unnoticed, to being invisible. "Aging is a double-edged sword," says Renae Bredin, an associate professor at California State University, Fullerton. "You do have much more freedom to do what you want—because no one is watching. Older women are invisible in our culture." This certainly validates what Carolyn Heilbrun, a retired Columbia University professor, has said. She jokes that she could burglarize any New York City apartment and not get caught. "If you aren't young and sexy, nobody sees you. You do become invisible. It's annoying at first. But it also gives you great freedom."

Well, I have a question: How do you ignore anywhere from ten to fifty women decked out in red and purple and sporting such accessories as red feather boas and rhinestone pins that spell out "QUEEN"?

Answer: You don't!

Wearing the bright, sometimes outrageous getups that some of us have begun to accumulate provides an opportunity for individualism and the expression of playful spirits. The wearing of the Red Hat Society regalia reminds us a lot of playing dress-up as children.

We loved doing that then, and we still love it. How *fun* is a fluffy red-feathered fan, or a pair of purple fishnet hose? And it is a lot easier to *act* silly when you are dressed silly!

This talk of silliness might sound, well, silly. But silliness is a very important part of the Red Hat Society. Just because we are no longer little girls does not mean that we are entirely grown-up! Those little girls hiding inside these mature bodies just love a chance to get out and play once in a while! So now, in accordance with the Red Hat Society's playful spirit, we have all decided that we are now queens, princesses, ladies, duchesses, et cetera. Expressing our importance as royalty (self-proclaimed though that royalty might be) is an element of the silliness that we all enjoy heartily. I had an early E-mail from one kindred spirit who said that her household consists of a wonderful husband and two teenage sons who need to be reminded, from time to time, that she is the queen of their house. So she keeps a tiara on her bedside table and never hesitates to put it on, lest they forget who she is.

It is not always easy to accumulate new friends as we get older. Some of us tend to put ourselves out there less often and just cling to the long-established friends and routines that we have known for years. But there can be great stimulation in adding new friends to your life and planning imaginative adventures with them. As any particular chapter adds friends of friends, many women get the opportunity to expand their own roster of good friends, whether they are newly discovered kindred spirits or old friends of other old friends. The Red Hat Society provides opportunities to meet new women, not only within one's own chapter but at area-wide and even nationwide events. The interplay and sharing among women who were formerly strangers can be very stimulating and lead to brand-new interests and explorations. I have heard it said that travel is broadening. So is making new friends. Our circle of friends and interests does not need to shrink as we get older; it can expand!

Spending regular time with your chapter members often leads to deeper ties, a feeling of sisterhood. We find that we have many life experiences in common, even though we have gone through them independently. This leads to mutual warmth and, oftentimes, to the development of close bonds. Then, as we continue through life, sharing with our new friends, we discover that we have developed a whole new support system of women who have come to genuinely care about one another. When the inevitable difficult times find one of us, she has a network of others to help her through them.

Having said all of this, I must now mention the attribute of the Red Hat Society that is cited first and foremost by Red Hatters themselves when questioned about their original attraction to the Red Hat Society: We have *no rules!* We have gotten used to functioning in every area of our lives within set structures, and we are weary of it. We established ourselves as a "disorganization," and as far as we possibly can, we are staying a disorganization. We don't want to fulfill the expectations of anyone or any institution. We want to fulfill some long-ignored needs of our own. We want to be free!

To sum up, the Red Hat Society fulfills these needs for its members:

• The need to play and enjoy the whimsical aspects of life
• The desire to dress up and find the "lost" little girl inside each of us
• The need for connection and communication with others who are at the same stage of life
• An appreciation for humor and the "sweetness" to be found in life
• The stimulation experienced by discovering the plethora of possibilities remaining in our lives
• Visibility as a relevant and active segment of society
• The fulfillment of the deep need that women have for fellowship with other women who have been through "the wars." We are through with competition. We need one another and are more than ready to admit it.

That is quite a lofty statement of attributes, isn't it?
I wish that I could say that I sat down one day and developed a

plan for this wonderful disorganization, but many of these benefits developed and revealed themselves only gradually. Now that they are clear, thanks to all of the wonderful Red Hatters who have helped me to clarify who we are and what we do, I have found a dream of my own. It is my hope that the Red Hat Society can promote and spread a countercultural message about women, and revolutionize the view of feminine aging in our society.

We are playing a game with room for an unlimited number of players. This game has *no rules,* no jobs, no responsibilities, and no penalties. You don't have to be brilliant, talented, or outstanding in any way to play. You just have to enjoy being with other women, playing dress-up, doing "girl things," and deepening your laugh lines. You have to practice lightening up once in a while, and let yourself learn how to find joy in the moment. You don't have to do it alone, though. We have our red-gloved hands extended. Grab hold! And use your free hand to slap a red hat on your head!

2

Ruby RedHat

I've acted old long enough. Now it's time for fun!

—Anonymous Red Hatter

He who laughs, lasts.

—Anonymous

The official mascot of the Red Hat Society is Ruby Red-Hat, a frisky, full-figured little lady, cleverly disguised as an adult. She represents the spirit of the little girl who is alive and well inside each of us. Ruby showed up on my daughter Andrea's computer screen in our early days, and she immediately charmed us all with her attitude. She is one sweet yet spunky little person, let me tell you. Over time, we have gotten to know her well, and her charm only increases with familiarity! Everyone who gets to know Ruby just loves her. And she reciprocates wholeheartedly. She may be small, but her heart is huge!

Ruby says she heard of the poem called "Warning" years ago and has been dressing appropriately ever since. She is partial to purple and has an entire wardrobe composed of various shades of it. She wears the requisite red hat (or something red) on her head at all times. I wouldn't be at all surprised to learn that when she curls her hair, she uses red rollers—she is that devoted to our colors. However, in her preference for comfort over fashion, she usually wears fuzzy pink slippers rather than high heels or any other less than comfy footwear. She says she is *so* done with pinchy shoes!

Ruby has to have most of her clothing custom-made, as she is severely height-challenged. (She insists that she is about one foot tall, but just between us, I think she's closer to ten inches.) In any case, that is a sensitive subject, so we try not to mention it. Her size, however, does make it harder to notice her when she attends our events. And her occasional fits of shyness don't help, either. Oftentimes, we will find one of her little pink slippers (which she has a habit of losing), which proves that she has indeed been there. But her low visibility has led some humorless doubters to assert that she doesn't exist at all. And, to the surprise of many, we have come to realize that not everyone can see her! Even Red Hatters themselves occasionally find her invisible, partly because she never stays in one place for long. It appears that only those who respond to the sparkly idea of red-hatted fun ever actually catch glimpses of her. She is similar to the famed leprechaun of Irish lore, a "now you see it, now you don't" little creature.

Ruby is the embodiment of the attributes and attitudes that Red Hatters admire and hope to emulate themselves. Here are Ruby RedHat's Top Ten Rules for Living, Plus One. (In her typical fashion, she says there's always room for one more!) While the Red Hat Society has no rules, Ruby's rules for living are worth listening to!

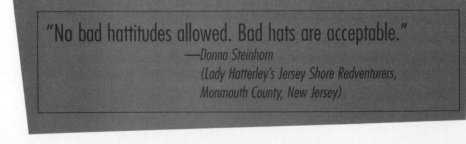

"No bad hattitudes allowed. Bad hats are acceptable."
—Donna Steinhorn
(Lady Hatterley's Jersey Shore Redventurers,
Monmouth County, New Jersey)

RUBY REDHAT'S TOP TEN RULES FOR LIVING, PLUS ONE

1. Accept reality and live in the here and now. Ruby can't be bothered with "what-ifs" or regrets. She says they interfere with her fun!

2. Accentuate the positive. Ruby always chooses to find the good in any situation she is faced with. She says she would rather develop laugh lines than frown lines.

3. Nurture yourself. Ruby listens to herself and provides for her own needs. When she needs a break, she gives herself one!

4. Indulge your sense of humor. Ruby heartily appreciates the value of laughter.

5. Play! Either Ruby never grew up all the way or she has regressed. In either event, she knows how to have a great time!

6. Dress up! Ruby adores embellishing whatever she is wearing with glitz, glitter, and glam.

7. Cultivate an openness to new things. Ruby will try almost anything.

8. Express your creativity. Ruby thinks "outside the hatbox."

9. Exercise compassion. Ruby loves to laugh and cry with others.

10. Have courage! Ruby knows she is up to the challenge of whatever may come.

11. Make up for the sobriety of your youth! Ruby says that she, too, was dutiful in her younger years and now she has a lot of quirky stuff that she needs to get done!

Any of us who choose to emulate Ruby strive to express, or develop, these same qualities. Let's take a closer look:

1. ACCEPT REALITY AND LIVE IN THE HERE AND NOW

We accept life, and people, as they are. When push comes to shove, we have to do that. The sooner we stop wasting our energy

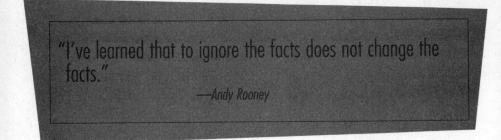

"I've learned that to ignore the facts does not change the facts."

—Andy Rooney

trying to change other people or inevitable circumstances, the sooner we can expend our strength on what we want to do with the rest of our lives.

For most of my life, I was a control freak. I thought that every last detail of the lives of my family members, and anyone else I was close to, needed my personal management. This attitude did not arise from grandiosity on my part, but, rather, from a deep need to hold back the chaos that seemed to result when I allowed events to take their own course, and people to make their own choices. I have receipts for several years of therapy to prove that I worked long and hard to rid myself of this undesirable trait. Anyone who has spent her life trying to shape everyone and everything except herself can attest to the deep feeling of relief that follows relinquishing universal responsibility and accepting things as they are. When you release the need to *make* things happen, you are free to find contentment with whatever *is*. The energy that once was squandered on things we could not change anyway, no matter how much effort we expended, is freed up to be used in more positive ways.

Marsha Harline, the "Mistress of Anxiety" of the founding chapter, and my longtime close friend, has told me that she always felt it was her responsibility to ensure that her husband and daughter made all the right choices. If they were not happy at any point, she assumed total responsibility. During therapy, she was given an assignment to try to learn to play. The counselor told her to buy an assortment of bubbles and bubble-blowing tools, take them to a park, and experiment. Marsha recruited both her husband and daughter to go with her and proceeded to teach *them* how to make bubbles in various ways. For several minutes, both Mike and Amy ran around trailing streams of bubbles behind them while Marsha sat on a bench and shouted directions. All of a sudden, they both froze in their tracks and stared at Marsha. Here she was, directing them to play, instead of learning how to do it for herself! Anybody recognize herself? I sure do.

A large part of accepting reality is doing the best we can within the boundary of the day in which we are currently living. (The truest cliché I have ever heard is "Take one day at a time.") Among the things we can never change is our past. Ruby loves to remember the good times she has had and the people she has loved, but she doesn't spend much time mulling over things she might have done differently. She knows that, as the poet has said, the past is "another country," and she cannot revisit it, nor can she change it. She no longer wastes valuable mental energy rehashing old mistakes and envisioning better choices she could have made. And she has also learned that the future is another dimension that she cannot inhabit, try as she might! Ruby says that she did a lot of worrying over the years about things that didn't happen, and failed to anticipate many things that did. Interestingly enough, this was one endeavor in which practice did not make perfect, so she has decided to stop trying to peer around all the corners and just see what happens when she gets there! I've been trying to emulate Ruby, and guess what? An old dog *can* learn new tricks.

2. ACCENTUATE THE POSITIVE

We have all heard it said that attitude is everything, and basically, it is. As I have connected with other Red Hatters over the past few years, I have seen that all of us have the power to shape and sculpt the ways we view the world and ourselves, and to adopt methods of coping with the inevitable ups and downs of life. We are nowhere near as powerless as we may think. We have lived long enough to learn from our own experiences (and maybe those of others) and we can see the power of choices we have already made, as they have affected our lives and the lives of those around us. We *do* have choices—in countless areas. The most important choice we can make is that of the attitudes we choose to adopt in the present and to take with us into the future. We can now choose to concentrate on the good things: what *has* been good in the past, what *is* good now, and what potential good we can create as we grow older. Red Hatters are making constructive choices to emphasize the positive aspects of life, to cultivate every bit of joy, love, and fun that we can find—or make!

> "Whatsoever things are true, whatsoever things are honest, whatsoever things are just, whatsoever things are pure, whatsoever things are lovely, whatsoever things are of good report; if there be any virtue, and if there be any praise, think on these things."
> *Philippians 4:8*

Choosing to concentrate on our gratitude for the good things in life makes an enormous difference in the way we see the world. It affects the way the rest of the world sees us, as well. No one wants to be around a person who continually bemoans past injustices, playing the eternal victim. This kind of attitude is very unhealthy for the complainer, as well. How much better to be like Jo Simon (Spring City Red Hatters, Waukesha, Wisconsin), who found a way to appreciate the good things left in her life after her husband of twenty-nine years walked out. She says, "I picked myself up, turned myself around, put a smile on my face, and headed down a new path. I asked God to help me discover a purpose in life and show me the direction to go so I could discover the road He wanted me to travel. Waiting for me was the perfect job, the perfect house, and all of it located in a perfect place." She says that becoming a clown and performing in church programs added "the cherry on top" to her life. When she heard about the Red Hat Society, she went to our regis-

> "I've learned that when you harbor bitterness, happiness will dock elsewhere."
>
> —*Andy Rooney*

tration page, "quicker than you could say 'purple,'" and became the queen mum of the Spring City Red Hatters. She says, "As I gaze around the room at my Red friends, hear the happy laughter and see the bobbing red hats, I'm reminded once again that life's treasures are people, not things. I am blessed."

Is Jo an unrealistic model? Is she too much of a Pollyanna? I don't think so. I am sure she has done her share of suffering. But she has chosen to get on with her life and emphasize the good that remains. And I will bet that her cheerful attitude is attractive to others. They probably gather around her inner fire to warm their own hands and hearts. The result is that she is not alone; rather, she is surrounded by people who care about her, and she has a full, vivid life.

Old Irish Blessing

*Always remember to forget the things that
made you sad.
But never forget to remember the things that
made you glad.
Always remember to forget the friends that
proved untrue.
But never forget to remember those that
have stuck by you.
Always remember to forget the troubles that
passed away.
But never forget to remember the blessings
that come each day.*

My husband had a great-aunt who lived to be ninety-eight years old. She was blessed with excellent health for her first ninety-plus years and had financial security, due to her late husband. But she was not a pleasure to be around. She spent most of her time finding fault with people, institutions, and religions different from her own. Her reaction to any new limitation imposed by her advancing age was one of intense anger. She constantly railed against the inevitable losses in her life, saying sourly to everyone, "Don't ever get old." I do not mean to set myself up as her judge and jury. I haven't gotten to her stage of life yet, nor do I know if I ever will. However, I do believe that an attitude adjustment would have done her a lot of good. What if she had decided to concentrate on the abilities she had been able to retain? She had lost her husband, but she still had relatives and longtime friends. She had lost some of her mobility, but she could still drive. She fell and dislocated her shoulder, but she was able to regain its function. She had her home and it was paid for. She was able to live off the interest of her husband's investments. She enjoyed nutritious meals delivered by Meals on Wheels volunteers. I have often heard that if you can't be an inspiration to others, you will just have to serve as a warning. I think about that . . . a lot.

3. NURTURE YOURSELF

At one time, I would have been the last person on earth to develop the Red Hat philosophy of life. The impetus for that first gathering at the tearoom arose, as I have said, from my reading of "Warning," and that tea was really nothing but a whimsical experiment, an aberration really, for me. But all of the responses to the *Romantic Homes* story, and the others that followed, made me suddenly conscious of the fact that there were an awful lot of women out there who resonated with this idea in a powerful way.

Speaking personally, I nurture myself by taking time for such things as long, lazy afternoons browsing in thrift shops and antique stores, taking long walks with my dog when I really should be accomplishing some task, or curling up with a well-written novel. Your particular method of self-nurture may be completely different—perhaps a trip to the opera (*without* the opera hater in your family), perhaps a 10K run. Whatever it is, do it. And, as often as you can, do those things in the company of other Red Hatters. We need to support one another in this sort of thing, reminding ourselves, and one another, of the value of self-care.

A few years ago, I began to see that it was mandatory for my mental and emotional health to allow myself to relax, to find ways to rediscover my childhood enjoyment of small things. I was good at urging others to do it, although not sure how to do it with any consistency myself. I wanted to learn how to do that, not only for my own benefit but also for the benefit of the women I was hearing from. I could sense their need to be encouraged to have fun and to take care of themselves. It was surprising to notice how many women seemed to be almost asking me for the permission to do that, not really understanding how to do it. How could I set myself up as an example if I couldn't practice what I was preaching?

Have you ever tried to *force* yourself to feel joy? Could there be a stranger oxymoron? Well, joyfulness may not have been an innate part of my makeup, but perseverance was. There had to be a way. As I received E-mails and letters from women asking me to explain the purpose of the Red Hat Society, I began to see the shadow of an answer. It was so simple: There *was* no purpose! This seemed to be a contradiction, but there actually *was* a purpose beyond the stated lack of purpose! It only appeared when I stopped reaching so hard for it. In the act of not doing anything, I began to grasp the idea of just being someone—at least some of the time.

A tremendous vision of peace, joy, and laughter gradually opened up to me. Fun is *good* for you! Most of you probably remember seeing *The Wizard of Oz* as a child. Do you remember that the early scenes were filmed in black and white? Then, as Dorothy opens the door into Oz, the entire screen suddenly blazes with glorious color, and her real adventures begin. In the same way, as the

Red Hat Society began to form, and I became excited by the knowledge that there were so many other women who wanted to play, too, I glimpsed a rainbow of colors through the door to our collective future. All of us Red Hatters would have the opportunity to find more enjoyment in life *just because.* Not because we were mothers, or wives, or retired, but because we finally were old enough to realize that we deserved it.

We matter just because we exist, not only because of our accomplishments and the services we perform. If you doubt that, look at your own loved ones. Do they matter to *you* only because of *their* achievements? Of course not! They are tremendously valuable in and of themselves! I began to relax a bit, in my frenzied search for relevance, and visit a few more of the rest stops along the highway of life. I saw that this lightening up can be serious business! And, as I developed contact with other newborn Red Hatters, I began to draw from them my own personal permission to slow down. Finally, I was able to write a statement of purpose for the Red Hat Society:

> The Red Hat Society began as a result of a few women deciding to greet middle age with verve, humor, and elan. We believe silliness is the comedy relief of life, and, since we are all in it together, we might as well join red-gloved hands and go for the gusto together. Underneath the frivolity, we share a bond of affection, forged by common life experiences, and a genuine enthusiasm for wherever life takes us next.

I put out a request to all Red Hatters to help me think up a good short slogan, and several excellent ideas were proposed. I put the best ones on the Web site and asked the membership to vote. The favorite,

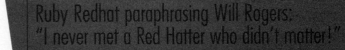

Ruby Redhat paraphrasing Will Rogers:
"I never met a Red Hatter who didn't matter!"

submitted by Gloria Clawson (the Selected Few, Lubbock, Texas), won by a landslide. It did a great job of expressing a lot of concepts in a very few words: "Red Hatters Matter." We do, ladies, we really do!

4. INDULGE YOUR SENSE OF HUMOR

Humor is as essential to Red Hatting as air is to breathing. As little girls, we found excuses to laugh all the time. But as we grew older and assumed the serious roles that accompany adulthood, we sobered up quite a bit—perhaps, we now think, a little *too* much. There is nothing like a broad grin or a deep belly laugh to lighten one's load. And we all know that these expressions of happiness are contagious. Some Red Hatters have nurtured the silly side of themselves all along, while some of us are relearning this art from others.

> "Think of the trouble the world would save if it would pay some attention to nonsense."
> —E. B. White

I suspect that Lady Vi Larimer was one of those in whom Red Hatted behavior had always been innate. Vi's daughter, Marjie Petroshanoff Segel (the Red Hotsie Totsies, Torrance, California), tells a wonderful tale about her mother's legendary sense of humor. Marjie flew east to visit her family, to be followed a few days later by her new beau, Norm, who was coming to meet the family. At Vi's instigation, the four members of the family who picked Norm up at the airport greeted him wearing Groucho Marx glasses, with huge noses and mustaches attached. Norm managed to keep a straight face, betraying neither surprise nor puzzlement. When the group arrived back at the house, Vi and Marjie's brother met them at the door, wearing the same glasses. Norm also greeted them, as if there was nothing out of the ordinary in their appearance. Shortly after that trip, Marjie accepted Norm's proposal. Since she valued her mother's opinion greatly, she called her mother for her approval. Vi's comment: "Honey, if you don't marry him, I will!"

Katie Graybeal (the La-Te-Das, Bristol, Tennessee/Virginia) sends this story about herself and her chapter mate Jane Daniel. They were on their way to a busy restaurant for a Red Hat luncheon, and Jane was telling Katie about the bargain purple suit that she was wearing, having bought it that morning at a thrift shop. She had not taken the time to try it on, and she had discovered when she got home that the jacket was her size but that the skirt was three sizes too big. Jane felt that it wasn't too much of a problem, since the jacket was quite long and covered most of the skirt anyway, and she could safety pin the skirt at the waist to keep it up, as she had done. When they parked at the restaurant, they jumped down from Katie's SUV. As Jane hit the ground, so did her skirt! She tried to halt the skirt's descent by spreading her knees, but to no avail. There she stood in her red hat, purple jacket, and panty hose, her skirt puddled at her feet. Katie says, "Speaking of puddles, I was laughing *so* hard that it was all I could do from making my own puddle on the ground! So I stood there, with my legs crossed, crying from laughter. Jane is a beautiful, true southern belle, and I will take to my grave the sight of her, all dolled up, with nothing but panty hose and heels on from the waist down."

Violet Lind (the Scarlet O'Hatters, St. Augustine, Florida) arranged to meet a man she had met through a personal ad in the newspaper. She chose a very public restaurant for safety sake. The gentleman suggested that she identify herself by carrying a yellow rose. Violet bought up every yellow rose in town and distributed them to every woman in the restaurant, then sat back to see what would happen. She says she wouldn't have been interested in a man who couldn't take a joke. He came through the door, looked around the room, and walked straight over to her, asking, "Do you have a yellow rose?" He claimed he never saw any other woman that night. They have been married for six years now.

Cheri Enters (Spring City Red Hatters, Waukesha, Wisconsin) is, in my opinion, our reigning queen of comedy, though she didn't wait for the Red Hat Society to set an example of her. Cheri's favorite place for expressing her sense of humor seems to be the airport, as she has sent me a number of stories about airport exploits. About ten years ago, Cheri's husband was due to arrive home from a business trip on the day of their wedding anniversary. Cheri persuaded her friends Jean and Mel Jones to help her meet him at the airport, dressed as a wedding party. Cheri and Jean outfitted themselves in a bridal gown and bridesmaid's ensemble, respectively, and Mel, after vigorous coercion, donned his tuxedo. Tim's flight was late, so the three of them had to stand around in the concourse for a while. They had time to gather quite a crowd of interested onlookers, none of whom could tear themselves away before getting the chance to observe Tim's face when he deplaned. When he finally exited the plane, he was met by a bride, two attendants, and about two hundred wildly applauding people. Tim is very used to Cheri's habit of surprising people by wearing costumes to the airport. His unruffled comment? "Oh, she's a bride this time."

5. PLAY!

I always drew and painted as a child, taking enormous pleasure in art. But when I reached college, I didn't choose art as my major, because I thought that it was rather frivolous, certainly not something "worthwhile." I got a degree in English, married, and started a family, all the while making little or no art. There was simply not enough time. When both of my children were in school, I returned

> "Girls just want to have fun!"
> —*Cyndi Lauper*

to the local college to take art classes, and began to dabble a bit. During those years when I was beginning to realize that art was an essential part of who I am and what I am, I became frustrated with my work. I was tied to the belief that the only *real* art was realistic rendering, at which I had become relatively skillful. But my favorite class during that time was entitled Exploratory Art, which didn't develop rendering skill but which forced me to experiment with odd materials (modeling paste, fabric, cardboard) and just improvise. Although I loved the class, I returned to the more accepted forms. Around that time, I was asked to judge some local children's art competitions, and I made an interesting discovery. The art of children from kindergarten through about fifth grade was generally just delightful, showing an enthusiasm for color, shape, pattern, et cetera. The children were relatively unconstrained by rules regarding what things really look like. But by about fifth grade, the students' art showed a preoccupation with producing work that looked real. These youngsters had become primarily concerned about how accurately they could reproduce what they saw. The work was now dutifully correct, and technical skill had become paramount. I realized that I was much more attracted to the joyful abandon and playful use of color found in the work of the younger children. But I couldn't produce that kind of work; I couldn't figure out how to "unlearn" my polished skills. I continued to turn out realistic renderings—but I did turn to more playful subjects, such as pinwheels, toys, and dancing shoes.

Finally, I gained enough confidence in my work to submit slides of some of my illustrations to greeting card companies. To my thrill and amazement, my designs immediately began to sell, and I found myself a bona fide freelancer in the greeting card industry. In the beginning, it was very enjoyable, but I quickly learned that the art directors preferred to assign the subjects for me to paint. They were not that interested in my ideas; they told me what they wanted, specifically and in great detail. And the commercial art market is just as subject to modern marketing strategies as any other business. Although I gave the detailed assignments my best efforts, the quality of my painting deteriorated rather steadily. Anyone who viewed the illustrations could pick up the decreasing passion in the work. I began to feel as if my nose were pressed to the grindstone once again.

Aside from the returning frustration, I felt shut in at home. Freelancing is a lonely way to work, as business is conducted primarily by phone and mail, and there is very minimal contact between the artist and the client. When I found out about a faux-finish/mural-painting business that two artist friends were starting, I quickly made a move to join them. My children were largely self-sufficient by that time, and this was my chance to get out of the house. After a bumpy start and a lot of effort, our business, Altered Interiors, began to provide us with steady work. We worked together for six years, painting the interiors of homes and businesses, hauling ladders and boxes of paints hither and yon. But the work was physically demanding, and eventually I bowed out of the partnership, intending to resume freelancing. Unfortunately, my earlier success was not repeated; the greeting card market had changed. Since it seemed unlikely that I was going to find a way to make money producing art at that time, I decided that I might as well experiment a little. There was no art director waiting to suggest changes and improvements. I figured that maybe I could try to set myself free! I took up a new medium (colored pencil) and began to render playful subjects—a cat in a jester's hat, a chicken family portrait. One day, while I was giving a presentation to a meeting of a chapter of the Colored Pencil Society, I just blurted out something that I had not consciously known I was going to say: "I guess I'm trying to *play* with my art." Here I was, using a "child's" medium, rendering "children's" subjects! At last it was clear! The playful little artist had finally staggered from the dungeon (where I had kept her) out into the sun! And there has been no turning back!

At about this time, though, the Red Hat Society zoomed into significance, and since then, my art has taken a bit of a backseat. I have made the time to produce a few more playful pieces and have had the opportunity to show them in a local gallery. To my amazement, they are selling! I guess the advice given to artists in so many magazines and books is true: Paint what you love and the work will reflect that, and your enjoyment of your subject will communicate itself to the viewer.

I have heard from many Red Hatters who have consciously realized their need for play. Apparently chronological age is no impediment when a "girl" just wants to have fun!

When we remember our girlhood, particularly our adolescence, one particular type of event stands out in a lot of our memories—the slumber party. Katie Sanstead (the Red Hattitudes, Tampa, Florida) threw herself a humdinger of a fiftieth-birthday bash, inviting many of her longtime friends to join her at her home for this event. She asked each guest to bring her jammies, pillow, blanket, beverage, a good joke, poem, or picture, and a yummy snack to share. After a buffet supper, they drank wine, told fortunes, shared humorous stories, and Katie opened her gifts. They used this occasion to launch their own chapter of the Red Hat Society—with Katie as queen, of course.

While slumber parties were great fun, parties of any kind were occasions for merriment when we were kids. Since when does one need an excuse to throw a party? Donna Syverson (Mobridge Red Hatters, Mobridge, South Dakota) has come up with some excellent spontaneous reasons to throw parties. She once gave one for friends on the day that England's Prince Andrew and Fergie were married. She had a wedding reception for them and required her guests to wear royal clothing. Just for fun, she also once hosted a party for seventeen women who shared her first name. Her friends were far from surprised when she invited twenty-seven of them to start a chapter of the Red Hat Society with her. They knew that she was very good at finding excuses to make her own fun.

If bigger is better, then a bigger party must be better than a small one. Sally Munson's chapter (the Matson Red Hat Society, Princeton, Illinois) held a wallflower prom (no dates) at a restaurant named, appropriately enough, the Red Door. Each attendee wore a prom dress, most of which were salvaged from thrift shops. Sally herself wore a dress with a bustier top, which laced up the sides, exposing at least an inch of flesh on each side. She called it her "coming out" dress, not because she was making a debut or coming out of the closet, but because she was literally coming out of her dress, which was glitzy purple, of course. They ate their dessert, Red Hat

Red Hot Cherries Jubilee, first, followed by Wild & Crazy Chicken Caccitore. They rented a karaoke machine and provided their own entertainment. According to Sally, that entertainment "ranged from yodeling to stuff that made the neighbors' dogs suffer greatly."

When we are invited to a party, we are usually given a fairly good idea of what to expect. But if your queen mother is Claire Turner (the Frankly My Dears, Memphis, Tennessee), you might have to be ready for anything. She gave her chapter the choice of a traditional tea or a mystery gathering, which would require them to go some- where they had never been. They opted for the mystery, and she took them, in their purple and red finery, to play laser tag, shooting it out with all those "little hoodlums," who thought the ladies were easy targets in their red hats. After that, they straightened their clothing and treated themselves to a marvelous lunch at a French restaurant, no doubt befitting the dignified women that they are!

Instead of a party, the Last of the Red Hat Mamas chapter, in Ellicottville, New York, chose a most unusual way to launch their chapter. They marched in the Ellicottville Mardi Gras parade as their inaugural event! According to one chapter member, Patricia Enger: "This daunting cluster of twelve, flaunting purple shawls, capes, robes, blankets, and ski jackets, displayed purple-trimmed red straws, red fedoras, red berets, red toques, red bandannas, and even a red golf visor . . . and a red tea cozy, also worn as a hat." Major Mama, the second in command, who has been a majorette and an instructor of baton twirling, tried to whip her group into shape enough to perform a few simple steps and a salute to the audience lining both sides of Washington Street. She met with varied success. At their headquarters, they proudly display a blue ribbon, which proclaims "First Place in the 2002 Mardi Gras Parade!"

"I've seen how hard I can work; now I'm seeing how hard I can play." —*Ruby RedHat*

6. DRESS UP!

The famous Dr. Phil, who appears regularly on his own TV show, has said that people seek ways to enhance their lives. One way of doing that, he says, is to revisit the things that gave you pleasure as a child. When I was little, my absolute favorite plaything was a big cardboard box full of old evening gowns and negligees that my mother had bought at a thrift shop. I remember those gowns as if it were yesterday. There were mounds of yellow, lavender, and green netting and shiny pink satin. There was a slinky black number trimmed in ostrich feathers. (No red or purple, though—not then.) Who knows, maybe flouncing around in those glamorous, fluttery ostrich feathers laid the foundation for my subsequent fascination with my big red-feathered boa. That box also contained old lace curtains and some hats that were rather the worse for wear. Wearing finery and having adventures still can give me the same feeling I remember having then. And, judging from my mail, I am not alone!

Queen Suzanne Birdenflight (Soaring Sistas, Downey, California) has carried parts of her regalia into her everyday wear. She says, "Lately, I have had the strangest desire to wear my ruby red rhinestone cat-eyed sunglasses everywhere I go. And it seems somehow quite appropriate to wear a goodly amount of my costume jewelry. I'm beginning to think *gaudy* is another word for *stylin'.*"

Permission (requirement?) to be more ostentatious in her choice of dress brought out a whole new side of Jill Davis (the Crimson Crones, Portland, Oregon): "Last week, after having lunch with another queen mother, I went shopping for, yes, another purple outfit. I was modeling an outfit for the saleslady, including my red hat, which I'd worn at lunch, when a customer came up to me and said, 'I like your purple outfit, but the red hat [shaking her head in the negative] just doesn't go with it.' I must have really surprised her when I started to laugh and thank her profusely. 'Good, good,' I said. 'Thank you, thank you.' Of course, I then explained my reaction. . . ." She told the other customer about the "Warning" poem and the Red Hat

Society, including our concept of "no rules." The other woman replied that not only was she familiar with the poem, but she had it hanging in her own home. Together, she and Jill decided that purple and red look great together. I think a big part of getting older is being able to look at things yourself—not the way society tells you to see things, but the way you yourself see things. From an early age, we learn that purple and red don't go together, but now that we're older, we can see that they do, in fact, go together just great.

7. CULTIVATE AN OPENNESS TO NEW THINGS

What is the surest antidote to boredom? I think it is the ability to be open to new challenges. Some people stay young by trying something they have always wanted to do. Red Hatter Fran Rafter (Girls Just Wanna Have Fun, Menifee, California) chose to mark

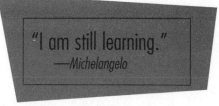

"I am still learning."
—Michelangelo

a major birthday by following through on a lifelong ambition: She parachuted out of an airplane.

Injecting newness into our lives can contribute greatly to our happiness and self-esteem, and give us a sense of joy. Some people might define joy as a frenetic, even frantic emotion. The kind of joy I am referring to might be better defined as a quiet, warm, peaceful satisfaction with one's place in life. I am talking about learning to be satisfied with who we are and with whatever stage of life we have reached. I've learned I will never be perfect, but I am good enough. I have plenty left to do and learn. I am good enough, and this good-enough person is not *done* yet! There is a great deal of happiness and fulfillment to be found in challenging ourselves to continue to grow and learn. That "been there, done that" attitude of bored disinterest is not for us Red Hatters. As long as we are living, there will be new horizons to seek. One sure way to find happiness is to pursue your passions, your deepest interests. Have you formed the habit of putting everything on hold "until . . ."? Have you fallen victim to the great "as soon as . . ." form of self-deception?

What have you always wanted to learn? Where have you always wanted to go? What have you always wanted to have (within reason)? If you are still waiting for the right time to get started doing something, or to acquire something, ask yourself this question: If not now, when? Ladies, it is high time to resurrect and explore old dreams. What were the things you were going to do as soon as you had time? Now *is* the time! If you are making the same old mental excuses that you have made to yourself for years, the time is ripe for action! Fear may well rear its ugly head, but we all know what Franklin Roosevelt said about fear, don't we? While it is true that we may not have the physical energy of our youth, we do have attributes that more than make up for that: determination, patience, humor, wisdom. We can make use of these qualities in the pursuit of our goals.

Here's an analogy: Ruby Redhat (see the sidebar) will help me illustrate my point.

She is demonstrating in a concrete way that each of us has domain over her own hot-air balloon. Sandbags, hung from

Ruby dropping sandbags

the sides of the basket, keep it on the ground. In the same way, we are kept on the ground, prevented from soaring, because we have sandbags (fear, low self-esteem, inertia) weighing down our balloons. If we cast off those sandbags one by

Let it go!

one, our balloons will begin to rise toward the sky, which is where they belong. Ruby says that she actually managed to do this for herself some time ago. She hopes to inspire us to follow her into the rarified atmosphere of freedom from self-limitation. She has certainly inspired me.

While I'm up here on my soapbox, I need to mention that modern bogeyman—the computer. Here is one of those new things that some of us have steadfastly refused even to consider learning anything about. As I have already mentioned, I was one of those naysayers for a while. But necessity forced me to become familiar with the little beast, and now we are fast friends.

I remember a letter I received from Barbara Merfeld (the Mad Hatters of Goldendale, Goldendale, Washington). She wrote that she was intrigued by the Red Hat Society but did not see how she could participate in it without computer access. She had discussed with her two sons the possibility of getting a computer. One son encouraged her. The other commented that it wouldn't be worth getting a computer just to stay in touch with a bunch of "loony toons." I wrote back to Barbara, saying that we could try to keep in touch via handwritten letters, although with the rapid growth we were experiencing, this might soon become impossible. Her next letter declared that she was slapping her red hat on and heading down to the computer store. The next time I heard from her, it was via E-mail! The Red Hat Society has become almost totally dependent on the Internet for its communications. Without it, how could we ever have hoped to form the vast network of connected women that we now have?

My son, Shane, is a computer engineer and software designer, and he told me that the computer industry initially assumed that women in our demographic would never be willing to learn to use its product, and it pretty much wrote us off. But surprise! I recently saw an article by David Andelman, reprinted from the *New York Times*, stating: "Women, ages 55 and older, are adopting the Internet faster than any other age group. . . ." As I keep saying, we are *not done*!

8. EXPRESS YOUR CREATIVITY

Don't stifle creative impulses, no matter how small. Find ways to try out "silly" ideas. How in the world do you know whether or not something will work if you don't try it? See what you can come up with when you bind and gag your inner censor!

The Red Writers (Fairfield, California) is made up of a number of writers. They have come up with a way to combine their talents in a unique way: They are having a terrific time writing a novel together. Each of them writes a few pages, then passes the work in progress on to the next member, who adds to it and also passes it on. In the first chapter of their very first novel, the ladies of an imaginary Red Hat Society chapter solve a murder! From the proposed title of the second chapter, "Chester Roasting on an Open Fire," there may be more imaginary mayhem to come! (Somebody better warn Chester.)

Michele Paiva (Seeing Red, Downington, Pennsylvania) says their chapter has found a creative way to work off the stress of PMS (or, if they are older, "phantom PMS"). They go to the local firing range and shoot at targets.

Some women have exercised their creativity by finding ways to give their original purple-and-red outfits extra flare. Jo Speakman (Wine and Roses, Ontario, Ohio) suggests a creative way to give one hat several different looks: "To give the appearance of having several hats (a change for each month), take a few hair bands and sew different trims on them. Slide one down the crown of the hat—and voilà—new hat in an instant." Aileen Fields (the Rowdy Raconteurs, Palm Springs, California) had much the same idea. She cuts lengths of ribbon to fit the hat's crown, glues pieces of Velcro to each end, and then attaches such things as berries, flowers, birds, or bells to each one.

And let's not forget holidays. They are a perfect excuse to embellish a hat for the appropriate special day. Cassandra Frazelle (the Wild Roses, Huntington Beach, California) wore a hat with an upturned brim to our last train hoot. Within the brim, there were Easter chickens and little plastic eggs nestled in bright green plastic grass. Some of us have snatched up small strings of lights with battery packs (easily hidden) to decorate our hats for Christmas.

My longtime friend and chapter mate Pat Judson found herself without any formal red head wear at a dressy banquet. She solved the solution by wrapping her red-feathered boa around her head, then securing it in several places with bobby pins. Instant Big Bird (except, of course, for the color). I suspect she had watched too many reruns of *Sesame Street* with her daughter!

Gail Fluskey, aka "Violet Bucket" (Vancouver Violets, Vancouver, British Columbia) tells the story of a lady in her chapter who missed a step leaving a Red Hat event and broke both ankles. Even in the midst of misfortune, she found a way to express her creativity. While the doctors and nurses were casting her ankles in the emergency room, she regaled them with tales of the Red Hat Society. Taking the doctor's facetiously offered advice, she opted for bright purple casts!

9. EXERCISE COMPASSION

Self-nurture does not preclude the nurture of others. Though we Red Hatters are learning to practice doing good for ourselves, we will naturally retain the desire to do good for others. And as a result of some self-nurture, we will probably have extra energy for that.

Red Hatters often show compassion for one another. Lavana Jeter (Red Hat Serendipity, Garfield, Arkansas) made a friendly farewell gesture to a neighbor who was about to move away and was a little frightened about her future. In order to create a good memory, and encourage her neighbor to face whatever came next with courage, Lavana dressed in her purple and red and showed up at her friend's door with a large basket containing all of the ingredients for a farewell tea: a teapot of tea, cups, teatime treats, small gifts, and even a crocheted shawl to use as a tablecloth. The ladies sat amid packing boxes and spent an hour sipping tea and tying up the strings of their friendship. Lavana says her friend got out her camera to record their little party and to help her remember the afternoon. She is glad that she followed through on her impulse to treat her departing friend.

Oftentimes, an entire chapter of Red Hatters seizes an opportunity to show one of its members how much it cares. Rose Marie Fischer (Red Hot Roses, St. Paul, Minnesota) experienced the compassion of her chapter mates after her home suffered serious fire damage. On the day of their next get-together, she was almost too depressed to go; she would have preferred to stay in the motel where she and her family were living. But she had promised to pick up another member, so she went, hoping that she could leave early. Before the tea was served, her chapter mates gathered around her and handed her a beautiful rosebud in a vase and a large gift bag. Inside the bag was a decorated shoe box containing thirty-seven beautiful cards—some handmade—expressing love and good wishes, and a coin purse containing money for her to buy a new red hat. It made her feel wonderful to know that these women, most of whom she had known only a short time, cared enough about her to express it so tangibly. Rose Marie writes, "For the rest of the time that we lived in that motel, I carried those cards around with me everywhere, and whenever I needed a pick-me-up, I just started reading my beautiful cards. My cards will be going into a special scrapbook that I can share with everyone as a reminder of how special Red Hatters are, and why the organization is growing so fast."

Marsha Allen (Purple Feathers, Dale City, Virginia) tells one of my favorite Red Hat Society stories:

I just had to share this remarkable experience with you:
On March 9, I was diagnosed with colon cancer, among other things. (The whole thing was a complete surprise. . . . I thought I was having a heart attack!) On March 16, I had sur-

gery to remove one third of my colon. At that time, we found out the cancer had spread.

Before all this happened, I had been talking to my family and some friends about the Red Hat Society and had decided it would be an outstanding idea to start a group here in Woodbridge, Virginia. I found a red hat for myself and then ordered an authentic one for my mother-in-law. (I have since ordered three more for some very supportive friends.)

My hat seems to have taken on a life of its own. When I found out I had to have surgery, my kids (all adults twenty-four to twenty-nine) brought my red hat to the hospital. It suddenly became very important to them to have me wear it as much as possible. I think it became a symbol of my still having fun despite the problems that kept coming up.

I looked absolutely awful in it because I couldn't wear any makeup and couldn't do anything with my usually lousy hair. But I wore it anyway. I wore it in bed while they ran all kinds of tests. At one point, I took it off and put it on a bedside table. One of my kids commented about that. I told him I wasn't particularly happy at that time. Well, the hat was put back on my head and I was informed that I needed to perk up and that the hat would help (as a matter of fact, it *did* help)!

I wore my red hat with my "attractive" hospital garb while waiting to be called to the OR. Quite a few people smiled at me, and I am sure it was because I looked awful!

While recovering from the surgery, I had to do the mandatory walking of the halls. I wore my red hat each time just for effect. It became, as I mentioned, a symbol of fun during hard times.

Anyway, quite a few people at my church were aware of the red hat because I had worn it several times before the emergency set in. Everyone I told about the Red Hat Society thought it was a great idea and wanted me to pursue the organization as soon as I was up to the task.

Today was the first time I was back at church since the surgery. I almost didn't go because I wasn't feeling all that great. Am I

glad I did go. . . . Because when I entered the sanctuary, I immediately saw one of my friends wearing a red hat and a purple
outfit. Then I saw another . . . and then another! I realized the
church was full of them. Overall, there were twenty women wearing red hats and purple outfits scattered throughout the congrega-
tion to support me in my fight against cancer! Isn't that just about
the nicest thing you have ever heard?

What a joy that was. . . . We all felt so good because of this
impromptu showing of support and caring!

Sadly, Marsha lost her fight with colon cancer a year later. During that year, she received the prayers and support from many Red
Hatters across the country, as her story was shared on our Web site.
Many of us came to feel that we knew her wonderful close-knit family, particularly her son Josh, who sent out regular updates on the
family's trials and joys throughout that year. Many of us grieved at
her passing. Not long ago, I received an E-mail from Marsha's
daughter Sarah. She said that she still enjoys reading the cards from
"the many, many groups who sent well-wishes during the last
months of her life." Could we change what Marsha had to go
through? No. But we could be there for her.

As our society has grown, the age range of its members has
expanded, and it now includes a significant number of ladies who are
not able to get out and go places like they used to. Some younger,
more active members of Red Hat Society chapters have spent time
and effort to take tea to some of these ladies. Rosalie Campbell (the
Scarlet Sippers, Canyon Lake, California) tells how her group put on
a Valentine Tea at Maple Ridge Retirement Home in nearby
Hemet. All ten members of the chapter came decked out in their
regalia and bearing baked goodies, teapots, and china. Many of the
home's residents attended in hats they had made in their craft class.
The following Valentine's Day, they treated the residents of a facility
for abused children with a party. Rosalie says that these events have
been the highlight of their outings and that they plan to complete
another "love project" each Valentine's Day. According to her, "Hav-

ing an outreach tea not only reaches out to others in love; it warms our own hearts."

When one is the recipient of compassion bestowed by others, the desire to reciprocate often arises. Fern Hartsell (the Razzle Dazzle Reds, Floyd County, Texas) is featured in her red hat and purple dress as "Miss April" in a calendar published by LifeGift, an organ-donation center located in her state. All of the photographs feature survivors of organ transplants. Fern has received a new liver, for which she is immensely grateful. These days, she concentrates on giving back the love that she received from her community supporters. She volunteers at health fairs, remains active in her church, and donates to an organization that distributes food and clothing to the unfortunate. She says she has found her purpose in life.

10. HAVE COURAGE!

Hey, we know that life is no bed of roses. But we aren't afraid of the tough stuff. We have lived long enough to make it through all kinds of trouble and we have discovered that we have what it takes to get through our miles of bad road.

Sometimes, those who have come through difficult and frightening experiences demonstrate an inspiring gutsiness. Carol Glindeman (Sizzlin' Red Hatters, Euless/Bedford, Texas) writes about one of her chapter members, a woman who demonstrated the results of her ongoing opera lessons at a Red Hat event. Though she had recently undergone a mastectomy, she insisted on participating. She says she wouldn't have missed it for the world.

Luckily, I haven't had to confront something as scary as cancer. But all of us, no matter if we've never held a job in our lives or ever raised our voices, have had to deal with uncomfortable situations. I used to be a timid soul. I knew that I needed to develop a more forceful way of confronting unpleasant situations, but my cowering inner core begged me not to push myself to change. Change is hard, and it hurts. But as I grew older, I longed to develop the courage to confront those who attempted to push me around or made it clear that they didn't respect me. When I entered a mural-painting business with two other artists, it quickly became apparent that none of us had sufficient backbone to compete in the world of business with the "big girls." Why was I afraid to defend Altered Interiors' prices to interior designers and home owners? Why apologize for charging fairly for our time, talent, and abilities? Where did this defensive attitude come from? It was time to practice being that sweetly assertive woman that I longed to be. I told my two partners that I wanted to step forward and deal with the crabbiest customers and the most demanding designers. With my interior coward screaming *"No,"* I began to take the hard phone calls and schedule appointments with the most penurious and disagreeable clients, willing myself to demonstrate the kind of courage I had always admired in others. Basically, I pretended that I was a confident, assertive person and practiced keeping my eye contact steady and my voice level. And I smiled a lot. Did it work? More often than not, it did. Did my level of confidence and courage grow? Absolutely. And my self-respect grew even more. Like the Cowardly Lion, I realized I'd had courage all along.

> "I am an optimist. It does not seem too much use being anything else."
> —*Sir Winston Churchill*

11. MAKE UP FOR THE SOBRIETY OF YOUR YOUTH!

Actually, the "sobriety" of our youth, as the poet puts it, had its good points, as we all agree. A lot of people around us benefited from our dutifulness. But we need to make it up to ourselves, ladies. As Ruby says, there is an awful lot of quirky stuff left to do.

Some may choose to start small, as Nancy Hasse (Vintage Tea Roses, Gainesville, Florida) did. She deviated from the narrow path in the area of food. For a chapter meeting, she ordered red-and-purple-swirled bread from a local bakery and later used some of the bread to make her husband a sandwich for his lunch pail. Purple-and-red bread in your husband's sandwich may not be the wildest way to deviate from the norm, but it is an imaginative beginning. I would guess that he had a bit of a time explaining his purple-and-red egg salad sandwich to his coworkers.

Tootie Krebs (Red Hat Classy Classics, Danville, Indiana) sent me the story of her own wake, which she threw on her sixtieth birthday. She said she wanted to do it while she was still around to enjoy it with her friends and relatives. She rented the local Italian club and decorated it with hundreds of red, purple, and silver balloons, and pink flamingos. She and her guests all wore red and purple. Her friends are still talking about her wake as one of the best parties they have ever attended.

Sheila Garner (the Ruby-Dooetees, Huntington Beach, California) had always longed to go to Paris. When she was laid off from her job, her husband gallantly suggested that she use his frequent-flier miles to fulfill her dream. She says, "I bought a Métro-rail pass and a museum pass in Paris, and had the most wonderful (and selfish) vacation I have ever had! Nobody asked me, 'Are we going to *another* castle today?' or '*Mooooooore* shopping?' Instead of healthy food, I ate French bread and cheese every day, because I loved it. . . . I did everything for me!"

For these women at least, making up for the sobriety of their youth involved nothing shocking or dangerous. It merely meant following the desires of their hearts and taking advantage of sudden opportunities, rather than stifling their impulses. This meant confronting that inner adult lurking within, who undoubtedly came up with all kinds of reasons not to take any chances. But they went ahead and took the opportunity to add a shot of joy and spontaneity to their lives, probably surprising those close to them as well as themselves. Let's hear it for unpredictability!

3

"And in a Supporting Role..."

Ladies and gentlemen, it takes more than one to make a ballet.

—Ninette de Valois

Say what you will, making a marriage work is a woman's business.

—Phyllis McGinley

For the most part, we women live our lives primarily in relationships with others. We are the caregivers of our society. Most of us have been wives. The majority of us have been mothers. A lot of us are now grandparents. We may now be divorced or widowed. Some are still caring for aging parents. The interesting thing about relationships is that although they are paramount, they are not static. We have had to learn to adjust how we relate to others in our lives in various ways as we have all grown older—and up. And the ways in which others relate to us have shifted significantly, as well.

We have also spent our lives working—some inside the home, some inside *and* outside of it. I guess if living is like climbing a hill, we have all reached a high-enough vantage point to be able to look back at where we have been, look one another in the eye, and smile. We did it! Let's give each other a high five!

What kind of woman is attracted to the Red Hat Society? Well, how much time do you have? Red Hatters have emerged from all walks of life and all sorts of backgrounds. In the areas of career, family structure, faith, and political leanings, there is as much variety to be found among Red Hatters as there is in society in general.

When we were little girls, playing with one another, we occasionally squabbled with our friends over differences, and sometimes we even picked up our toys and went home. When we were teenagers, we often competed with one another, mostly over boys. Well, we are grown-ups now and we don't do those things anymore. We freely acknowledge our differences. But we passed through childhood experiences into adulthood during roughly the same era. We have all been exposed to similar familial and cultural messages. We have a large reservoir of common experiences and attitudes. We share so much! We have come to understand one another in ways that render many differences of opinion relatively unimportant. We choose to place our emphasis on all that we have in common, all the ways in which we are basically alike. We Red Hatters have spent years learning to play on the same team.

So, if we disregard differences, what experiences have we shared?

MARRIAGE

Generally, Red Hatters grew up in an era where marriage was a given. Most of us were raised within a nuclear family of some sort and automatically assumed that we would eventually marry and establish a family of our own. That was the model we were used to, and there were strong cultural expectations placed upon us to follow that model. If your childhood took place in the first half of the twentieth century, you probably accepted this pattern and, more than likely, you fulfilled it. The major question was not *whether* you would marry, but *whom* and *when* you would marry. We married at a significantly younger age than many women do now. Most of us grew up before the sexual revolution. We could argue about whether the cultural changes seen since then have been beneficial or harmful to society, but that argument is a bit beside the point. I am merely describing the way things were.

Most of us learned how to live with another person, how to adjust and change in an intimate relationship with a man. Some of us were able to build mutually nourishing long-term marriages; some of us were not so fortunate. Every marriage is a story unto itself. As young wives, we learned that living with a man was totally different from living in a nuclear family or with a female roommate. Although we tried to develop friendships with our husbands (in addition to sexual intimacy), we discovered quite early that, for the most part, a husband, just by virtue of his maleness, cannot relate to us in the same way a good girlfriend can. Men and women, while being essential to each other, are just too different to fully understand the opposite sex. It is for this very reason that the Red Hat Society has grown so rapidly. The similarities found among women are a given. What is it they say? "It takes one to know one."

> "I now have an opportunity to celebrate me, with no other purpose but to relish my women friends. This in no way diminishes our love of spouses, children, or others, but it does provide us with a joyful self to present to them."
> —Judy Davenport
> (Parkville Red Pepper Popsies, Parkville, Missouri)

It has been very interesting to hear of the typical reaction of husbands of Red Hatters. Many men have asked why I don't start a society for them. I always reply that it would take a man, exercising his innate understanding of men, to do that, and I suggest that they get their own group going. Sadly, few have expressed much interest in this, although I have gotten wind of some men's auxiliaries forming here and there. The special way that women bond is fascinating for men to watch, but it's hard for them to emulate. There have also been a number of occasions when men have asked to join Red Hat chapters. I believe that some of them have been dead serious. The Red Hat Society is for women only, although there is no rule against planning an occasional event that may include men. Dottie Manross (the Little Biddy Buddies, Erie, Pennsylvania) says that her chapter occasionally includes their men, but they require them to wear plaid clothing and sloppy slippers. The men call themselves the Silly Slipper Society!

I have heard from several women who experimented with taking husbands and significant others along on their outings, but they felt that the men's presence totally changed the atmosphere, with the women lapsing into deferential roles, trying to ensure that their husbands had a good time. No, ladies, we love our men dearly, but the Red Hat Society is for women! Remember the old cartoons of the little boys in the tree house with the sign, nailed at a haphazard angle, that said NO GIRLS ALLOWED? Well, reverse the sex and the age, and you get the Red Hat Society!

In spite of their exclusion, most of our husbands, and most men in general, are supportive of our participation in our fabulous disorganization. Sid Fields gets my vote for husband of the year—for coming up with a wonderful way to make his wife, Margaret, feel good about reaching her fiftieth birthday. He threw her a surprise party and arranged for her to be presented with her own charter for a new chapter of the Red Hat Society, which, of course, automatically made her a queen mother. She was delighted, and she very quickly established the Valley Drive Venerable Venuses, in their hometown of Albermarle, North Carolina.

O'Naria Youngblood says all of her chapter members' husbands rallied behind the effort of the Red Hat Dollies of Jessup (Jessup, Georgia) when they were preparing for their first meeting. Her husband even ironed a purple outfit for her to wear. I name him runner-up, second only to the marvelous Sid!

Elaine McDonough (Red Hot Red Hats Too, Evanston, Illinois) credits the Red Hat Society's silliness with helping to resurrect a bit of her husband's old wit, which he seemed to have lost after suffering a stroke. She says that he enjoyed listening to her read aloud her E-mails from other Red Hatters, and she read him one concerning a "reduation" ceremony. He asked her what that was, and she explained that it was a graduation ceremony conducted by Red Hatters for their members' fiftieth birthdays. He then asked her why she had never had a reduation. She explained that she hadn't become a Red Hatter until well after her fiftieth birthday, and thus it had been too late to "reduate." She reports that he replied more quickly than she'd expected, saying, "Well, you weren't 'hatriculated'!" He then commented that she was "grandmothered" into the Red Hat Society. Both of them got a good laugh out of that, and Elaine says her heart was warmed by this glimpse of her husband's old self.

Angel Burke (the Improper Bostonians, Boston, Massachusetts) says that her husband is the biggest advocate of the Red Hat Society around. He encourages women who visit their ice-cream shop to join, explaining all about our activities. She says Danny is responsible for several of their new members!

Lucinda Denton (Nonpareils, Knoxville, Tennessee) took the time to summarize her view of this support phenomenon and jotted down the following comments from her chapter members:

"My husband thinks this is the greatest thing I have done since retiring."

"Well, my husband called twice from a hat shop in Vienna, Austria, to see what my head size is. I actually had to measure my head, and he had a red hat made to order."

"Do you know that we stopped at *every* mall between Portland and Boston to find red hats? He didn't complain one time."

Lucinda went on to relate a story about an E-mail she received from someone who called himself "Hubby." This story brought tears to my eyes because of the selfless love this man obviously had for his wife. The man was interested in helping his wife get connected with the Red Hat Society. Although her own chapter had exceeded a manageable number, Lucinda invited the wife to be a guest at their next function and later followed through by helping her start a chapter of her own. Later on, Lucinda learned that this wonderful man had recently received a discouraging medical diagnosis and was looking for ways to build up support for his wife so that she would have people who could help her cope with the challenges that lay ahead of her. This man obviously loved his wife very dearly and understood women's immense need for companionship.

I think men are happy when they know that their wives are happy. While kindness and attention from one's husband is always welcome, we Red Hatters receive similar treatment from other men wherever we go.

Georgia Smith (Blushing Bonnets of Brea, Brea, California) tells of a gentleman whose wife had recently passed away. He approached their group as they toured a museum garden and asked about them. Georgia told him that they were part of a group of ladies devoted to having fun, and that they were required to wear purple outfits with red hats, combinations that didn't match. He responded that his late wife would have loved that: "She would have been right in the middle of it, probably one of the leaders." Georgia asked him if his wife would have met the age requirement, and he replied, "She would have just made it!" As he walked away, he told them, "Enjoy every day, ladies. . . . Enjoy every day." Georgia's answer is, "I do. . . . I do!"

It seems rare indeed to hear of a husband who is *not* highly supportive. In fact, many men seem fascinated and delighted with our group. They enjoy seeing their wives in lovely hats and brilliant clothing. I also think they appreciate the sparkle that they see in their wives' eyes and the playful side that emerges as their wives really get into Red Hatting.

One Red Hatter, who shall remain anonymous (her husband

might kill her if she named him), has a husband who apparently approves *very* heartily of her involvement in the Red Hat Society. She says that she placed a mail order for two boas, one red and one purple, then hurried home every day, hoping that they had arrived. Her husband was enlisted to check with the post office daily to see if the package had come. Every day for almost two weeks, she was disappointed. Then, one day, she hurried home and called out as she entered the house, "Did they come?" She received no answer. She rushed into the family room, to find her husband dancing on the coffee table, wearing her two boas and *only* her two boas! Alas, he refused to have his picture taken in this ensemble! She says that she is considering ordering more boas, just so she can see an encore of the "boa dance"!

Even young single men think that we Red Hatters are "totally cool." Kathy Langley (D.A.M.S.E.L.S., the Villages, Florida) relates that the security guard who works at the same bank as she does actually went to the Red Hat Society Web site and ordered her a CD of our theme song as well as a Red Hat Society T-shirt for Christmas! Kathy says, "Even a twenty-five-year-old bachelor respects the Red Hat Society."

MOTHERHOOD

It is often said that a good mother is one who works herself out of a job. So most of us are now empty nesters. But we have shared the trials and tribulations of motherhood, as well as the deep satisfactions and joys, and this commonality forms a strong bond among us. In his novel *Brave New World,* Aldous Huxley portrayed motherhood as such a negative thing that the very word *mother* conveyed disgust. And it did seem, at least for a while, that motherhood was going out of style in this country—at least full-time motherhood. Those of us who had chosen to stay home, perhaps putting budding careers on hold, were made to feel undervalued and unappreciated by our society, if not by our families.

But we all know that our child-rearing years were among our best. We were the bakers, the laundresses, the chauffeurs, and the den mothers. We were there to serve them ginger ale and crackers when they had the stomach flu and to put Band-Aids on their boo-boos when they fell.

What is there in the process of becoming a mother, raising children, and nurturing a husband and family that changes a woman so profoundly? We learn to give unstintingly of ourselves, putting our own desires aside, often not even taking the time to discover what those desires might be. This giving of oneself is a very beautiful thing, and those of us who have done it would not choose differently if we had that choice to make again. Deep down inside, we know that what we did was right and good and that it made us better people.

There was a story in *National Geographic* several years ago that illustrated the instinctive way that mothers (of whatever species) shield and nurture their young. The story dealt with the aftermath of a forest fire in Yellowstone National Park. A forest ranger came across a small bird on the ground, covered with ashes. When he prodded the little body with a stick, it fell over, revealing three tiny chicks, alive and unharmed, which the little mother had sheltered with her wings while the fire raged around them. Do mothers routinely do that sort of thing? Yes, they do. Are they glad to have that opportunity? Yes, of course.

This adorable story by an anonymous author circulated on the Internet not long ago:

Angel

Up in Heaven, a child was ready to be born. The child asked God, "I know you are sending me to earth tomorrow, but how can I survive there? I am so small and helpless."

God replied, "I have chosen a special angel for you there. She will love you and take care of you."

"Here in Heaven, Lord, I don't do anything but sing and smile. What will I do on earth? I won't know how to sing the songs down there."

"Your angel will sing for you," God replied, "and she'll teach you how to sing, too. And you'll learn to laugh as well as smile. Your angel and I will take care of that."

"But how will I understand what people say to me? I don't know a single word of the language they speak."

"Your angel will say the sweetest things you will ever hear, and she will teach you, word by word, how to speak the language."

"And when I want to talk to you?"

"Your angel will gently place your little hands together and teach you how. That's the simplest language of all. It's called prayer."

"Who will protect me there, God?"

"Your angel is soft and gentle, but if something threatens you, there is no stronger force on earth than the power she'll use to defend you."

"I'll be sad, not getting to see you anymore."

"I will always be next to you, even though you can't see me. And your angel will teach you the way to come back to me if you stray."

Then it was time to go. Excited voices could be heard from the earth, anticipating the child's arrival. In a hurry, the babe asked softly, "Oh, God, if I must go, please tell me my angel's name."

And God replied, "You will call your angel Mommy."

It is a beautiful thing to be a mother. But it isn't always easy or fun. And when we remember our years as "Mommy," some of the memories may be less than sentimental. I vividly remember a conversation that took place between my daughter, Andrea, and me when she was about four years old. We were discussing her older brother's firmly declared intentions of becoming a doctor when he grew up. Since the age of three, he had been carrying a little metal box around, which he referred to as his medical kit, filled with

Band-Aids and a jar of Noxzema. When the neighboring children suffered scrapes and bruises, they came banging on our door for "Dr. Shane," and he left the house in a dead run on his mission of mercy. (Later in his life, an interest in computers nudged aside the ambition to have a medical career.) I asked Andrea what she wanted to be when she grew up. She scrunched up her little face thoughtfully and declared, "I want to be just like you, Mommy. I want to be nothing." I think I might rather have been punched in the stomach at that moment. Of course, part of me realized that my little girl loved me and thought I was valuable, but another part of me reeled a little from the knowledge that she thought I didn't really do anything.

I wasn't content with her answer, so I decided to ask my eight-year-old son what *he* thought I did. His answer was very quick in coming: "You clean things—the house, our clothes, and me." Ouch! This led to some soul-searching on my part. How could I possibly let myself feel so bad as a result of listening to my precious children's opinions of me? Well, of course it wasn't their words alone; it was the reinforcement of my fears that society as a whole didn't much respect my career choice.

That same summer, my husband, by virtue of his skill as a sales-man, won a trip to England. During the course of a boat trip on the Thames, our tour guide was encouraging conversation among our group, and she asked each person what he or she did for a living. When she came to me, I answered, "I am a wife and mother." Her smile froze, and she very abruptly turned to someone else. She seemed embarrassed for me! I can still feel the diminishment of self that I felt at that moment.

I feel fairly certain that a lot of us who stayed home when our children were small had experiences like that. It is unpleasant to sense that your chosen career is seen by others as insignificant. Even though we knew, in our own hearts and minds, that our job was highly important, the disrespect still smarted. This unattributed story, also found on the Internet, expresses one woman's unique solution to feelings of insufficiency:

Go, Mom!

A few months ago, when I was packing up the children at school, another mother I knew well rushed up to me. Emily was fuming with indignation. "Do you know what you and I are?" she demanded. Before I could answer, she blurted out the reason for her question. It seemed she had just returned from renewing her driver's license. . . . The woman recorder had asked her to state her occupation, saying, "What I mean is, do you have a job, or are you just a . . ."

"Of course I have a job," snapped Emily. "I'm a mother."

"We don't list 'mother' as an occupation," said the recorder emphatically.

I forgot all about her story until one day I found myself in the same situation, this time at our town hall. The clerk was obviously a career woman, poised, efficient. "And what is your occupation?" she probed.

What made me say it, I do not know. The words simply popped out. "I'm a research associate in the field of child development and human relations."

The clerk paused, ballpoint pen frozen in midair, and looked up as though she had not heard right. I repeated the title slowly, emphasizing the most significant words. Then I stared with wonder as my pompous announcement was written in bold black ink on the official questionnaire.

"Might I ask," said the clerk with new interest, "just what you do in your field?"

Coolly, without any trace of fluster in my voice, I heard myself reply, "I have a continuing program of research [what mother doesn't?] in the laboratory and in the field. [Normally, I would have said indoors and out.] I'm working for my master's [the whole darned family] and already have four credits [all daughters]. Of course, the job is one of the most demanding in the humanities [any mother care to disagree?] and I often work fourteen hours a day [twenty-four is more like it]. But the job is more challenging than most run-of-the-mill careers and the rewards are in satisfaction rather than just money."

There was an increasing note of respect in the clerk's voice as she completed the form, then stood and personally ushered me to the door. As I drove into our driveway, buoyed up by my glamorous new career, I was greeted by my lab assistants—ages thirteen, seven, and three. Upstairs, I could hear our new experimental model (six months) in the child-development program testing out a new vocal pattern. I felt triumphant! I had scored a beat on bureaucracy! And I had gone on the official record as someone more distinguished and indispensable to mankind than "just another mother."

The emotional rewards of motherhood have been so great that this lack of respect from our culture has paled in comparison. The special bond that forms between a woman and her little children is priceless. Some of the warmth that I refer to is expressed in the following essay, written by my friend (and Red Hat queen) Jean Hedrick (RH Society Gals, Whittier, California):

> The special bond of Mother's Day caused me to be reminded that this most sentimental of holidays encompasses many phases. Our daughters, each of whom is a mother, are in a particularly delightful stage of motherhood. Of course there is that first Mother's Day, when you are convinced that you deserve every accolade that comes your way. But the rewards are greater as time goes by. Let me explain.
>
> Lori, our firstborn, came into church this past Mother's Day in a nice summer dress and heels, wearing necklaces that were obviously plastic. After a hug and greeting, I inquired about the necklaces.
>
> "Mother's Day gift?" I asked.
>
> "Yes," she exclaimed. "Amber and Nathaniel gave them to me. They even glow in the dark."
>
> It seems her children had been saving their Chuck E. Cheese

coupons for a couple of years and were able to turn them in for two whole packs of heart-shaped glow-in-the-dark beads.

When I complimented Amber on the necklace at dinner, she explained further: "We strung a pink one, then a blue one, then a yellow one, then a green one." She was so proud. She told how they had gotten the beads and how she and her brother had worked together to make this memory for their mommy.

That necklace will be one of Lori's treasures for the rest of her life. It brought back memories of some of my treasures—a garden rock paperweight painted brightly with the word mom on it, a felt needle holder tied with a shoestring. Why is it we never want to get rid of those treasures?

As I commented to Julie, our second-born child, about the necklace, she asked me if I had seen her brooch. As a matter of fact, I had noticed a nicely shining lapel pin. Upon close scrutiny, I discovered the pin had been made by five-year-old Tessa from three or four puzzle pieces. She had glued them together and added glitter, making a lovely pattern on the top piece. A small pin was glued to the back, as well.

"Tessa gave it to me this morning. Isn't it great?" Julie asked.

I agreed it was eye-catching and that it totally belied its humble origin. I received the loveliest cards and scented gifts from my three children—cards that spoke of gratitude, of modeling, of closeness, and love. They were wonderful. I felt duly honored.

There is just something about glow-in-the-dark necklaces and puzzle-piece pins.

Those of us who raised families, whether we also worked outside the home or not, have all had the experience of learning to live with another person, bearing and caring for children, and helping craft a family. Most of us have felt the pangs of separation as our children gained confidence and left us to embark on lives of their own. So now, parenting is done. All of us can identify with the strange period of silence that we had to live through while we acclimated to this next stage of life. Perhaps we did a bit of mourning.

I remember when my older child, Shane, was about to leave for college. I shared his rising excitement about the new stage of life that he was entering. We shopped together for dorm necessities and discussed class schedules. We visited the campus of his chosen school and strolled its wooded paths. My husband and I accompanied Shane to a weekend orientation for new students and their parents, and we were able to get a clear preview of the adventures that awaited our son. The day came to deliver him and his mound of possessions to the dorm, help him get his first groceries, and set up his computer. Then we hugged good-bye and set off with our daughter on the hundred-mile drive home. Later that evening, I went into his old room, sat on his bed, and listened to the silence. The walls were bare of the usual posters. The shelves were empty, save for a few discarded remnants of his boyhood. I felt a heaviness in my chest as I realized that all of our excited preparation had led, inevitably, to this reality: There was one less child in our home. He would be only a visitor from now on. I felt great pride in his accomplishments, in his successful embarkation upon a college career, his growing self-sufficiency. But this warm glow was tempered by a visceral feeling of loss. One child launched, one to go.

Four more years passed like a blur, and it was time to deliver Andrea to *her* dormitory! The experience of sitting on the bed was repeated, but with an even greater sense of finality. There were no more children to raise. Neither the phone nor the doorbell would ring so much any more. And the house was very, very quiet.

I have read many wonderful, witty pieces on the joys of getting one's children launched, and, in my more reasonable moments, I agree completely. But any mother and father will testify to the pain that parents must endure for a certain period of time when their children make the inevitable separation from the family home.

My friend Jean Hedrick recently shared another of her special poems with me. It describes the torrent of emotions she felt when she unearthed a tiny plastic soldier while digging in her garden. It had obviously been lost years back by her now-adult son. She took it into her kitchen, washed it, and placed it where she would see it whenever she prepared meals.

Buried Treasure

The little soldier on the windowsill
    stands brave and stoic
    poised and ready
      rifle steady
        . . . always still.
Fallen in days of Flower Garden Wars
    fought in furrow trenches
    and rocky ridges
    arrayed in olive drab plastic
    from helmet to heart.
Buried by little boy hands
    amid great pomp and pretend sadness.
Resurrected as years brought change to the flower
    garden, only to remind that change comes to
    the boy, as well.
Now the little soldier on the windowsill
    stands brave and stoic
    poised and ready
    rifle steady
      . . . always still.
Risen to remind not of flower garden wars
    but present battles of the mind
    battles of a different kind—
      of calculus and chemistry
      loneliness and love
      careers and mates and broken dates
    as parents' prayers become the ally of
The little soldier on the windowsill
    brave and stoic
    poised and ready
    rifle steady
      . . . always still.

We continue in our long-running role of mother as we grow older, but we find ourselves functioning in an advisory capacity only (and only when asked, at that). We are now our children's peers, and we must work for a way to relate to them in new ways, without the mantle of parental authority.

When my husband and I participated in our son's first parents weekend at his college, a speaker mentioned that parents often make a mistake when relating to adult and near-adult children by appearing to lean on them too much for support. He said that kids will call home less and less if they get the impression that their parents are too dependent on them. They feel much freer to get on with their new lives if they know that their parents are busy with their own activities and are not just sitting by the phone, waiting to snatch up the receiver and complain of their loneliness. I would imagine, since the speaker emphasized this point, that this is a common mistake parents make. I am sure that no parents want to feel like a millstone around their children's necks. We want our children to seek us out when they genuinely want to communicate with us, not just when they feel guilty.

What do our children think of our participation in the Red Hat Society? I often hear from women whose children and grandchildren wholeheartedly support them in their membership. Our children love to see us involved in life, growing as we experience new opportunities. When we do talk to them, they enjoy it when we have stories of our own experiences to include in the conversation. They like knowing that we have plenty of peers in our lives to help fulfill our need for companionship, and plenty of activities to stimulate us and occupy our attention. We Red Hatters often have interesting, amusing stories to share with our younger relatives, and it reassures them to see us living full lives. There is no question that they find us more fun to be with. I doubt that any mother wants to saddle a child with the guilty responsibility of filling her time for her.

Sara Knight (the Yellow Roses of Texas, Howe, Texas) posted the following on the Red Hat Society Web site:

When I was fifty-four, I was diagnosed with MS. At that time, my son, Dustin, was only twenty. I set out not to let my illness affect how he lived his life. I wanted him to make decisions based on what he wanted to do with his life and not on how he thought it might affect me. I didn't want him to worry about me or, worse yet, to feel sorry for me. I never wanted to see pity in his eyes, only love and respect. When I founded the Yellow Roses of Texas chapter of the Red Hat Society and Dustin saw me planning and going to luncheons, talking about shopping for red hats and purple clothes, telling him about all the happenings on the Queen Mother Board, I could tell that he was glad for me, but also relieved for himself. He never said anything, but when he talked about his plans for himself, he was able to share them with me without feeling bad about leaving Texas and me. Dustin left this morning, driving a U-Haul with all his stuff and dragging a trailer with his motorcycle, headed toward Phoenix. . . . He can leave knowing that his mom is out doing things and having a good life.

Sara says that we need to live our lives to the fullest, and give our children and other family members permission to live their lives with gusto, too: "The Red Hat Society gives women the opportunity to *live life large.*" I am sure that Sara has grieved Dustin's going. But she is justifiably proud of herself for enabling him to claim his freedom guilt-free.

Fortunately, there is a wonderful compensation waiting for many of us who have said good-bye to our children.

GRANDMOTHERHOOD

Unfortunately, the mothers of both my parents passed away long before I was born. All of my life, I have wondered what it would have been like to have a grandmother. I remember feeling a longing bordering on envy when I saw my playmates interact with their grandmas. Just the word *grandma* sounded beautiful to me. Perhaps I may have idealized grandmothers, but I do believe that little children derive very special affirmation and support from their grandmothers (and grandfathers, too, of course). From what I saw, grandmas had time to rock their grandchildren; they had time to "waste" with them, too, perhaps gathering colored leaves in the fall or reading a beloved book three times in a row.

Modern grandmothers may not be quite as available, at least on a full-time basis, as were the grandmas of old. But the ones I know still deserve the magical status that their grandchildren accord them. My friends who are already grandmothers consider their grandchildren one of the greatest gifts that come with advancing age, and I think I understand what they mean.

Many Red Hatters have fond memories of their grandmothers. Marcia Cloyd shares some of her memories about the years her grandma lived with her family. She says that her granny outfitted her and her sister and two brothers with hand-knit slippers and presided over their races up and down the freshly waxed upstairs hallway. Grandma's pride in the "mirror shine" of the floor was an extra benefit. And every Sunday, after noon dinner, her granny would take Marcia upstairs to her room for a few of her special candies and a session of trying on granny's hat collection. Marcia says it was the red one that she especially liked to wear. When her grandmother passed away, she left a note for Marcia tucked into the red hat. It said, "Marcia, I'm leaving you your favorite red hat and want you to know that as you grow up, you will have to run in many a race. You'll go to school and college and you will have to compete to get ahead and accomplish the things we've spoken of. I believe that you will grow to be a woman of conviction and competence and yet still find time to try on the red hat. I hope so. Love, Granny." Years later, as a single mother, whenever she felt particularly discouraged, Marcia would sit at the small dressing table her granny had left her and put on the red hat. She says that it made her feel "strong, smart, and even, at times, pretty all over. . . ." Grandma's red hat still warms her heart, as well as her head, and it has also come in handy for Red Hat Society outings!

The following story, related by Phyllis Mosher (D.A.M.S.E.L., the Villages, Florida) also expresses the special quality of a grandma, this time from the viewpoint of the grandmother herself:

> My two eight-year-old granddaughters were going to meet in Florida at my house for a reunion. They had not seen each other for two years because one family was living in Australia. I wanted this to be a memorable occasion for both girls. Since they both love horses (don't all little girls?), and I am only a few miles from Ocala, Florida, which is horse country, I made my plan. I would combine my love of the Red Hat Society and their love of horses. I bought the girls lavender outfits with pink hats, with all of the accessories for a dress-up party. Of course, I wore purple and my red western hat. I rented a red carriage, which was pulled by a Clydesdale named Bill. We were taken on a tour of several horse farms. After our exciting carriage ride, we had lunch at the Horse and Hound, where all the horsey people eat. We then proceeded to downtown Ocala to view the life-size horses that were painted by artists and displayed in the community. That evening, I put out all of my red hats, boas, gloves, and jewelry and the girls put on a fashion show for the rest of the family. I am sure that I have two future Red Hatters with memories of a very special day.

Although Phyllis and her granddaughters are separated in age by many decades, Phyllis was able to draw very close to them in spirit—closer perhaps than those who were nearer in chronological age. Perhaps her involvement in the Red Hat Society, with its attendant encouragement to find and nurture her inner child, enhanced her ability to connect with her grandchildren and, by extension, to make wonderful memories for (and with) them. Certainly the Red Hat Society's fondness for dress-up links us, in spirit, to our grandchildren.

Another red-hatted grandma, Ginger Stimson (Royal Rubies, Fredonia, New York), recently welcomed her daughter, her husband, and their two boys into her home. They had moved away from the Manhattan area after September 11, 2001, in search of a haven in another state. She says that what she enjoys most about this arrangement is watching her grandsons learn about life and their world: "Everything is new to them and they want to know about everything around them. They don't like to be rushed, so we operate on the same speed a lot of the time. They are very inquisitive about nature, and I love teaching them about how birds build nests, how the squirrels store acorns for the winter, and the best way to pick flowers for a bouquet for their mommy. I took them to the library for the first time to share my love of books, and I got to take them fishing for the first time to share my love of nature. Now they love to read and just love fishing in the nearby creek. I help get them off to kindergarten and day care in the morning and get to hear all about their little problems, which seem so important to them. And one of our favorite times is helping them get their bath in the evening. Their smiling faces and sparkling eyes make my heart smile and fill me with an indescribable joy. While this may seem ordinary and boring to some, seeing life through a child's eyes gives life a beauty that I had lost."

Observation: Grandparents + grandchildren = magic!

CAREERS

A lot of us have added careers to the already-full lives we have had. Here again, Red Hatters have done it all. Sally Ann Eaves (Tea Time Tootsies, Arvada, Colorado) spent many years in the air force, and eventually she attained the rank of brigadier general (all the while also caring for a husband and three sons). She says she has traded a flight hat for a red hat, dress blues for a purple outfit, and combat boots for satin slippers.

Another former member of the air force is Winnette Reck Payne (Les Rouges Chapeaux, Fort Collins, Colorado). She was a certified parachute rigger for the air force, and she later learned to fly. After time out for mothering, she went back to school and earned a degree in English, which enabled her to teach, earn her master's degree, and coordinate a language-arts program.

Red Hatters have held an extremely wide variety of jobs, some of them in groundbreaking fields for women. One member was one of the first women to become an installation-repair person with the telephone company. She says, "Yes, I did climb telephone poles and install service to people's homes and pull drop wires and all that stuff. . . ." She later launched a second career in the field of health care.

When I say that our members have held a variety of jobs, I couldn't be more serious. Some of them still hold those jobs. Diane Jones (the Leading Ladies, San Antonio, Florida) is especially proud of two of her members, Sister Helen and Sister Irma of Holy Name Monastery, Order of St. Benedict. She sent us photos of the two nuns. In one, dated 1956, they are shown as novitiates; in the other, dated 2002, they are shown as Red Hatters. Diane has even written an original poem to commemorate their membership in her chapter:

Our Sisters

Lest you think the life of a nun
Is all prayer, work, and no fun,
Let us put that rumor to bed,
Here're our Sisters in purple and red!

Our ranks include dentists, doctors, professors, secretaries, teachers, and attorneys. We have saleswomen, judges, accountants, artists, and business owners. You name the job; we have a Red Hatter who has done it, or is still doing it. The work world is yet another thing many of us have in common.

So at this point in our lives, many Red Hatters have experienced childhood, marriage, motherhood, and perhaps careers, as well. And yet there is another of life's challenges that many of us now face. We are aware that many of our members are empty nesters, but now these women are called upon to spend much of their time as caregivers for their elderly parents. They desperately need some self-care, and Red Hat Society gatherings give them a much-needed, lighthearted break.

Interestingly, some Red Hatters have found a way to integrate caring for elderly mothers by having their mothers join a chapter right along with them. Billie Shalvey (Darlin' Dames, Amarillo, Texas) says she was having trouble getting her eighty-two-year-old mother out and about . . . "until we joined the Darlin' Dames! Now she is kicking up her heels and asking where we are going next!"

Donna Madrid (California Red Queens, Chatsworth, California) writes that she joined a chapter initially for the benefit of her eighty-five-year-old mother, who has Alzheimer's disease. Donna writes: "She is getting worse, and there is nothing I can do about that. But once a month, she puts on that purple pantsuit and that red hat and she is ready to roll. . . . She laughs the afternoon away. She doesn't remember the next day, but it doesn't matter, as I have pictures of each gathering for her scrapbook, and as she sits all day (on days I must work), she can go through that book and see all of the fun she was having and remember it all over again. She had a Red Hat Birthday, with all the guests attending in their regalia, for her eighty-fifth. What fun!"

VOLUNTEERING

There is one more way in which a great many of our generation have nurtured others—volunteerism. Many of us have spent countless hours serving on committees, attending meetings, making phone calls, and taking collection envelopes door-to-door. We have been room mothers, den mothers, meal deliverers, and everything else you

"Altruism: the principle or practice of unselfish concern for or devotion to the welfare of others."
—*The Random House Dictionary of the English Language*

can name. This is another area of activity for which we can, and should, give ourselves credit. Our members continue to give liberally of themselves in the service of many charitable causes, both in their churches and communities. We are by no means finished giving.

The same dictionary quoted above defines the opposite of altruism as "Egoism: the valuing of one's personal interest above that of all others." Red Hatters plead "not guilty" to this! The Red Hat Society was not formed in *opposition* to altruism. What it *does* provide is a *recess from* it. You may have heard it said that "All work and no play makes Jack a dull boy." Well, it makes Jill a dull girl, too! We don't believe that carving out playtime for ourselves should be viewed as selfish, either by ourselves or by others. Play and silliness put some spice back into our lives and enable us to resume our caregiving with renewed energy and enthusiasm—just as soon as we get back from recess!

Marge Miller (Quirky Ladies, North Tustin, California) writes about her chapter members in a way that illustrates the need many of us have for this recess. She says that they have a queen mother who is always busy and is an inspiration to all of them. They have a member who took care of her parents for fourteen years in order to keep them out of a nursing home. One of their members is a single mother who has devoted her life to many foster children, as well as to her own child. One of their ladies is a victims' aide, who goes to the scene of accidents and helps the friends and families of victims who have no one else to help them. Another regularly delivers meals to shut-ins. One entertains for the elderly. One does charity work for a children's hospital, and another sews teddy bears and pillows for children with cancer. As Marge puts it, "So many ladies doing for others all their lives and now taking time for themselves, while still doing for others."

Having said this, I need to add that some Red Hat Society chapters do commit group acts of kindness from time to time. That generosity just leaks out sometimes. And far be it from the Red Hat Society to dictate that any chapter *can't* perform good deeds. As I've said, we have no rules.

The Red Hot Flashes of Greenville (South Carolina) painted a house, which had been built entirely by women, for Habitat for Humanity. They contributed a new washer and dryer for the new home owner, as well. As Queen Dianne Batson writes, "I think it is important for all to know that even though we thrive on the fun part of Red Hatting, we actually go much, much deeper than that."

Several chapters have visited their local nursing homes and brightened the residents' lives by sharing the Red Hat spirit with them. Queen Linda Leopold of Bodacious Babes (Amarillo, Texas) sent a description of the special Mother's Day Tea they gave at a nursing home. She says that they sang songs about mothers, read a "Mothers Prayer," and drank tea and ate strawberries dipped in chocolate. Two of the guests asked if they could join their chapter.

Since great minds think alike, I guess great hearts also feel similar emotions.

Marilyn Young-Pruter's chapter, the Cape Dames (Cape Coral, Florida), joined two other chapters, the Red Hat Madams and the Red-Crested, Double-Breasted Purple Chickadees, to serve a special tea at the Coral Trace Nursing Home. They gave each lady an honorary membership, a red hat, and a corsage of red carnations and purple ribbons. They also took pictures of each resident in her new red hat and put each photo in a special frame as a gift. The next day, when Marilyn returned to pass out additional frames, she was touched to see rows of ladies attending their Sunday church service wearing their hats and their corsages again. She said she experienced a sensation flow through her body that felt "like the touch of God." There is certainly no denying that giving grants the reward of great satisfaction to the giver.

There are plenty of ways to help others while showing yourselves a good time. Queen Bee Barbara Haltenhof (Jewels of D.E.N.I.A.L., St. Louis, Missouri) says that three of their members are breast cancer survivors, and their chapter participated in the Komen Race for the Cure, the ladies decked out in their "jewel"-encrusted red ball caps and their purple shirts. This provided them all with a way both to support an excellent cause and to get to enjoy the great outdoors with their whole group.

There are many other stories that demonstrate even more varied ways Red Hatters have found to enjoy one another's company while giving to others at the same time. These more serious undertakings have their place within the Red Hat Society as a whole, but they are usually pretty disorganized and sporadic, which is just fine! It occurs to me that maybe even just showing our colorful outfits and bright spirits in public promotes goodwill in and of itself as we spread cheer and smiles among those who encounter us!

So, the message is: Do as your spirits move you, Red Hatters. If you enjoy committing an occasional act of kindness in your red-and-purple regalia, you are encouraged to do so! On the other hand, if you want to do your contributing to society on days when you don't happen to be wearing a red hat, that's just hunky-dory, too! Once again, may I remind you: *No Rules!*

4

The Old Gray Mare Just Ain't What She Used to Be

Time may be a great healer, but it is a lousy beautician.
—Anonymous

Wrinkled was not one of the things I wanted to be when I grew up.
—Anonymous

Nature gives you the face you have at twenty; it is up to you to merit the face you have at fifty.
—Coco Chanel

The Red Hat Society began as a disorganization for those of us who have reached the half-century mark. Now here is something every one of us is in on: We are now, as the poem says, "practicing" to be old. But Dr. Pauline Abbott, the director of the Ruby Gerentology Center (notice the serendipitous name), affiliated with California State University, Fullerton, has shared fascinating information with me. She cites studies that show that older women, particularly baby boomers, do not want to be perceived as old in the same way and at the same age as our mothers were.

Women who are over fifty in the twenty-first century are quite different from women over fifty in the past generations in terms of our function in society. We have been having our children later; many of us have combined careers with marriage and children. We are staying active and involved in the outside world longer, and are not considering ourselves "over the hill" nearly as early. Now, as we grapple with midlife issues, we find ourselves victims of the pervasive atmosphere of the "culture of youth" that some of us helped to perpetuate when we were young. I think baby boomers have always considered themselves special. It was they who coined the phrase "Never trust anyone over thirty." Since I missed being lumped in with them by a couple of years, I remember feeling as if I was leaving my own youth behind when I turned thirty, as though life was going to be all downhill from that point on.

We need to find new, more palatable ways to age. Since we have no role models to show us how to do this, we are peer mentoring, looking at one another and saying, "Now, how do we do this?" We are watching and consulting one another, figuring out how to age without acting old. Surely, we can reinvent the process of aging to suit ourselves, or at least find a way to make it more user-friendly. Choosing our attitude toward the inevitable aging process is challenging. But here again, we do have a choice. As I see it, there are three aspects of human beings: the physical, the mental, and the spiritual.

PHYSICAL AGING

Even though we have all grown up surrounded by older women—mothers, aunts, neighbors—the changes in our own bodies still seem to come as a bit of a shock to us.

A few years ago, I was brought up short when I went shopping with my sister, Jane Farrington, for summer clothes. She and I bear a strong resemblance to each other, having the same coloring and similar faces and figures. What looks good on one of us probably flatters the other, as well. I was trying on a sleeveless garment and Jane, sitting in the dressing room with me, exclaimed in dismay, "Oh no, we're getting old arms!" Whose arms do you think she was looking at right then? Strange as it seems to me now, I remember feeling a jolt of shock and surprise. I wasn't old yet! How could this be happening? I realize now that, without consciously being aware of it, I had thought of old age as a place we all eventually wind up—not as the final step in a gradual process of aging. Up until that time, I had felt pretty good about myself. I had kept my weight down (but now it was creeping up); I wore makeup conscientiously every day; my hair didn't have much gray in it (or did it?). Some part of me must have assumed that if I didn't give in to the aging process, it wouldn't occur until I was *really* ancient! (I wonder, if pinned down, how old I would have said that was.) Why is it that we somehow perceive ourselves as being immune from the inevitable?

Once the veil of denial was lifted, I slowly found the courage to face some other unwelcome truths. The veins in my hands were becoming unattractively prominent; my never-perfect thighs had gone from a five (on a scale of ten) to a two; when I parted my hair and examined the part and the hair at my temples, there was more gray than I had noticed before. I needed to stop this train of thought immediately. It was just getting too depressing! We have all been there, right? We need to *get on* with it.

I began a mental struggle with myself. As had happened before many times in my life, I had seen a new reality that had to be faced and somehow accepted, so I could just proceed with my life. I needed to make peace with myself and my body. How much of what I was seeing was it possible for me to change? Well, the hair color was a no-brainer, thank goodness. At first, I just covered the gray with dye that matched my original dark brown hair color. In the last couple of years, this earlier solution has given way to shades of dark blond and lighter brown because all that dark hair was too harsh for my face. I wasn't ready to be gray, but it did make sense to follow nature's example and go lighter. So this was really just a modified method of accepting reality.

The weight? My wonderful female gynecologist, who is in the Red Hat age range, too, tells me that a certain amount of weight gain is almost inevitable for a postmenopausal woman on hormone-replacement therapy (that would be me). But she says it shouldn't get out of hand if I make good food choices and control my sweet tooth and my portions. (Oh no, common sense!) But even if a woman in our age group manages to control her weight, we all know that the body's shape *will* change. The waist will thicken, the breasts will sag, and the facial muscles will slacken. Gravity will have its way with all of us. This is getting a little grim; the truth often is! But we are brave, courageous Red Hatters. The truth about physical aging may be a bitter pill, but the sooner we get it down, the sooner we can forget about it and determine to concentrate on the many wonderful things that we have in our lives here and now.

It is interesting that it is only our physical appearance that reliably betrays our chronological age to others. So whenever the subject of aging arises, one's appearance is the first thing to be noted. We forget that this aspect of a person constitutes only one-third of one's being. The other two-thirds, the mental and the spiritual, cannot be so easily detected or understood. So the fear of aging seems to be primarily the fear of looking old, or being thought of as old and irrelevant by those around us. As women, we see physical aging as the enemy. After all, it concerns the steady, inevitable deterioration of the face and body. Those two things have been extremely important to us ever since childhood. Like it or not, women in our society are automatically pigeonholed on the basis of those attributes. Who wants to be judged a two on a scale of one to ten? Yikes! Could there be anything worse for a female in our culture?

The relentless self-criticism to which we women subject ourselves begins early in life. My daughter, Andrea, began modeling professionally at the age of fifteen. Over a period of years, I accompanied her to countless auditions and photo shoots, where I was able to observe first-hand the self-doubt that this atmosphere produces in attractive young girls. Time and time again, I watched a roomful of beautiful girls submit themselves for consideration for a single job. Eventually, one girl would be chosen. Lovely as all of those girls were, their self-esteem rarely jibed with their appearance. They were mercilessly critical of themselves, each seeing the others as more attractive than she was. The girl chosen was made up and coiffed to within an inch of her life by professionals, then photographed to the best possible advantage by highly trained photographers using the best lighting techniques. Any tiny imperfections that survived the cosmetic process were airbrushed away for the final advertisement. And remember, the average age of these gorgeous young women was usually between fourteen and twenty! It is such photos that make up the standard that the rest of us compare ourselves to, not only when we are young but also as we get older! Not even young models look that good, and yet we think that we should.

As we get older, we continue to have difficulty learning to have mercy on ourselves. Maybe we accept the fact that we cannot look like the girls on the covers of fashion magazines, but we still set impossible standards for ourselves. There are quite a few publications that have appeared in recent years that are supposedly aimed at midlife women. One of these magazines publishes in each issue a statement guaranteeing that all of their models are over forty. Okay so now we get more realistic images to emulate, right? No. We get great beauties, women who turned forty last week, work out with personal trainers, eat nothing but lettuce, and are the beneficiaries of the best hairstyling, makeup, lighting, and photography techniques—and sometimes the best plastic surgery. These models pose for photo illustrations for articles that declare it is possible for us to look great after thirty, after forty, and even (gasp) after fifty! That's where the assurances usually stop. What is the implied message for those of us who exceed those limits?

There was a clever piece, entitled "Midlife," that circulated on the Internet a couple of years ago. It managed to be funny and brutally honest at the same time. Some of the comments included:

Midlife is when you realize that if you were a dog, you would need a control top flea collar.

Midlife is when you bounce (a lot), but you don't bounce back. It's more like splat!

Midlife is when you go to the doctor and you realize that you are now so old that you have to pay someone to look at you naked.

Even great beauties eventually have to come to terms with the gradual fading of their features. Isabella Rossellini was the "face" of a famous cosmetics company for years, but she was eventually replaced by a younger model. She responded by coming out with her own line of makeup, which emphasizes good skin care but does not promise to prevent normal aging. She has been quoted as saying that she objects to "beauty terrorism," which holds up the unattainable goal of beauty frozen in time. Women must be allowed to age gracefully, without being made to feel somehow ashamed of themselves for doing it. Speaking of freezing, the actress Susan Sarandon has also commented on this problem, saying, "In my business, there is a lot of pressure to freeze at a certain age. . . . Do you really expect me to say gravity hasn't taken its toll?"

My friend Jean Hedrick has written this vignette, illustrating the difficulties encountered during the aging process:

Recently, it was time to renew the old driver's license that I had carried for twelve years. I was really looking forward to having one of those shiny new colored ones, but I was not prepared for the jolt when I arrived at the DMV. You see, in twelve years, a lot of things change, and I found that only two items on the identification part of my license were the same as before—birth date and eye color! Height, weight, and hair color all had to be changed. It wasn't too much trouble until I came to the hair color.

Now, I knew that I was graying, but how do you put that on a driver's license? "GRNG" would never get the point across. I had considered my hair color of late as "pewter." I didn't want "PEW" to describe anything on my ID, and "PTR" could be easily misunderstood. All the while I was in line, I pondered the question, and when it was my turn, I decided to ask the man behind the desk. You will probably agree that DMV personnel are not always the most chatty, but this man was indeed helpful.

"I don't know what to put down for hair color," I said. "What would you call this? I call it pewter."

"Well," he said, looking me over carefully, "I'd go with brown one more time."

What a guy! He really knew how to make points with the over-fifty set. As I left, I thought, You really know you're getting older when you like your old driver's license, especially when you think the picture isn't too bad. Now it's time for the new one.

The biggest challenge we face is finding an acceptable balance between the goal of being as fit and attractive as we can be (without resorting to desperate measures) and learning to accept gracefully some of the signs of aging. I say, let's do an about-face on matters about faces!

An anonymous E-mail widely circulated a couple of years ago began with the oh-so-appropriate heading "Warning!" It went on to say:

I don't skinny-dip... I chunky-dunk.

My thighs were stolen from me during the night of August 3 a few years ago. It was just that quick. I went to sleep in my body and woke up with someone else's thighs. The new ones had the texture of cooked oatmeal.

Who would have done such a cruel thing to legs that had been wholly, if imperfectly, mine for years? Whose thighs were these? What happened to mine?

I spent the entire summer looking for them. I searched, in vain, at pools and beaches, anywhere I might find female limbs exposed. I became obsessed. I had nightmares filled with cellulite and flesh that turns to bumps in the night. Finally, hurt and angry, I resigned myself to living out my life in jeans and Sheer Energy panty hose.

Then, just when my guard was down, the thieves struck again. My rear end was next. I knew it was the same gang, because they took pains to match my new rear end (although badly attached at least three inches lower than the original) to the thighs they had stuck me with earlier. Now my rear complemented my legs, lump for lump. Frantic, I prayed that long skirts would stay in fashion.

Two years ago I realized my arms had been switched. One morning while fixing my hair, I watched, horrified but fascinated, as the flesh of my upper arms swung to and fro with the motion of the hairbrush. This was really getting scary. My body was being replaced, cleverly and fiendishly, one section at a time. In the end, in deepening despair, I gave up my T-shirts.

What could they do to me next? Age? Age had nothing to do with it. Age was supposed to creep up, unnoticed and intangible, something like maturity. NO, I was being attacked, repeatedly and without warning.

That's why I've decided to share my story; I can't take on the medical profession by myself.

Women of America, wake up and smell the coffee! That isn't really "plastic" those surgeons are using. You know where they're getting those replacement parts, don't you? The next time you suspect someone has had a face "lifted," look again! Was it lifted from you?

Check out those tummy tucks and buttocks raisings. Look familiar? Are those your eyelids on that movie star? I think I may have found my thighs . . . and I hope that Cindy Crawford paid a really good price for them!

There is a current trend in home decoration, started by Rachel Ashwell in her best-selling book *Shabby Chic*. The gist of her idea is that a lovely home may be appealingly furnished with treasures unearthed at flea markets and garage sales. The worn finishes and chipped paint common to old cupboards and tables are considered highly desirable evidence of a past marked by loving use and faithful service. Sometimes, these finds are repaired and spruced up a bit, but often they are left as is. Finishes are described as having acquired the "rich patina of age." Vintage fabrics are prized for recycling as pillow covers and upholstery. Now, I ask you, if this standard of beauty is prized in our homes, why can't we apply this standard of beauty to ourselves? We all bear evidence of wear caused by years of loving service, too. Many of our wrinkles testify to years and years of tears and smiles. Why can't we, too, be considered "treasures," good enough just as we are?

> "[People age better] when they respect and take care of their bodies, but are not obsessed with the loss of physical beauty. This is partly because they're less stressed. Aging is not the enemy. Illness and inactivity are much more dangerous."
> —Dr. Joyce Brothers

The following E-mail came to me from a woman in New Zealand:

> I know so many amazing, intelligent, beautiful women in their fifties and sixties who are just so brainy and creative—and yet the veneration of youth that our society is based on has the effect of making many women feel that one is on the scrap heap at fifty! It's great to see that something is happening that encourages women to feel positive about getting to *that* birthday—and in a way that is informal, wacky, quirky, and irreverent. Just exactly what is needed to inspire energy and creativity. I remember on one occasion hav-

ing a blinding flash of realization about how we need to appreciate the whole spectrum of womanhood in a different way. I sing in a barbershop singing group (Sweet Adelines) and I remember an occasion when I had been to a weekend convention. Two of the musical directors working with us were wonderful, energetic women, so knowledgeable in their field, very impressive. They were large women, and both in their fifties, not the conventional image of "beauty." But they were so inspiring in their power and energy. When I returned home that same day, I went to a fashion show with my daughter, and the image that was being presented there was: lots of young girls prancing around onstage in the way that they had been taught—lithe and nubile, beautiful, exuding an image of confidence, but also self-conscious in the way that teenage girls are. And I remember thinking, Is this the image of womanhood that we're meant to aspire to? It was so different from the beauty, power, and energy of the women I had just been with.

Ladies, I have a proposition to put before all of you. Let's all agree that it's okay to *look* older as we *get* older. It's the truth! We don't need to be ashamed of, or make excuses for, our aging faces and bodies. Each one of us should decide (here we are, choosing again) just how much time, effort, and money she will expend on herself to keep looking as good as possible. And whatever she decides will be fine and dandy with the rest of us. I propose that we grant ourselves and others some tender mercy, and abstain from passing judgment on anyone on the basis of her appearance alone.

FIVE STAGES OF FEMALE LIFE

1. To grow up
2. To fill out
3. To slim down
4. To hold it in
5. To hell with it

MENTAL AGING (MATURATION)

> **"The trick is to grow up without getting old."**
> —*Frank Lloyd Wright*

Jimmy Buffet wrote a song that I just love, it's entitled "Growing Older but Not Up." Obviously, he was not talking about remaining a child in a literal sense. The song does suggest, though, that we should attempt to retain the best aspects of the children we once were. When I talked about physical aging, I said we face the fact that no matter how we try, we can't freeze our physical appearance in its youthful stage; as we age, so will our bodies. But it is interesting that, if we are not careful, our mental attitudes and outlooks *will* freeze, sometimes as solidly as granite. We can allow the hard knocks life has dealt us to harden our hearts. We can stop challenging ourselves to learn new things, make new friends, and try out new attitudes. We can build nice solid little prisons for our brains, keeping them safe from the tedious exercise of facing new challenges and ideas, and allow our lives to shrink steadily, until they are very, very small but very, very manageable.

I am a longtime fan of Dr. James Dobson's radio program, "Focus on the Family." I remember his personal observations about the years of his mother's life that followed the loss of her husband. He said that she lived her life as if she were in a large house, constantly retreating farther into the bowels of that house, closing doors behind her, until she was safely ensconced in a tiny windowless room. He went on to state that many people do that sort of thing as they get older, steadily discarding activities they once enjoyed, people they once associated with, and opportunities for mental exploration of any kind. One by one, they shut the windows and doors to the outside. Once his mother reached that tiny room, she just settled in and waited for her life to be over. He said that it broke his heart to watch her.

In his book *Return to Wonder*, Arthur Gordon shared his recollections of the southern town in which he grew up. He said that most of the adults he knew seemed rather staid and sober, with the exception of Miss Lucy, a widow, who lived with her prim and proper sister, Clara:

> One day Miss Lucy—in her 60's—asserted that she could still stand on her head. When we looked doubtful, she clamped her skirt between her knees and did so, beaming at us upside down.
>
> "Oh, Lucy," said Clara. "Do be your age!"
>
> Miss Lucy righted herself. "What sort of nonsense is that?" she asked. "How can anyone be anything other than their age? The trick is to love your age. Love it when you're young and strong and foolish. Love it when you're old and wise. Love it in the middle when the challenges come and you can solve some of them, maybe most of them. If you love your age, you'll never go around wishing you were some other age. Think about that, Clara."

A study of adult development at Harvard Medical School followed groups of healthy people born in the 1920s, 1930s, and 1940s and came to the conclusion that one's attitude is the deciding factor in how well one ages. This directly contradicts the commonly held assumption that mental decay necessarily accompanies physical aging. It was determined that the brains of people who were in their fifties were actually better developed and "sharper at emotional tasks" than those of people age thirty. The self-nurture that we provide ourselves as we age is critical. Participating fully in life is crucial. The study, summarized in the *Los Angeles Times*, cited four attributes that are shown to be connected with successful aging:

1. Orientation toward the future. The ability to anticipate, to plan, and to hope.
2. Gratitude, forgiveness, and optimism. We need to see the glass as half-full, not half-empty.
3. Empathy. The ability to imagine the world as it seems to the other person.
4. The ability to reach out. We need to keep our doors open to others.

There was a time when I had a fixed idea of the elements necessary for a good piece of art. The subject matter should be recognizable, the colors should be applied exactly as they appear in nature, and the perspective must be painstakingly accurate. I held this view for the first several decades of my life, until, when my daughter entered kindergarten, I reentered college part-time to study art. Although I was stubborn about compromising my view of what was and what was not good art, I gradually learned how narrow my view had been. Objects can be beautifully represented in abstract as well as in excruciatingly realistic art. Color can be applied subjectively. In fact, there was an entire school of artists in twentieth-century France called the Fauves, who dazzled the eye with gorgeous paintings of red trees and pink and blue animals! Perspective can be deliberately distorted to serve design goals; an artist of no less stature than Cézanne demonstrated that principle. I was forced to retire my prejudices and embrace a broader view of what constitutes good art.

If you feel the doors to your mind slowly begin to close, prop them open! Learn something. Try looking at things from a new vantage point! Notice that I am not advising anyone to discard firmly held views without carefully considered reasons. In many cases, we may not choose to alter our attitudes. (There are still plenty of examples of so-called modern art that I will probably never enjoy, understand, or accept.) But I *am* suggesting that new or different viewpoints are worth considering.

SPIRITUAL AGING

Physical aging must be accepted. Mental aging must be vigorously combated. But what can we say about spiritual aging? I have come to the conclusion that the phenomenon we might describe as "spiritual aging" is to be eagerly sought after, if we define it as the willingness to continue to grow in spirit and to continue to seek wisdom and truth.

> "A cheerful heart is good medicine, but a crushed spirit dries up the bones."
> —*Proverbs 17:22*

As we enter midlife, and venture beyond, we recognize that we are now closer to the end of our lives than we are to the beginning. When we were young, we yearned to be older. Now that we are older, we need to guard against the yearning to be young. Most people I know say that they would love to revisit their youth, but only if they could take with them the hard-earned knowledge and wisdom that experience has taught them. There are probably few of us who would like to relive our youth if that meant having to reexperience its attendant naïveté and anxiety. In any case, we have no choice but to live in the present, since that is where we find ourselves.

> "Feed your faith and doubts will starve to death."
> —*Anonymous*

But this is an excellent time to do some reexamination and reevaluation. It is time to sit down with the puzzle pieces of our memories, opinions, and beliefs and try to assemble them into a coherent whole that hangs together well and makes sense to us. What do you believe? Why do you believe it? Have you fully integrated your belief system with your behavior, or do you detect gaps? That is, do you *do* as you *say*? Has life taught you anything that you could or should pass on to others? After all, as I keep emphasizing, we are not *done* yet! There is still time to seek clarification if we haven't settled on core beliefs. There is still time to make course corrections and to apply more fully the fruits of our hard-earned wisdom.

The Red Hat Society is composed of women of all faiths. Mem-

> "For is it not true that middle age can be looked upon as a period of second flowering, second growth? Having shed many of the physical struggles, the worldly ambitions, the material encumbrances of active life, one might be free to fulfill the neglected side of one's self. One might be free for growth of mind, heart, talent, and free at last for spiritual growth."
>
> —*Anne Morrow Lindbergh*, Gift from the Sea

bership in our disorganization is not based on any specific one. Anyone who has reached the half-century mark or beyond has probably realized that certain questions must be dealt with by each person individually. Why are we here? Upon what standards do we base our moral codes? Is there something higher than ourselves? Some sort of framework for our lives is necessary, even more so as we age. We need values, a relationship with a higher power, a guide and a reason for living. I do not presume to dictate any specific standard for anyone, but I have chosen mine. I am a Christian and have come to base my life on a relationship with Jesus Christ. This lays the foundation for everything I do, and gives my life meaning. But whatever faith one chooses, one finds a basis for believing that life is valuable and that each person matters. If we can value and nurture ourselves, we can more easily value and nurture others. We can extend respect to others, as we learn to respect ourselves. We are good enough, and we are choosing to be better. We are all still travelers on the road to whatever lies ahead. We are engaged in life, and we are excited!

The following story came to me in a newsletter from the late Mary Lou Heard, owner of a very special plant nursery in my area. It concerns a woman who was complaining to her mother about the difficulties of her life. She said she was tired of dealing with continual struggles and felt like giving up. Her mother took her to the kitchen and placed three pans of boiling water on the stove. Into the first pan, she dropped some carrots; into the second, she placed eggs; and into the third, she put coffee beans. After a few minutes, she removed the items from the water and put them in separate bowls. She asked her daughter to touch each item. The carrots were soft, the eggs hard-boiled, the coffee now a rich aromatic liquid. She pointed out that each of these substances had reacted differently to the boiling water, in much the same way each of us reacts to the adversity in our lives. The carrot had gone in strong but came out soft and weak. The egg had gone in fragile but developed a hard shell as well as a hardened interior to protect itself. The coffee beans were different. They had changed the water itself into something fragrant and aromatic. The boiling water (adversity) had caused the beans to release their inherent flavor, thus actually improving the water. She asked her daughter how she responded to trouble—as a carrot, an egg, or a coffee bean. It's worth asking ourselves the same question.

Aging happens. Laugh and enjoy life with your red-hatted friends, but also consider learning to love and to trust one another enough to share the deeper things of life. There is never a reason to be totally content with the status quo. Find ways to stimulate one another's mental and spiritual growth and to enrich one another's lives. And, of course, have fun doing it!

5

Connecting the Dots (and the Lindas and Dianes)

No man is an island . . .
—John Donne

No woman is an island, either.
—Sue Ellen Cooper

*L*ife is just not much fun if you are all alone. It is common knowledge that we all function better within the structure of safe, nurturing relationships. In years gone by, women found this sort of community in quilting bees, where they would stitch relationships together, sharing bits and pieces of their lives while they fashioned beautiful heirloom quilts from scraps of fabrics. Though such things as sewing circles and quilting bees are rare today, women remain reasonably good at building circles of friends, within which they find intimacy. Linda Nargie (the Hat Pack, Santa Barbara, California) writes: "There is a bond between women that is so intense that we find ourselves knowing a new face inside and out as though we have known that woman forever. Men can never figure out how we find so much to talk about. . . . We can have a never-ending conversation, one subject leading to another. We feel each other's moods, joys, needs, loneliness, happiness, sorrow, and pain."

"Blessed are they who have the gift of making friends, for it is one of God's best gifts. It involves many things, but above all, the power of going out of one's self and appreciating whatever is noble and loving in another."
—*Thomas Hughes*

As we all know, the pressures of family and career often leave us little time for adequate upkeep of a support system, even if we have built one. But if friendships are not nurtured, they wither. I have often heard it said that children spell the word *love* T-I-M-E. So do adults. In her book *Best Friends: The Pleasures and Perils of Girls' and Womens' Friendships,* researcher Ruthellen Josselson, Ph.D., says:

> Every time we get overly busy with work and family, the first thing we do is let go of friendships with other women. We push them right to the back burner. That's really a mistake, because women are such a source of strength to each other. We nurture one another. And we need to have unpressured space in which we can do the special kind of talk that women do when they're with other women. It's a very healing experience.

The Nurses' Health Study, which was conducted by Harvard Medical School, found that the more friends women had, the less likely they were to develop health problems as they aged, and the more likely they were to be leading happy lives. It is apparent that friends are so important that the lack of them is actually detrimental to women's health. Being a part of a community of caring friends is not a luxury; it is essential.

"By putting on that red hat, I have instant sisters. Everywhere I travel, there is always a group of like-minded women that I can instantly relate to. With my sisters, my inner child feels free to come out and play. . . . Yes, I am of age to wear a red hat, and proud of it."
—Queen Linda Leopold (Bodacious Babes, Amarillo, Texas)

Another study, conducted at UCLA, has shown that women, unlike men, respond to stress "with a cascade of brain chemicals that cause us to make and maintain friendships with other women." *Brain chemicals?* Well, whatever! Dr. Laura Cousino Klein, one of the study's authors, says that this chemical solidifies bonding among women and produces a calming effect. (I'm pretty sure most of us could have told them that!)

We have been told that many doctors all over the United States have written prescriptions advising their patients to join a chapter of the Red Hat Society. They see membership in our group as an antidote to the depression that can descend on an aging woman who feels disconnected and useless.

Over the course of time, established friendships can fade, or end entirely. Nothing stays the same forever in this world. In the natural order of things, all of us may well find our circle of friends shrinking as we get older. How do we fill the empty spaces? It is not as easy as it once was to gather a new community of girlfriends around us after we pass fifty, partly because there may be fewer places to find them easily. We don't have children at home anymore, so we don't meet the parents of their friends during the course of school and sports activities. More and more people work full-time and fill their leisure hours with other forms of business, leaving less and less time for interaction among neighbors. Sometimes all we see of one another is our cars, coming and going.

Most of us who have worked outside the home have found new friendships that flourished independent from the job. Many times, we automatically lose casual workplace relationships whenever we leave a particular job. And is there time for the give-and-take required to build meaningful friendships with coworkers while pursing a career? Marlene Wright (Ruby Amethyst, Eagan, Minnesota) says, "My background is corporate, where you don't see women supporting women—I'm sorry, you just don't." She contrasts this problem with her Red Hat Society experience: "This is positive. These are very classy women."

As we age, we also run a risk of losing other supportive relationships. Some marriages end in divorce or widowhood. Friendships with coworkers may phase out with retirement. Children may move far away from us. At this time in our lives, we may also find our energy dwindling a little. We just don't have as much time and energy to develop new friendships from scratch with those with whom we lack a shared history. We find ourselves wanting to pick and choose whom we spend our time with because our time is perceived as more precious. Making new friends can be labor-intensive. So how can we go about it?

> "We must be willing to get rid of the life we've planned, so as to have the life that is waiting for us."
> —Joseph Campbell

The spirit of the lady in the poem "Warning" has inspired us in the Red Hat Society to begin to please ourselves and seek fun more often. But the women of the Red Hat Society differ strongly from that lady in one highly significant way. Whereas the woman in the poem seems to be a bit of a lone eccentric who can no longer be bothered by what others think of her, we are not at *all* interested in being loners! We are tuning in to one another more and more, and finding, to our communal delight, that we are all on the same frequency! We might indeed go out in the rain in our slippers, and we might even learn to spit, but we will not do it independently; we will do it together! And, in regard to the impressions we make on others, we are benignly indifferent. We are not performing for an audience; we are entertaining ourselves. And we are very good at it!

It is said that the whole can be more than the sum of its parts; nowhere is that concept more evident than within our group. Every single woman who has joined has

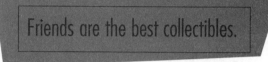

Friends are the best collectibles.

contributed some of her essence to the Red Hat Society mix. There is a picture book, which I read to my children when they were small, that illustrates my view of our group beautifully. It is called *Stone Soup,* and it was written by Marcia Brown. It tells the story of three starving French soldiers. Returning home from war, they enter a poor village, trying to find something to eat. The villagers, also starving, claim that they have no food, so the soldiers announce that they will have to make a pot of stone soup. They set a large kettle over a fire to boil, then add three stones as their contribution. Each villager goes to his home and returns with a small bit of food, scavenged from his meager provisions. One brings a cabbage, one a scrap of meat, another a couple of carrots and a few potatoes. As the water boils, each peasant drops his contribution into the pot, and eventually they all enjoy a celebratory feast of hearty soup.

Each woman who has joined the Red Hat Society has brought something of herself to the "pot," and all of us have benefited from the wonderful stew that has been the result. As a group, we all reap the benefits of the rich mix of ideas and personalities that, blended together, have come to make up the Red Hat Society. As we come to know one another, in our communities, on the Internet, and at both large and small events, we enrich one another and increase the value of the Red Hat Society as a whole. Connections, both deliberate and accidental, are made. Something larger than any one chapter, or group of chapters, has begun to take shape—of its own accord, without premeditated orchestration by any of us.

I like to think of this phenomenon as akin to a spiderweb. It is spun of many unique fibers, some even flimsy, but it is an amazingly strong, resilient structure as a whole, by virtue of the number and strength of its filaments. Every time I hear of a connection made between two individual Red Hatters who didn't know each other before they joined us, I am just thrilled! Every time two or more chapters plan a joint event, the invisible web grows stronger. All of us enjoy sharing our lives and experiences with one another, and I sense excitement among all of us as we watch our disorganization grow in size and scope, reaching far beyond what any of us could have envisioned.

The Red Hat Society has become a wonderful place to form new friendships, based on all the things we have in common. Cindy Cross (the Wild Orchid Society, Glendale, Arizona) has this to say: "Since I have been in the Red Hat Society, I have met thirty-five new people whom I call my friends. I just don't know anywhere else you could make thirty-five caring and loving friends so fast. When our group had our first meeting, we all felt like we had known one another before. I plan some kind of icebreaker so new members can share some interesting things about themselves with the group. Friday night, I was eating dinner with the ladies and they were sharing about their lives, and I realized Red Hatters are like having a friend, sister, and mother all rolled up in one."

Agnes Curran-Tonkin (the Red Cardinal Chapeaus, Havelock, North Carolina) says that the sisterhood that has developed among their members reminds her of connections she made over the years her husband was in the military: "My deceased husband was in the U.S. Marine Corps for twenty-four years before retiring. On many, many occasions when he was overseas without the family—off on deployments, or when I was hospitalized, or when the children were sick, et cetera—other women came to my rescue. I learned early on that the only way to repay these kindnesses was to pass them along to others in the same boat. Moving around the world, living in strange places, having to go out and meet neighbors and other people—all of this was difficult, but I knew I was not alone and others had done this before me. I think the Red Hat Society reflects the established model provided by many military wives who experienced the blessings, kindness, and love of other women when they were so far away from home and parents who could help. We just didn't have a name to call ourselves. Now I find I'm back in the role of extending friendship, kindness, and understanding to younger military wives, new people transferred to our area, new young families coming to our church, et cetera. Isn't this just what the Red Hat Society symbolizes? Sharing and reaching out to others, creating friendships, and helping those who just need a friend—it's all the same. Now I have a red hat and purple dress to identify me, and a title of 'Queen,' but really, nothing has changed. Our group (mostly retired military wives) has experienced it all, and it's our turn to help those coming up the ladder."

Some Red Hat Society chapters are made up of established groups of longtime friends. They use membership in our group as a vehicle for making sure they get out together and enjoy one another's company regularly. In these instances, the Red Hat Society is an effective way to stay in touch. But there are a great many chapters that have been initiated by women deliberately stepping outside of their immediate circles and drawing in women they have not met before. Some of these women have simply run little newspaper ads, or just spread the word, or gone out in their outfits and gathered interested onlookers into their chapters. They are actively eager to meet new women and expand their number of friendships. After all, as we have already established, we have so much in common. All we really need to do is get to know the particulars of one another's lives, and we will often form a natural bond in the process.

NICE TO MEET YOU

Many serendipitous stories have come my way from women who discovered underlying links between themselves and other women that they might never have known about if they hadn't joined the

Red Hat Society. Some connections are revealed by chance. A visitor at a Red Hat Society event (Red Hat Highlanders, Sebring, Florida) wrote that she is a retired journalist and a life member of the National Federation of Press Women. At one of her chapter luncheons, someone passed around newspaper clippings about the Red Hat Society that they had received from family and friends in other states. She automatically checked the bylines and discovered one of the articles had been written by a friend and colleague of hers who had retired and moved to Tennessee five years earlier. She says it's a small world and that the Red Hat Society is helping to make it smaller and friendlier.

Joyce Senatro (Port Orange Mad Red Hatters, Port Orange, Florida) was prowling the aisles at a local swap meet, looking for a red hat to wear to her first event. At the very last booth, she found hats—including the perfect red one—waiting for her. She tried it on and said to the husband/wife proprietors, "I have to have this!" While she was paying, she asked the pair, who were Asian, where they were from. They answered, "Vietnam." Joyce says, "I recalled having met many wonderful Vietnamese families in the 1970s, when I worked with their resettlement to the United States. I was a social worker with Catholic Charities. The couple looked at each other, then at me, and asked, 'You Joyce? We are Lee . . . remember?' What a thrill for all of us! Thanks, Red Hat!"

See what I mean about magic?

It doesn't hurt to conduct a lighthearted search for links, though, instead of waiting for them to pop up. Deb Johnson (the Red Hot Hatitudes, Mankato, Minnesota) writes that the queen of her chapter poses a get-acquainted question each time they meet, asking the ladies to take turns answering the question of the month. At one particular luncheon, each member was challenged to share an embarrassing event from her past. One new member shared an event that she had been part of fifty-five years ago in a distant town. Amazingly, the story caused another woman at the table to recognize the storyteller as an old childhood friend. She jumped from her seat, exclaiming, "Was that *you*?" Their names had changed due to marriage, of course, and their faces had altered due to age, so they might never have recognized each other! They say it was an awesome reunion and they have become fast friends once again.

I need to mention here that not every woman is blessed with the knack for making friends with ease. Some women, for whatever reason, have had little experience with warm friendships with other women. The Red Hat Society, through our policy of *in*clusivity rather than *ex*clusivity, has proven itself to be a place where those who have been so deprived can find something they need desperately.

Sue Champagne (the Beach Rubies, Jacksonville Beach, Florida) tells a tale of one such woman, who stood up and shared her story at their very first get-together. She said that she had raised her daughter by herself, after leaving her alcoholic husband when their child was only five years old. In the hustle and bustle of supporting them both, she had had little time to develop friendships of her own. Now her daughter was leaving for college. Her family was several states away. She said that she had seen a newspaper notice about a Red Hat Society chapter starting, and she'd gone and outfitted herself, having every intention of joining. But it had been so long since she had sought out other women her age, she'd underestimated how emotional a step this would be for her. Sue says, "She told us that she drove around the block many times, trying to get up the courage to come in. Then she parked the car a bit away and watched as other women came up—some by themselves, some in pairs, but all with smiles on their faces. After a quick prayer, she approached the door and timidly rang the doorbell, her heart pounding. She said that once she stepped inside the foyer, her fear and apprehension just evaporated." This woman has not missed a single gathering of the Beach Rubies.

Lucinda Denton, who lives in Knoxville, Tennessee, went out of her way to reach out to a woman who obviously longed for connection but was fearful. She sends a touching story of her experience with a woman unskilled in friendship: "A feature article about the Nonpareils chapter appeared in our local paper and inquiries about membership began pouring in. One lady, who wanted to remain anonymous, continued to send E-mails, and as I answered her and she replied over the months, we became friends. Whenever I encouraged her to join our group, she cited health problems and family obligations with an elderly father. I finally got her to agree to meet with me, just me, for lunch one day. From her E-mail messages, I pictured her as a svelte, elegant woman, who, at age forty-nine, probably wasn't ready to hit fifty and adopt the Red Hat image. The purple tent dress and red rain hat were the only clues that my new friend was walking in the restaurant door the day we met. Her feet were so swollen that she wore bedroom slippers. She was unkempt and grossly overweight. I realized her hesitation to join our group was based on an unfounded worry that she wouldn't fit in.

Lucinda soon dispelled the woman's concern and persuaded her to agree to attend their next event. But before her next chapter meeting, Lucinda learned that the woman had been hospitalized. Lucinda says, "I spoke daily by telephone with my new friend in the hospital, but cancer, complicated by other ailments, quickly took its toll. She said that she wasn't ready to have visitors, but I ignored her wishes, and after the next Red Hat Society event, which would have been her first, I arrived at the hospital in my Red Hat attire. She was sedated and laced with IVs and oxygen tubing, and I wasn't certain that she was even aware that I was there. But I had made a miniature red hat, and I pinned it to her pillow. The nurses and staff wanted to hear the entire Red Hat story, and I assured them that their patient was now an official member. She died that night, so I was never certain if she knew, but when I attended her funeral, wearing a purple suit and red felt hat, her grieving father greeted me, saying, 'Oh, *you* are the wonderful Red Hat lady my daughter told me about.'"

One other woman's story must be told, but she asked that I withhold her name. She says she was invited to join a group by the one person she knew well enough to call a friend. At each monthly luncheon of this chapter, the queen passes out numbers indicating where each person will sit, thus ensuring that eventually they will all get to know one another. Gradually, they are all getting acquainted. This woman finds her new friendships particularly precious, as she has been told by her doctor that she has less than a year to live, due to her recurring cancer. She says, "When the time gets closer, all my Red Hat sisters will be told, but for now, I love it that I can have 'normal' warm relationships with these women without the burden of pity." In this life, friends can be the most valuable assets we have. We don't have to be alone.

WIDENING OUR CIRCLES

Though some coincidental connections have been discovered, there are far more connections being deliberately forged by enthusiastic women who have seen the Red Hat Society for what it is—a terrific way to connect with other women, some of whom they might never have met otherwise in the course of their normal lives.

Sue Green (Lone Star Red Hat Society, Nederland, Texas) says, "I give the Red Hat Society so much credit for the wonderful friends I have made and will have for the rest of my life. I correspond regularly via E-mail with Red Hat Society friends here in Texas and other states, such as Iowa, Illinois, Washington, Oklahoma, Delaware, Michigan, and Alabama. It would not have been possible for me to have met these wonderful women if you hadn't started the Red Hat Society." Sue and her husband, Al, have become such fast friends with another Red Hatter and her husband, who live in Iowa, that they travel to each other's homes on vacation!

How do you connect with other Red Hatters when you are on the road all the time? Mary Boehm (Red Rovers, USA) and her friend Ruth, both widows, travel often with a group of RVers and thus have had trouble becoming part of a Red Hat Society chapter. They are never home long enough to get acquainted with the members of their local chapters or attend regular functions. Mary says she came up with a solution "during a fretful but exciting bout of insomnia." She and Ruth started their own chapter for ladies who are RVers, traveling with or without husbands. She posts notes on paper in the shape of a hat, filled out with first name, date of arrival and departure, and the RV site number, and places them on the RV park entrance's message board. Any interested traveling Red Hatters can stop by to visit, knock on the door of her RV, and get acquainted! She plans to keep in touch with other Red Rovers via E-mail, posting itineraries and recording new members, for those who travel with laptops. She is also considering a Web site.

The wearing of the red and purple can actually serve as a signal to others, and allow for some very interesting revelations and opportunities. As the Red Hat Society continues its spread, more and more little spontaneous connections are made. Sharon Sims (the Red Hat Classics, Augusta, Georgia) was vacationing in Myrtle Beach, Florida. While sitting on the beach reading a book, she glanced up and saw a lady with a purple outfit topped by a red-feathered hat strolling along the surf. Sharon could not resist approaching her and asking if she was one of "us." She was indeed! She said that this was her last day of vacation before she returned home to Maine, and she had decided to "show her colors" to see if she could connect with any Red Hatters in Florida. Sharon was amazed to learn that she was the *ninth* Red Hatter who had approached this woman that very morning! She says, "Hopefully, she ran into several more Red Hatters. I mean, we are everywhere!"

Even when there is no actual meeting, Red Hat Society connections can be observed and celebrated. Why not use every opportunity to link up, even if it is only for a moment? Nancy Hasse (Vintage Tea Roses, Gainesville, Florida) was driving back to her home from Ocala, where she had gone to shop, when she passed a cute PT Cruiser and noticed four ladies in it wearing red hats. She quickly changed lanes, positioning her car in front of theirs, and waited for them to notice her license plate holder, which identified her as a Red Hatter. She says, "It wasn't long till they blinked their lights on and off at me! And, as I got off at my exit a few miles down the road, they passed by me, waving! I thought that was just the best thing that happened to me that day!"

Carol Shifflet (Lidias Red Hat Society, Sigourney, Iowa) says that when she was in Iowa City, browsing through the clothing racks in a thrift shop, she struck up a casual conversation with another woman shopper and mentioned that she was trying to find something purple. The other woman asked her if she already had a red hat to go with it! Carol says, "So, we had fun looking for dresses together, as sisters would."

The extension of the red-gloved hand of friendship is beginning to occur deliberately among chapters. Red Hatters vacationing in areas far from their homes are taking the time to contact Red Hat Society chapters there and perhaps attend one of their events as a "visiting dignitary." Marilynn Krafft (Ornery Upbeat Crimson Hatters, San Diego, California) was going to Florida to visit her daughter over the Christmas holidays and contacted the Kiss-Im-Me Red Hats queen, Joanne Lupa. Marilynn asked if she could possibly attend one of their events while she was there. Joanne shot her an E-mail right back, saying, "Of course you can . . . and if we don't have an event going on while you're here, we'll make one!" That demonstrates a *very* Red "Hattitude"!

Even arranged meetings sometimes reel in extra Red Hatters, innocent bystanders, so to speak. Barbie Lesiak's chapter (the Queen of Hearts, Elmwood Park, Illinois) arranged to meet a member of a Wisconsin chapter in Chicago for a bit of Christmas shopping. While enjoying one another's company as they trailed through various stories, they ran into yet another Red Hatter, a tourist from Denver, Colorado, and then another from a different Wisconsin chapter! They decided to top off their day by paying a lap-sitting visit to yet *another* (unofficial) Red Hatter whom they ran across—Santa Claus!

Christine Morrison (Red Hat Eastsiders, Punta Gorda, Florida) says that her chapter is composed of women who work, or have worked, at East Elementary School. One day a month, they all wear their purple and red to school to identify themselves as Red Hat Society members. All of the little girls are encouraged to go to school in lavender and pink, just to emphasize the link between women of all ages. Christine says that the bonds that are developing among teachers and girls are "awesome." In some ways, this reminds me of the mother/daughter clothing that was once popular, when little girls enjoyed dressing like their moms. How wonderful if they can learn to be proud to be girls and anticipate a future as productive women.

A little initiative can result in some fascinating surprises. Barbara McDonald (the Dixie Dames, Foley, Alabama) writes that a Red Hatter from Ohio contacted her. She was hoping to connect with other Red Hatters when she, a snowbird, traveled south to her second home in Alabama. She and Barbara met for lunch and later began to correspond regularly. It was not long before they discovered that one had a son and the other a son-in-law, both of whom were in the navy active reserves, and both stationed at the same base in New Orleans. When they checked with their "boys," they discovered that the two of them were already friends! Those young men might have been a little bewildered, I would imagine. Can't you hear one of them asking, "You met this lady *where*?"

Five members of the Red Hot Flashes from Greenville, South Carolina, took a trip to Nashville, and arranged to stay overnight at Lucinda Denton's (Nonpareils, Knoxville, Tennessee) house on their way, having gotten acquainted on the Internet. The get-together resulted in a lot more fun than they had envisioned. Lucinda says, "Margaritas had barely been sipped when I was presented with an honorary membership certificate in their chapter!" They also presented her with a lovely purple cut-glass flower bowl as a hostess gift. After dinner, which was topped off with cookies in the shape of red hats, they all climbed into their pajamas and prepared for bed. But, as Lucinda writes, "It was not to be! The day's rain had stopped, the temperature was nearly seventy degrees, so we walked down to the dock for a *midnight* boat ride!" Lucinda's husband awoke to total silence, then found all the lights on in the house and the doors standing open. He feared at first that someone had been rushed to the hospital, but then he heard singing as the boat came back into the cove! It's hard to imagine these previous strangers having such a good time together if they weren't all Red Hatters.

Whether an onlooker actually joins one of our chapters or not, there have been cases in which our red and purple have brought about wondrous connections among people. Sometimes I believe that there is some kind of glittery magic inherent in our very spirit, and the brilliant colors we wear emanate a glow, revealing that magic to others. Sue Harrison (Madhatters of NW Indiana) tells a heartwarming story about a woman whose life was touched by their chapter. About twelve of the Madhatters were visiting a crafts fair at the Kane County Fair Grounds in St. Charles, Illinois. Sue recounts that one of their members had "really taken the purple to heart," and had dyed even her bra purple. Sue was playfully making sure that her friend's bra strap showed, pulling it out of her sleeveless blouse and draping it down her arm, when they were approached by a woman who looked to be about forty. Sue says, "She told us that she had terminal breast cancer and that she had always loved lace panties and bras. After her last treatment, she had gone shopping with a person she had considered to be her best friend, and her friend had commented, 'Why would you spend so much on fancy bras, knowing you have breast cancer?' Naturally, this crushed her. She wanted us to know that she was so inspired by our group that she was going to go home and dye all her lacy bras *purple*! Several of us cried, hugged her, and wished her well. We pray for her and hope that she will be a survivor and become a Red Hatter someday. This is a true testimony to our organization and the real reason that it has been so contagious."

Over and over again, it has been demonstrated that one of the best ways to find connections, even the most unlikely ones, is just to mention the Red Hat Society within the hearing of others. You never know what might happen. Bobbi Johnson (Red Hot Mommas of Gulf Harbors, New Port Richey, Florida) tells of a jamboree being planned by thirty-three chapters in Florida. She knew, from reading my Friday broadcasts, that the founding vice mother, Linda Murphy, was now living in Florida, but she had no idea how to track her down and invite her to their jamboree. The day after she decided to try to do that, Bobbi was socializing on the sidewalk after church services, explaining to two friends how they could start a chapter. A man standing next to her overheard, turned to her, and asked, "Excuse me, but did you mention the Red Hat

Society?" He then beckoned to his wife and said, "This is the original vice mother!" Bobbi says she shrieked with delight and asked
if she was the *real* Linda Murphy! "My friends and I giggled and
carried on like children who had just met Santa Claus! She lives
right here. Is that not *wild*?" Well, actually, we Red Hatters are no
longer surprised by these delightful coincidences. Thrilled, yes,
but not surprised. Red hat magic rules!

MOTHERS AND DAUGHTERS

Red Hat magic has even extended its red-gloved fingers into
those close yet complicated relationships many of us have—that of
mothers and daughters. Terry Santore (the Crimson Sages, Wallace,
North Carolina) says that when she began her Red Hat chapter, her
twenty-two-year-old daughter would roll her eyes, as if to say, Oh,
here she goes again! But then an interesting thing happened. Terry
started working on a Red Hat Society scrapbook, and Gina commented, "You know, Mom, this is just like my sorority in college. We
had a scrapbook, and sisterhood. . . . You are just older!" Gina
hauled out photos of her own, sat down beside Terry, and began to
catalog her European trip. She noticed that Terry's group was having a lot of fun, and when Christmas neared, she said to her mom,
"Of course you are planning a Red Hat tree, right?" Well, of course
she was! Then, for Terry's next birthday, Gina gave her a purple
sweater with sparkles on it. To quote a happy Terry, "Today she will
meet me and three of my chapter members in our full regalia at a
tearoom in Raleigh, North Carolina, where she now lives . . . and she
won't even blink an eye at our outfits. It's okay now to be this zany!"
A year or two later, Gina became involved in an alumni chapter of
her sorority. After sitting through a meeting to discuss rules, regulations, and requirements, Gina decided to start her own alumni chapter and pattern it after the Red Hat Society—no rules, no
regulations, no requirements. Flattery? They say imitation is its
surest form.

"What I love about Red Hatters most is that this group keeps reminding me that everything is connected. Somehow, some way, it all fits together. I find comfort in this idea."
—*Brenda R. Murphy (Red Hat Mamas, Lilburn, Georgia)*

Diantha Grant shares the news that her seventy-seven-year-old mother and she (age fifty) have Red Hatting in common. Diantha and her husband moved to Jacksonville, Florida, a few years ago to be near her parents. When she heard about the Red Hat Society, she knew it was perfect for both of them: "My mother is a ham, and I inherited the same trait—so what could be a better place to be ourselves than in the La Tea Das? We love the Red Hat Society and plan on being a part of it for a long time to come."

Some daughters may not be quite as receptive to our little idea as others, and a lot of that may depend on age. Mickey Jo Smith, the founding mother of the Red Magnolias (Frankfort, Kentucky), has a teenage daughter still at home. Mickey Jo's daughter thinks that she has "totally lost it" when she puts on her purple scrubs and her red-glitter Hawaiian-print hat to go to work as a registered nurse. I have a feeling she will eventually come to be proud of her mom!

6

Why Little Girls Love Pink

And young and old come forth to play on a sunshine
holiday.

—John Milton

I have had playmates, I have had companions in my days
of childhood, in my joyful school-days."

—Charles Lamb

*W*hat exactly
is a Pink Hatter? When the
Red Hat Society first began to
gain momentum, I was sur-
prised to receive an occasional query
that went something like this: "I am not
fifty yet, but I would love to play with you ladies.
Why do I have to wait until some arbitrary age that you have
selected?" More than one woman stated that for the first time in her
life, she wished she were older! From others, I heard similar statements: "My best friend is only forty-seven and I want her to be a part
of my group. Is that okay, or does she have to wait for three years?"

Here were younger women actually clamoring to be allowed to join with us "seasoned citizens." Well, what fun!

But to be honest, the first few times these kinds of questions were asked, my vice mother and I hesitated. Shouldn't there be certain perks associated with getting older? Wasn't it only right to make these spring chickens wait outside the door of our imaginary clubhouse until they had chalked up a full fifty years, the age we had stipulated was necessary to wear the red hat? Wouldn't that make fifty something to look forward to, rather than something to be dreaded?

Well, yes, but then another thought struck me almost immediately. Wasn't this reluctance to allow younger women to join us rather unbecoming to a group that claimed to be nonexclusionary? Maybe the wearing of the purple and red *should* be reserved for those of us of "a certain age," but what about the developing concept of sisterhood spanning the age gap? How would that be served by any needless exclusions? The solution presented itself quite easily: I decided to open the door to any woman who was inclined to want to be a part of our burgeoning group. Come one, come all! But the fact is, we *did* feel that one needs to earn the right to wear the deep jewel tones by having lived a certain number of years, with all their attendant experiences, and reached the magic age of fifty. (Why? Because I'm the queen, and I said so!) I couldn't help but think of the beloved children's story *The Velveteen Rabbit*. The stuffed toy horse has to learn that he cannot become real until he has belonged to a child long enough to have his plush fur worn thin and his stitched seams frayed by years of "tough love" from the child who owns him. We Red Hat Society members feel that younger women have to complete fifty years of being worn by living in order to don the red and purple. We who have passed that landmark birthday are justified in wearing the real colors, as we have lived a bit longer and perceive the Red Hat Society colors as a badge of honor, worn for all to see. These younger women could come out and play with us, but they would have to wear diluted, paler colors of pink and lavender. They were, after all, the same colors, just not as vivid—just not yet!

Now, I saw a chance to develop other types of relationships

within the confines of the Red Hat Society. Perhaps some Red Hatters would begin to stand in as mother figures for Pink Hatters whose mothers didn't live close to them, or perhaps were estranged or dead. I mused about my own mother, who was only four years old when her mother passed away. As I grew up, I remember hearing her hazy recollections of her mother. She obviously never got over the hole that her mother's loss had left. I have read studies and articles about girls who grow up without mothers; the consensus seems to be that most of them express a lifelong yearning for their mothers, mourning a vital relationship that was cut far too short. How wonderful it would be if some younger women could bond with others fifteen to twenty or even thirty to thirty-five years older than they! The mutual benefits could be enormous.

Occasionally, someone will just sort of slide into red and purple a little early, sometimes even semilegally. (Remember, we have no rules.) One such Red Hatter, Chris Zambito, is the youngest member of the Red Hat Mommas of Clackamas County (Portland, Oregon). She writes that she moved to Oregon in her forty-ninth year, after spending her entire life in upstate New York. She joined a Red Hat Society chapter to help her get acclimated to her new life. She says that the Red Hat Mommas lovingly took her in, although she was shy of being fifty by about six months. They gave her extra credit for her recent hysterectomy and let her "reduate" early!

Another interesting phenomenon has taken place in some Red Hat Society chapters. A mentoring relationship has sprung up between younger and older women as a result of the wide variety of ages found within some chapters. We refer to our Pink Hatters, variously, as "postulates," "ladies-in-training," and "Red Hat wannabees," and we undertake to "reducate" them in the ways of Red Hatting, so that they can "reduate" when they reach the magic age of fifty (more about that later). We believe that we have an opportunity to set positive examples for younger women, including our daughters, about how to accept the aging process in good spirits and surprise the world with our playfulness and vitality at the same time. We all know that "Do as I do" is a far superior method of modeling behavior than "Do as I say." If you have trouble setting yourself free once in a while, ask yourself how you would advise your daughter to live, if your roles were reversed. Someone needs to show her now how to add a little variety and spice to her life, as well as how to head off a dawning fear of aging. She and her friends are watching us. We have shown them how to be wives, mothers, and career women. Let's show them how to play!

Judy Whitney (Rootin' Tootin' Tootsies, Tucson, Arizona) says that she lives in a development composed largely of people over fifty, and she found herself, at age forty-seven, very depressed about approaching that age herself. She didn't think it took much imagination to see that the battle against going downhill was about to begin. One day, a friend invited her to a luncheon and told her nothing except that she would have to wear lavender clothes and a pink hat. When she got to the restaurant, she stood still, amazed to see many, many women wearing purple clothes and red hats. She says, "They weren't sipping lemonade, and they certainly weren't watching life pass them by. These ladies were laughing, playing kazoos, blowing bubbles, entertaining one another with jokes and stories, and even dancing with the waiter. . . . Good grief, everything I had been told all my life about old ladies was now about to go up in a poof of red and purple!"

Though we had decided to admit younger women to our red-hatted ranks, not everyone got the word right away. Remember, we are a disorganization, and we sometimes live up to our name rather well. In any event, April Brown (Wild Women, Hartford, Connecticut) wasn't fortunate enough to hear about the special dispensation we were willing to grant Pink Hatters. She says that she waited two years from the time she first heard about the Red Hat Society to begin her chapter, just yearning to be old enough. She threw her own fiftieth-birthday party, during which she gave her closest friends red hats and other gifts. She says it was a wonderful day, and the anticipation of becoming a Red Hatter made the planning all that much more special! We're just glad that she doesn't hold grudges.

Barbara Owens (Red Hat Mommas, Kingston, Washington) writes that her daughter has been encouraged by the older women within their chapter. She has been a stay-at-home mom and has had trouble finding career women of her own age who understand her situation. The older women *do* understand, and they offer her support and encouragement to realize that there will be a future waiting for her when she is through raising her children. She has begun checking books on photography out of the library and planning for the years ahead, when her children will be gone. Barbara says, "Of course, the fact that *I* finished college and taught school for twelve years after *she* left home had never clicked in her mind. But seeing the Red Hatters and hearing of their adventures has given her a vision for her own future."

We were happy to receive the following testimonial from an enthusiastic Pink Hatter, Michele Paiva (Seeing Red, Downington, Pennsylvania). Michele, who earned the title "Mrs. Pennsylvania 2002," has this to say: "Here I am, a grateful Pink Hatter. Never underestimate the importance of a Pink Hatter who embraces the friendship of Red Hatters. Why is pink so important? Because we know that we are just around the corner from wearing our red with pride. We learn from the Red Hatters, who embrace life . . . and we choose to tell our silly nonqueen friends all about the joys of life in our society. Some may scoff. Some may not get it, but in the end, we will all be a hatter of some type, as the clock is ticking and the world is turning. . . . It is my choice to embrace my youth at thirty-five as I hope to embrace my youth at fifty-five, or sixty-five, or, God willing, ninety-five. . . . Am I promoting the Red Hat Society? Yes. Am I a committed chapter president? Yes. Am I the future of the Red Hat Society? *Yes!* And those who don't understand our zest for life? I pity them. Commoners!"

"We're all on the same ladder; we're just on different rungs."
—*Ruby RedHat*

It has gradually become apparent to all of us that sisterhood has absolutely nothing to do with age. Some of us may function as big sisters, some as little sisters. Whichever way it works, it works! The Main Street Madames (St. Charles, Missouri) is composed of a group of shop owners whose stores all line up along their town's historic Main Street. Robin Fogarty Bowman says, "We have realized one thing very early on in this group. Age certainly does not matter! I am the youngest, being thirty years old. And we have members who, at the very least, are old enough to be my mother. And we all get along as splendidly as if we were all a few months apart in age! We have many common interests—namely, our businesses and our love for our charming and historic city. And those common interests have made us begin to get close already. . . . I cannot wait to see what the years ahead will bring to us!"

None of us should make the error of assuming that younger women would not be interested in joining us. One Red Hatter says that she was telling a colleague at work about the chapter of the Red Hat Society she was starting. Her friend just stood there. Then, after a long pause, she asked if she could join, too. The Red Hatter says, "She had no idea what she was in for. She has come to every tea and has also included her mother. We have a great time. I had no idea that such a young gal would be interested." Well, we fascinating older women have just been underestimating ourselves, right?

The Ruby Red Hots (Bakersfield, California) had a similar experience. They hired a limousine to take them on a tour of wineries in Paso Robles, north of their Bakersfield. They managed to peruse antique and junk stores and visit six or seven wineries in their ten-hour day. They demonstrated Red Hatting so efficiently to the forty-one-year-old limo driver that she bought herself a pink hat and signed up to be a part of their chapter. Obviously, this Red Hat virus can be extremely contagious!

It is no longer a rare thing to catch wind of whole chapters made up entirely of Pink Hatters. According to Laurie Foster, the Crazy Crimson Crabettes (southern Maryland) have but one Red Hatter. The Ragamuffins (Hendersonville, North Carolina) is also made up entirely of Pink Hatters. Their queen, Cynthia Fore, says that their oldest member has approximately four more years to go before her fiftieth birthday, so they have a long time in which to plan a rousing celebration in her honor. She adds, "Till then, we'll just stay young with the rest of you!"

And just when I thought I had heard it all, I got word from Connie Hyde, queen bee of the Dallas Divas (Dallas, Texas) concerning one of their nine Pink Hatters. They are having a baby shower for one of their "Pink Princesses"—she is expecting a "Petite Princess" this coming year. Talk about starting them out young! I'm thinking a pale pink baby bonnet and a lavender sleeper!

There is no need to wait for younger women to ask to join us. We may know a few of them who we would love to include. Joyce Dilda (Ravishing Reds of Roanoke, Roanoke, Virginia) says she is strongly encouraging her chapter to recruit Pink Hatters: "After all, they will be the ones to keep this going! *And* . . . pushing our wheelchairs someday!" Hey, there's another motivation for recruitment. Let's train these young ladies right.

7
She Ain't Heavy... She's My Sister

In everyone's life, at some time, our inner fire goes out. It is then burst into flame by an encounter with another human being. We should all be thankful for those people who rekindle the inner spirit.

—Albert Schweitzer

It is great to have friends when one is young, but indeed it is still more so when you are getting old. When we are young, friends are, like everything else, a matter of course. In the old days we know what it means to have them.

—Edvard Grieg

*O*ur society is less than supportive of aging women. Therefore, it is in our interest to band together and create our own support system. The Red Hat Society will always be indebted to Jenny Joseph's poem. The poem concerns a solitary eccentric who plans on pleasing herself from now on. It is clear that she also plans to give her husband a lot of space, for she turns to him, in reverie, and says that *he* will be able to "wear terrible shirts and grow more fat." The tone of the poem seems to indicate that the two of them will enjoy not only their liberation *from* the expectations of others but also the liberation from too much society *with* others. But we find ourselves irresistibly drawn, first to the spirit of the Red Hat Society and then to one another. Rather than each of us wandering off by herself, we have begun to gather together at every opportunity to celebrate sisterhood and demonstrate solidarity. I believe that the Red Hat Society arose first and foremost from women's love and need for one another. Originally, we gathered together to play and kick up our heels, but we soon found that we were developing friends who would also stay around and hold our hands when our laughter turned, as it sometimes will, to tears.

Pauline Vetter (Duchesses of Bedford, Fairfax, Virginia) wrote to tell us about one of their members, Rita Lockwood, who fell and injured both of her arms. She attended her chapter event wearing a splint on one arm and a cast on the other. I mentioned her in my Friday broadcast, which I send out to all of our members weekly, and suggested some of our members might want to wish her well. Many members responded with loving support. As the "get well" E-mails poured in, Rita's husband was heard to remark that there must be something wrong with their computer!

While we Red Hatters emphasize the need for fun and play, we are not living in La-La Land. We are well aware that life holds sadness and tragedy for all of us sooner or later.

I Shall Be Glad

If I can put new hope within the heart
Of one who has lost hope,
If I can help a [sister] up
Some difficult long slope
That seems too steep for tired feet to go,
If I can help [her] climb
Into the light upon the hill's crest
I shall begrudge no time

Or strength that I can spend, for well I know
How great may be [her] need.
If I can help through any darkened hour,
I shall be glad indeed.
For I recall how often I have been
Distressed, distraught, dismayed,
And hands have reached to help, and voices called
That kept me unafraid.
If I can share this help that I have had,
God knows I shall be glad.
                    —**Author Unknown**

Empathy is a beautiful emotion. I believe it is such a comfort to know that someone else has been in our shoes and genuinely understands what we are going through. It may not always be possible to *do* anything to improve the lot of one of our sisters, but we can certainly be there, quietly placing a hand on her shoulder.

I remember participating in a study of the biblical book of Job. Job was a man who was beset by a hoard of problems, none of which was of his own making. Friends gathered around him and began to analyze his situation, most of them trying to find someplace to lay the blame for his suffering. As the book progresses through a number of chapters, nothing changes. Job continues to suffer and the friends continue to speculate on whose fault it is. Interestingly, by the end of the book, it has become apparent that there is no way to discern the cause of the suffering of another person. And even if that were possible, it would still be impossible to alleviate it. Job's best friends turn out to be those who really do nothing but sit there with him, comforting him with their quiet, caring presence, assuring him that he is not alone.

This story was passed along to me by Herman Weiskopf, a writer and husband of Queen Jo-Ann Weiskopf (Ravishing Red Hatters, New Hope, Pennsylvania). A farmer was plowing his field with his tractor, when he got bogged down in the mud. No matter how he tried, he couldn't get it moving. His neighbor happened by in his truck and volunteered to pull the tractor out. They hooked the truck up to the tractor with a rope and gunned the truck's engine, but to no avail. After several tries, the truck also became totally bogged down in the mud. The neighbor sat down on the running board of the truck, next to the farmer, and exclaimed, "Well, I guess all I can do now is just sit here with you."

Of course, being women, we will add one element to this idea of sitting together—we will talk to each other, too. There is a great catharsis that results in just explaining your situation and your feelings about it to an uncritical, caring listener. That is priceless. So we will be there for one another, and we will listen, and that is a gift—to give, and to accept, as well.

Some women, married or not, experience great loneliness, some even within the context of marriage. Some mates are emotionally distant or consumed by their work. Jean Hedrick expresses the loneliness a neglected wife can feel in this poem that she wrote.

The Old Shoe

the old shoe lay by itself alone
out of style
scuffed
and worn
invisible behind the dust bunnies and boots
wear wrinkles pressed deeply across the toe
disregarded in favor of the latest fashion
shiny
polished
and new
it only needed a little care
a shoemaker's heel
a bit of polish
a careful shine
but where is its mate?

it waits
ready for usefulness again

but then it's discovered
the hole in the sole clear through
and it needs the shoemaker again
still the old shoe lay by itself alone
and in a world of pairs
you always need two

where is its mate?
where in the world is its mate?

Estrella Pfaff (WOW! Red Hats, Cameron Park/Shingle Springs, California) writes that her chapter mates listened to her when she shared the heartbreak caused by marriage to an abusive husband. Her health, finances, and emotions were at the breaking point. Her friends not only listened; they helped her to see that she was endangering her very life by staying with this man. One of her chapterettes said to her, "Estrella, if money is the only thing standing in your way, keeping you from getting out, don't worry. I have some money you can use. Do what you have to do." Imagine what that meant to Estrella. She walked out the door on May 24, 2002. Estrella says, "With the help of Michelle and many other women, I have reclaimed myself and my life. I moved back into my home . . . after a judge ordered him out. Since then I have been creating a new life with the continued support of my friends who wear red hats and purple dresses."

At our stage of life, many of us will, unfortunately, endure the loss of our parents. Maggie Hawk (Red Hot Flashes, Greenville, South Carolina) says she had no idea what she was getting into when she joined the Red Hat Society. After the recent death of her mother, she says, "I have gotten much more than I expected. The outpouring of compassion and love I received in the past few weeks from my Red Hat sisters has been beyond belief. I heard numerous stories about the women and their mothers and what they mean to them. I can't express how much this means to me. My mom was a great lady and she would have loved the Red Hat Society. Actually, I think she may be joining the heavenly chapter."

> ## "I get by with a little help from my friends."
> —the Beatles

One of the things that many of us face is the fading or loss of our health. Pris Price (Absolutely Fabulously Friendly Little Rockers, Little Rock, Arkansas) filled much of her time after her retirement doing volunteer work in an elementary school, which she loved. But her doctors ganged up on her and made her give it up; she was picking up too many viruses from the kids, and this was aggravating health problems she already had. She says that every idea for filling her time that she came up with was discouraged by her doctors. A friend suggested that she check out the Red Hat Society Web site, and she immediately started her own chapter, which quickly grew to twenty-five women. She writes, "I am feeling better now than I have in years. I've loved the meeting of new people and shopping for purple outfits." She has made and given away several hats and is in the process of making several more. She has dusted off her "poor neglected sewing machine" to make purple satin pajamas for an upcoming pajama party. Pris says, "If you have someone reluctant to form a chapter, send 'em to me!" And her cardiologist says her membership in the Red Hat Society has given her a new lease on life.

Health worries can put such a damper on our lives, and the caring companionship of dear friends can be a great antidote to fear, if we will let them into our lives. Susan Burkholder (Rosie Hattitudes and Rootin' Tootin' Tootsies, Tucson, Arizona) says that she recently learned she had a tumor in her kidney. As treatment progressed, she lost enthusiasm for her Red Hat Society activities. She had not decided whether to attend their next get-together, doubting that she could muster up the spirit. But their chapter's "Mother Nurturer" urged her to go, so she did. "With little luster, I donned a purple T-shirt, old scarf, a jean jumper, and my red straw hat.

Before, the best part had been putting together an outfit, but not that day. As my friends arrived to chariot me to the luncheon, I wondered how I could have a good time. Was I crazy in even going? Silently, I rode along, hoping that this would end quickly. But Mother Nurturer had contacted my Red Hat sisters, and they honored me at the luncheon. There were many bright gifts, wrapped in red and purple or in flashy gift bags. The words of care and concern were so genuine; I could not believe what was happening. It is easy for me to give a gift, and yet very difficult to accept them. This was overwhelming. Yet I loved the heart pillow with bright red wings that I was given to take to the hospital to remind me of my sisters. There were nightgowns, robes, coloring books, crayons, notepaper, and even a red rose pin for my hospital gown. I arrived home and didn't fall into tears. Instead, the Red Hatters' sisterhood had turned a very bad day into a wonderful memory. With great appreciation, I wrote thank-you notes. . . . They had taken my hand to help me through a terrible crisis."

"There is nothing better than the encouragement of a good friend."

—Katherine Butler Hathaway

Among the illnesses that we all fear, cancer seems to be the most prevalent. It has become the common enemy of many of us, and I have heard from large numbers of women who have weathered it, with the support of their red-hatted sisters. Here are a few of their comments:

I was diagnosed with breast cancer in March of '01, had the mastectomy in May '01, and in August '01 found myself with a red scarf tied around my bald head . . . enjoying the company of the Seattle Diva Dahlings.

—Roz Kenney
("Lady Limey")

Two years ago, I developed breast cancer and had a mastectomy. . . . This disease has given me a new perspective on life. . . . I read in the paper about a new chapter of the Red Hat Society starting in Memphis, and I went to the Internet to learn more about the group. Wow! . . . Just what I needed to lighten up my life!

—Natalie Turner
(Antique Teenagers,
Memphis, Tennessee)

Some people want to run from the word *cancer*, but that is when we need one another the most. Since I have started our Red Hat Society chapter, I am meeting other women who seem to have a real need to connect with others. We have become stronger, gained wisdom, and have so much to offer one another. No matter what we are going through in life, if we can put on a red hat and laugh together, our burdens will be so much lighter.

—Sharon Haught
(the Strawberry Preserves,
Winfield, West Virginia)

I recently had a mastectomy, and when I got home from the hospital, one of the ladies called and told me they would deliver dinner to my house for three consecutive nights. . . . The dinners were still hot from the oven. . . . I didn't even know I had so many friends, and all because of being a member of this wonderful *society*!

—Shirley Deardorff
(Sizzlin' Red Hatters,
Euless/Bedford, Texas)

Genuine sisterhood perseveres to the very end—and sometimes goes even beyond. The funeral of a Red Hatter can give her sisters a chance to support her family. The first time I heard of a link between red hats and funerals was when I received an E-mail from a woman named Sue Smith. She had never heard of the Red Hat Society before attending the funeral of her husband's sister. Sue writes, "Someone placed a large red hat with purple flowers around the band in her coffin, just above her head, only fifteen minutes before the funeral. We never knew who had placed it there." The donor's name may never be revealed, but she was obviously someone who cared enough to send a message of condolence and sisterhood.

Delilah Horsfield (the Villages First Red Hatters Chapter, the Villages, Florida) writes that her chapter was asked by the family of a red-hatted sister's chapter to attend the lady's funeral. Delilah says, "It really didn't matter that some of us didn't know her; she was a sister, and we needed to honor the request. Nineteen ladies turned out, and all nineteen felt not that they had done their duty, but that it had touched their own lives to have the opportunity to show respect to her and to her family. She was attired in her purple dress, according to her wishes, and her red hat was on display. Perhaps, as one Red Hatter suggested, she had turned in her hat for a halo."

Some of us are involved in ongoing situations that are quite demanding. It is good to have a group of people to play hooky with and know that they don't mind if we occasionally break down. Bonnie Lang (Red Hot Red Caregivers, Milwaukee, Wisconsin) started a Red Hat group for those who take care of severely ill kidney patients. As one new member began sharing at a gathering, she burst into tears. The poor woman said that she was almost embarrassed to return next time, after bringing herself and everyone else to tears. But at their next Red Hat event, the tears were from laughter, and she was among those laughing! Bonnie says that she has been asked by the organizer of a large caregivers' conference to wear her purple and red to the conference, with a button saying ASK ME on it. The Red Hat Society may well be a great help to caregivers.

Saundra Rae D'Arcy (Ozark Scarlet Women, Cherokee Village, Arkansas) tells of a conversation she struck up with a salesclerk in a department store. She was amused by a print she saw on a shopping bag for sale. The illustration on the front of it depicted several women in hats, and Saundra Rae laughingly explained the Red Hat Society to the clerk. The woman suddenly became emotional. Wiping away tears, she said, "You know, this is just what I have been looking for." As Saundra Rae was leaving, the clerk said, "I am so glad you came into this store today." Saundra Rae says, "We never know, in all our silliness, what opportunities we will have to share the fun and friendship of sisterhood with others. When we least expect it, we come face-to-face with someone who believes this is something they need in their life." It never hurts to be on the lookout for someone whose day you can make, does it?

Marge Williams, who is coqueen with her twin sister of the Prominently Purple Red Hatters (Bay City/Essexville, Michigan), is a working nurse and also cares for an extremely ill husband at home. Her prescription for coping with the stress of one crisis after another? She says we can do it "with a strong faith, lots of prayer, and also a much-needed sense of humor. . . . Many in our chapters are overwhelmed at times by the stress of watching our loved ones suffer as we try to make life more comfortable for them, and we *need* a break from time to time, to get out and laugh in the company of our fellow Red Hatters."

Sometimes a situation that was assumed to be temporary morphs into something permanent, and it requires added strength for the long term. Karen Zawada (the Red Hat Ladies of Sterling Heights, Sterling Heights, Michigan) raised five children and enjoyed being a mother immensely. She says she knew that when they grew up and left home, she could have a life of her own. But that has not happened for her, as her fourth child was born with cerebral palsy and is severely impaired. Karen found that over the years she had lost the ability to find ways to just let loose and have fun: "I just barred the wild and crazy Karen deep down and decided that she would never be able to roam this world again. . . . That sounds kind of sick, but truthfully, it's how I felt." The Red Hat Society concept gave her "an opportunity to dig up the old Karen, dust her off, and send her back into the world. I have been smiling ever since."

AN EMPTY BED

Widow. Just the word is sad. The concept is frightening. But it is a reality that many Red Hatters have to face. Most of us have already learned to live in a house empty of children. How much emptier must that house feel after the loss of one's husband?

> "As a recently appointed queen mother of the Rowdy Rocks of Plymouth, I wish to acknowledge that this treasured privilege has given me the impetus to regain a balance of fun in what has been a life full of blessings and challenges. I am widowed, after losing my husband and life partner to Lou Gehrig's disease . . . dealing with the loss of my dearest partner, my home, my business, my source of income, my career as I had known it, and what happens? My sense of self, my priorities in life, and the humor that sustains me have all been recovered, thanks to the sisterhood of the Red Hat Society."
> —Susan McNichols

Jean Hedrick wrote this description of adjusting to loss:

What Do You Do in a House All Alone?

What do you do in a house all alone when you cough?
　　Do you cover your mouth,
Say, "Excuse me" and "Please" and "Be there in a
　　minute"
　　When no one has asked you to come?
What do you do with those 4,000 words?
　　Do you talk to yourself and then

*Get in a fight, hold a grudge and make up with
          Yourself again?*

*What do you do in a house all alone when you cry?
          Do you say "You OK?"
Put your arms 'round yourself and hold on tight
          And wait for a better day?
What do you do with those bumps in the night
          And you wake up wanting to cling?
Do you wonder if bumps in a dream sound as loud
          'Cause awakened you can't hear a thing?*

*Well, you talk to your kids, clean out the garage
          Fix the plumbing, too
And you work so hard when you go to bed
          You can't help but sleep clear through.
There's time for a friend, for reading a book
          And talking to God all day.
Time to start a task, and finish a task without putting
          The pieces away.
There's time to think and time to grow and time
          To look back and reflect
That life is good and no matter what state
          I can truly say I'm content.*

The Morning Glory Sisters of Pleasant Prairie is a chapter of the Red Hat Society composed of women who met in a support group for widows and widowers. Mary Ann Smith says that some of the women thought she was a little nuts when she brought up the idea of starting a chapter of the Red Hat Society, but, after talking about it for a while, they decided it might be fun. Sister Mary Ann is the faithful adviser of their chapter of women aged fifty to ninety. She writes, "I think the more we get together, the more we realize we can have fun at any age and think about ourselves for a change. This group is just another good way we are working on healing ourselves."

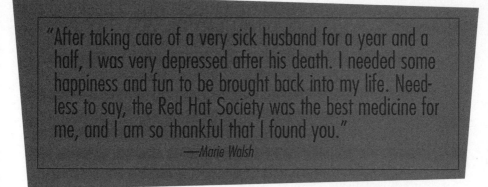

> "After taking care of a very sick husband for a year and a half, I was very depressed after his death. I needed some happiness and fun to be brought back into my life. Needless to say, the Red Hat Society was the best medicine for me, and I am so thankful that I found you."
>
> —*Marie Walsh*

Jerianne Payne (the Mah-jongg Dragon Ladies, Spring Hill, Florida) says that her chapter also was born out of a bereavement group. There were ten ladies who had been nurturing a wonderful group friendship for ten years. "When we saw the article in a magazine about the Red Hat Society, we knew immediately that was us," she says.

Martie Hobson (Red Hot Retirees, Hemet, California) has been a "birthing consultant" for the Red Hat Society, helping new groups get started in her area. She says that within one year, there have been thirteen chapters established in their small town. She recalls that one woman called to inquire about our group: "She said that her husband had passed away two years ago and she hadn't been out of the house until she came to our Spring Fling. She told us later that she had such a good time, and this had brought her out of her shell, and life was worth living after all."

A member of the Bodacious Babes (Phoenix, Arizona) says that she and her husband loved to travel. When she lost him, one day short of their thirty-eighth anniversary, she feared that her traveling days were over. But when she learned that the Babes were planning a trip to Hawaii, she was overjoyed to realize that she still had traveling companions.

Yes, there is a lot of trauma in the average life. But traumas come in all sizes, don't they? Sometimes, an event that might seem small when viewed over the span of a lifetime can assume huge proportions at the time of its occurrence and make life seem horribly difficult. One such event took place during the Red Hat Society's first national convention in Chicago. Vice Mother Elaine Williams and her queen, Joey Lambert (Aged to Perfection, Orange, California) met several new red-hatted friends on the first evening of the convention. They were having so much fun talking that they went out for a late-night snack. To her horror, when Elaine reached for her purse to pay her bill, the purse was gone. She had been carrying an unusually large amount of cash, which she had saved for the convention activities, and was so devastated at her loss that she didn't get up to attend the Pajama Breakfast the next morning. But Queen Mother Carrie Shepard and her roommate, Loretta Batliner of the Kentucky Ruby Reds (Louisville, Kentucky), had had trouble sleeping, just thinking about poor Elaine. At the breakfast, they asked that Linda and I share the story from the podium with the other Red Hatters. Within a matter of minutes, a spontaneous collection was taken up and delivered to Elaine's room. Joey Lambert was thrilled when she heard what had transpired a few minutes before her arrival at the breakfast. "My heart was overflowing and joyful tears rolled down my cheeks! This was a very emotional experience for Elaine and still is to this day."

Do any of you remember sitting around a blazing campfire at Girl Scout camp, singing camp songs? Do any of you remember taking your playmate a box of cookies after her puppy died? How about sharing your dolls with a friend who didn't have one? Let's do it again.

8

Queens for a Day

A man's home is his castle—until the queen arrives.

—Anonymous

s little girls, we usually chose to play princess because the title conjures up images of satin gowns, filmy netting, and glittering tiaras. Isn't it interesting, though, that the princess of most childhood fantasies is usually a young person of glamour and privilege, one who sashays about in lavish finery and receives gifts and homage? I can't recall that the young princesses whom I have known (or the one I used to pretend to be) were particularly interested in power, though. They were too busy dressing for the part and playing princess to have duties or bother themselves with any lowly subjects. I think there is a good reason little girls play princess rather than queen.

Now, a queen is another matter. While she will also gussy herself up within an inch of her life, her persona is a more commanding one. She will probably wield a scepter and make pronouncements. She is a reigning sovereign, not to be toyed with or ignored, a force to be reckoned with. Well, here you have it. Does this not, once again, perfectly play into the fact that we older women are disinclined to disappear quietly from the stage? A queen commands notice and respect simply by existing, does she not? And she has a backlog of deeds and accomplishments to add luster to her reputation. Thus, it is not the least bit surprising that many of us have decided to become queens. And how is that rank attained?

In the days of yore, the rank of queen was attained through inheritance and/or bloody battles. These days, in the Red Hat Society, one simply declares oneself queen and then acts the part. After all, there is a precedent for this sort of self-coronation. The story is widely told of Napoleon's coronation. He became impatient with the overlong ceremony, grabbed the crown, and placed it on his own head. Power? We queens of the Red Hat Society become power-mad in much the same manner (though with our tongues tucked firmly in our cheeks). We make pronouncements and remind everyone of our significance every chance we get. What fun!

The Red Hat Society members are known for their flurry of self-bestowed titles, royal and otherwise. Hey, if one of the girls is going to play queen, the other kids are going to want special names, too, aren't they? And shouldn't they be able to claim any title they want to? Since the Red Hat Society has no rules, there is no rule against this, either. In the true spirit of little girls' play, some chapter members are *all* queens, refusing to reserve that special title for just one of their number. A chapter may have a "Queen of Manners," a "Queen of Clean," and a "Queen of Naps," among others. In any case, the founding queen of a chapter should be preeminent. But here again, there are exceptions. Some chapters have coqueens, and, in some, members even take turns being queen.

Why do you suppose this concept of being queen is so popular? There have been images of queens and crowns on thousands of products as long as I can remember. There are queen bath towels, queen of this and that T-shirts, and queen plaques, signs, and bumper stickers. In the last few years, a great many wares have appeared for princesses, as well. While there may be fewer and fewer bona fide queens left in the world, the appeal of the office and its trappings remains strong. Artist Mary Engelbreit, one of my idols, has contributed to the American scene many humorous greeting cards and other products using this queen theme.

> "You are only young once. After that, you have to think up another excuse."
> —*Anonymous*

Lucinda Denton, queen of the Nonpareils (Knoxville, Tennessee), found herself extremely interested in this queen concept. She had seen playful queen references many times before, and she found herself analyzing the role of women who have founded Red Hat Society chapters. These women often add an extra word to their titles, declaring themselves to be the "Founding Queen Mother." It seems that they like the distinction of being the one who got the chapter started, especially if their chapter was the first in their area. Lucinda's fertile brain eventually served up the following treatise, which says a lot about both her and the Red Hat Society:

The Role of the Founding Queen Mother (FQM)

Do you remember the portrait of Liberty with a flowing gown, one of the most familiar symbols in America? As a child, I visualized this woman as the one who provided the freedom we enjoy as citizens. She epitomizes FQMs in the Red Hat Society! Miss Liberty, this time wearing a red hat and a purple outfit, assures the freedoms of her chapter's membership. There are freedoms to plan events, function without rules, enjoy without causes or obligations; there are also freedoms from having events that are out of the price range of members, discrimination, committing the group for social action or fund-raisers. Assuring these freedoms is important in the role that FQMs have chosen to play.

Queen Mother Liberty assures her subjects that they are free to participate in a variety of planned activities without being compelled. They are free to assume responsibility, but only when they want to. Red Hat members are free to form their own chapters if they are not satisfied with the one that they are in, and they are free to mold the image of a group. My favorite discovery includes the Florida ladies who have a nudist group.

Perhaps each FQM has her own list, but some of my favorite "freedoms from" include: formal meetings, officers, rules of order, fund-raisers or causes, requirements for membership, and fulfillments of expectations of members. And, best of all, no more cookbooks and bake sales ever again—at least for the Nonpareils!

When I mentioned that some of us participated in a Walk for Alzheimer's, the immediate reply was, "But I thought there were no causes." I think the difference is that we are free to participate, although we do not initiate the cause, nor require or even expect attendance. The freedom and fun of doing something with the group made the walk fun, as well as worthwhile. A member is free to plan entertainment for residents at a nursing home with a Red Hat fashion show. The models provide hats for the elderly ladies. But none of this is required or even expected in order to be a Nonpareil. Spreading the Red Hat joy is a freedom, not a demand.

At our first convention in Chicago, I learned that the complexion of groups is quite varied. Some enjoy the ridiculous and absurd, from their attire to their activities. I saw a hat made out of a red tank top, a feathery red purse made from a bra, ladies dressed identically in knit hats and matching shirts. How wonderful that our organization provides freedom to look or be as outrageous or as sophisticated as the membership desires. The FQM plays a leading role in this.

To me, the greatest pleasure in our chapter is that we have evolved into elegance and sophistication. We do things that are "different," such as riding a vintage bus in holiday parades. We take theater trips, boat rides, and behind-the-scenes tours. Members take pride in being properly dressed for each occasion, and I feel that the FQM has a role in the direction that the chapter takes. Just as a teacher taking a school class on a field trip, it would be difficult for the FQM to be embarrassed by the dress or behavior of her group.

Thanks to the foresight of the first Red Hat Society chapter, ladies are not bound by "must do" and "can't do." There are no rules and regulations, no constitution and bylaws. Each group is its own entity, although still a part of the larger flock. When walking into the Chicago hotel for our first convention, the reality dawned: I am free to be me. I am welcome to partake of something bigger than me, and I have the freedom to share this wonderful experience with other women. Red Hat queens aren't in competition, but together in liberty. I maintain the theme with our members, "You, too, are a Queen." The FQM has the freedom and the chance to make every member a queen in her chapter.

> "Don't treat me any differently from the way you would the queen."
> —Anonymous

We have established that being a princess or a queen is good. But it is also very good to assume the importance of other titles. Perhaps one of us may prefer to be a duchess or a countess, or maybe a lady of something. We are well aware that there is a formal pecking order among royals, but we disregard this sort of thing just as cavalierly as we do all other rules. Valerie, who works in our office, has declared herself to be an empress. Honestly, I am not at all sure which is more important, a queen (that would be me) or an empress. But as Rhett Butler said, "Frankly, my dear . . ." Suffice it to say that we are both royalty, and as such, we are equals.

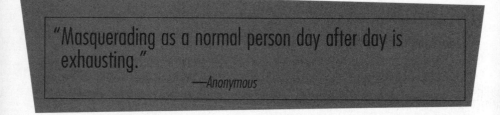

"Masquerading as a normal person day after day is exhausting."
—*Anonymous*

Gertrude Stein said, "a rose is a rose is a rose is a rose." But would a Red Hatter without a title have nearly as much fun? With a title, one can define oneself anew. If I don't feel like doing anything, why should I not call myself "Duchess of DoLittle," as does a member of the Vintage Tea Roses (Gainesville, Florida)? If I feel like throwing my weight around and being humorously full of myself, why not dub myself "Lady Know-It-All"? Choosing a title is a great opportunity to express your new self. Here is a sample of what some creative women have come up with. Hopefully, they'll give you some ideas for creating your own royal title.

The "Crowd Pleaser" is the temporary title for whoever hosts the event of the moment for the Improper Bostonians (Boston, Massachusetts).

The "Baroness of Bargains"—Barbara Scott-Cannon (Divine Order of the Woo Woos, Charlotte, North Carolina) says, "Anyone can pay retail; it takes a real shopper to get it on sale." There are a lot of us who pride ourselves on our shopping expertise. The hunt is so much more fun than the capture. Don't you agree?

The "Nanny of the Royal Money Bag" keeps track of her chapter's "fortune."

Some titles are not self-bestowed, but are given by one's chapterettes. "Baroness Barbara de Beethoven" of the Akron Red Hat

Flashes earned her name by agreeing to play the piano for some spontaneous singing at a chapter get-together. "Dame Purple Paparazza" is the chapter's official photographer.

"Presiding Perpetrator" Wanda Hoyles (Personalities in Purple, Freemont, California), is the founder of her chapter, but she prefers this title over "Queen." Taking her cue from Wanda, the second in command calls herself the Vice Perpetrator. That sounds even more threatening than "Vice Mother," doesn't it? I'll bet *she* gets a lot of respect!

"No Count Duchess" Cathy Smith (Crawford County Cuties, Van Buren, Arkansas) keeps track of the days and months of each member's birth, but in her great mercy, she doesn't keep track of the years.

Perhaps Gayle Willard (Chapeaux of the Purple Prairie Flames, Manhattan, Kansas) found the job of heading up a chapter somewhat confusing. She titled herself "Floundering Queen Mother." Her chapter also boasts "Queen Keeper of Creative Memories," who will create a memory for anyone who can't remember anything, and a "Catty Countess of the Cave," who apparently intends to remain devoted to technophobia. I guess if she stays in her cave, she won't have to learn to use a computer. Maybe we can toss notes through the cave door.

Marge Williams and Elaine Embrey (Prominently Purple Red Hatters, Bay City/Essexville, Michigan) call themselves "Tween Mothers," as they are twins and they share the rule of their chapter. (I wonder if they are the first twin queens in history? Do they carry matching scepters?)

"Queen Bee" Marcy LaSalle heads up the FUN-Key Flint RHS (Flushing, Michigan). She says she isn't anybody's mother, and doesn't intend to become one at this late date.

"Major Mama" (Last of the Red Hot Mamas, Ellicottville, New York) once taught baton-twirling to majorettes—hence the name. I'll bet she never dreamed she would be twirling and high-stepping in parades again at this stage of her life.

"Sister Superior" (the Red Writers, Fairfield, California) fines any member who attends a function without her colors. Remember, although we have no rules, we do frown dramatically on those who are out of the properly hued uniform.

"Lady Runamuck"—Judy Blankenship (the Red Hattitudes, Decatur, Illinois)—says that she is trying to get back into running (she took a twelve-year break), and her husband thinks this name is appropriate whether she actually runs anywhere or not.

An "Ac-Countess Receivables" collects cash.

"Lady-in-Weighting"—do we want to know?

"Duke of URL" (we pronounce it "Earl") is the title my husband has given to himself. Though men cannot be official members of the Red Hat Society, my husband, Allen, has, rightfully, I think, given himself a title anyway. After all, he is my consort. What does URL stand for? you may ask. Universal resource locator, an Internet term. Allen has been up to his eyeballs in our computer and Internet-related technical challenges almost from the beginning, and he continues to be very useful. (I have made him extremely aware that a queen outranks a duke, and he must never expect to be king.)

LAWS ARE FOR COMMONERS

While there are no rules (royalty, after all, doesn't abide by rules), the Red Hat Society offers three (*extremely* strong) guidelines:

1. Women fifty years of age or older must wear red hats and purple clothing at all official Red Hat Society events.
2. Women under fifty must wear pink hats with lavender clothing at all official Red Hat Society events.
3. Members of the Red Hat Society must promise to have *fun* and treat one another with kindness and consideration.

Failure to comply with these suggestions *may* result in "deCAP-itation," according to Pat Enger (Last of the Red Hat Mamas, Ellicottville, New York).

So much for guidelines.

Since we are so averse to anything that smacks of *Robert's Rules of Order* in any way, the Red Hat Society does not hold "meetings." The very word *meeting* conjures up images of agendas, motions, and committees. We prefer to participate in "gatherings," "get-togethers," "events," or "activities." We try not to prepare any more fastidiously for one of these events than is absolutely necessary. Obviously, in the case of large groups, reservations may be preferable to just winging it. Times, decorations, or menus may have to be arranged. But we try to do those things in a light spirit—and as little as possible. In my opinion, too much rigid scheduling tends to stifle serendipity. Sometimes it is kind of nice to leave wiggle room for spontaneous additions or deletions in a plan. But I have to admit that attention to detail sometimes avoids disaster. Only the most intrepid of us dare to dispense entirely with some degree of preparedness. As one of those people, I am qualified to warn you against the failure to think ahead at least a little. But each group is perfectly free to indulge its own level of comfort in this area, as in all others.

Now, having said this, I must be impeccably honest with you. Some Red Hatters have heard all my twaddle about not going to too much effort, and in typical Red Hat fashion, they have decided to discard this advice and suit themselves, which sometimes leads to undeniably hard work. The types of gatherings that I had originally envisioned were far too modest in scale for them. I had pictured two or three chapters in the same area coming together now and then in some low-key way that called for minimal planning. You know, something like just putting the word out on the Web site: "Hey, let's all of us Fullerton chapters go see *Divine Secrets of the Ya-Ya Sisterhood* at the Bijou on Tuesday night. Hope to see you there." Because the Red Hat Society is all about not working, I assumed that everyone else would be as hesitant to plan on a grand scale as I was—at least in the earliest stages of our development.

Well, no. Some women just couldn't resist the urge to plan large-scale gatherings on city, county, or statewide levels. My assumption that everyone else would be as comfortable with my "less is more" philosophy was wrong. It has been interesting to observe some of the major hooplas that have been planned here and there across the country. The photos and descriptions pour into our office and we just marvel. Never underestimate the power of several women who are absolutely determined to plan and present major productions! Obviously there are some of us who were just born to organize. When these women were little girls, they must have been like the people in those old movies who shouted, "Hey, let's put on a show right here!" That is undeniably a great boon to the rest of us, I admit.

There is one little nicety that we do not eschew, however: manners! "No rules" does not translate to "no RSVPs" in the Red Hat Society dictionary. Courtesy and consideration are not to be discarded by Red Hatters. In fact, because we think so highly of one another, we find mutual courtesy more desirable than ever before! Elaine Embrey (Prominently Purple Red Hatters, Bay City/Essexville, Michigan) said it very well in her communication to her chapter: "We realize that *everyone* cannot necessarily make *every* activity that is planned. This is meant to be a 'fun' group and not 'one more thing to dread.' So, having said all this, we all agree to RSVP promptly to each activity to give the 'planner' an accurate and prompt count ASAP, so that she/they can make reservations for the correct number of ladies for that activity in a timely manner. That's easy enough! Right?" My sentiments exactly. When one is called upon to give a credit-card number to secure a certain number of spaces, this kind of thing is absolutely essential.

THE *DUMBO* PHENOMENON

The first E-mails I ever received were from women who were attracted to the Red Hat Society concept but who had no idea how to begin to join the fun. At that time, there was no Web site, no brochure, no materials available to help them get started. So I spent a lot of time explaining our concept to one woman at a time, on-line, on the phone, and by mail. In the beginning, the only way newcomers could participate was by starting their own chapters, so that's what the majority of them did.

Later on, a lot of E-mails started coming in from women who had gotten their chapters going. They were full of enthusiastic gratitude! I heard wonderful comments, such as these: "You have changed my life!" "Bless you for starting the Red Hat Society!" "What a wonderful thing you have done!" Needless to say, this warmed my heart. But I knew that I, personally, had done very little. The Red Hat Society was started on a whim, and it grew with very little direction from me. I had never envisioned that the tiny seed I had planted would grow like a kudzu vine in the South! Most of the credit for the joy the Red Hat Society has brought to so many belongs to the hundreds and thousands of like-minded women who impulsively seized this tiny seed of an idea. They planted it in the fertile soils of their own imaginations then nourished it with their own ingenuity and creativity.

Do you remember the Disney movie *Dumbo*? Oh, how I loved that movie as a child! Do you remember Dumbo's discovery that he can fly? He thinks that this ability is bestowed upon him by a feather that has been given to him by his new friends, the crows. He believes that he needs to have that feather clutched firmly in his little trunk in order to fly. During the big circus fire, which comprises the film's climactic scene, he accidentally drops the feather, and he discovers, to his amazement, that he can fly under his own power! It's not the crow's feather that enables him to soar; it's his own ears! This story illustrates my belief about the success of the Red Hat Society. Women all over the world were inspired by our idea; they merely seemed to need permission or encouragement to try finding the merriment themselves. By calling upon the creativity, wit, and resourcefulness inherent in their own personalities, they have found the impetus to fly on their own! Each new Red Hatter already had the capacity within herself to come out and play with the rest of us. She just needed a little encouragement. Because this analogy seems to work so well, our office now sends out little purple and red feathers with every new chapter charter. When those envelopes are opened, tiny feathers flutter out, along with the charter and membership cards, serving as a reminder that the new queen and her members can find the joy on their own by setting their hearts and imaginations free.

I am extremely grateful to be able to be the spokeswoman for the disorganization as a whole, and I enjoy playing the "Exalted Queen Mother" to the hilt! But the Red Hat Society is not about me. It is the sum of every one of its red-hatted, purple-clothed parts!

9
Party Hardy (What Do We Really Do?)

All work and no play makes Jack a dull boy.

—Proverb

All work and no play makes Jill a dull girl, too.

—Sue Ellen Cooper

I have a news flash for all of us: There will *always* be something productive to do, something that we feel we should accomplish. For years, we have lived with the illusion that we would eventually finish every bit of work we could possibly find to do. Then and only then, we tell ourselves, we will take time for leisure activities. Oh, what fun we will have then!

What a mean trick to play on ourselves!

It has become obvious to me that, in our culture at least, it is considered highly suspect to, at any time, do nothing. Aren't we always supposed to do our best and give it all we've got? We insist that everything have a purpose, don't we? But I would like to promote the idea that it is occasionally okay (even better than okay) to spend time just being a human *being*, instead of a human *doing*. And I suggest that said human being should be enjoying herself!

I have been fortunate to do a lot of media interviews over the last few years, and there is one question that reporters invariably ask me: "So what exactly is it that you *do*?" I usually pause before making my reply: "Nothing." This is followed by an even longer pause on the part of the reporters. Then comes the request for clarification: "I mean, do you raise money for scholarships, or . . . ?" I reply, "No." This is followed by a further question: "Then what is your purpose?" After another pause, I take pity on whoever is asking the question and say that we get together solely for the purpose of *fun*-raising, not *fund*-raising! Of course, then I am asked what sort of fun I am referring to. This leads to varied answers, depending on the latest information I have gleaned from my E-mails. There is always a wonderful story or two to use to fill in the blanks.

As I see it, there are actually three aspects to the question of what we do:

- What job(s) do we do (have done or are still doing)? This question will have to be answered by each individual for herself.
- What does a Red Hatter do within our disorganization?
- What do we plan to do with our lives as we go forward?

Do we do charity work? Do we raise money for scholarships? Do we serve our community? Do we serve on committees, boards, et cetera? The answer is yes. But just as children don't do schoolwork on the playground at recess, we don't do volunteer work during our chapter gatherings. The Red Hat Society exists solely for the purpose of having fun together! Charity work is more suited for other areas of our busy lives.

What do we plan to do? Continue to schedule recesses together. We are nowhere near done with living, growing, seeking out new experiences, or new friends.

Dust If You Must

Dust if you must, but wouldn't it be better
To paint a picture or write a letter,
Bake a cake or plant a seed.
Ponder the difference between want and need?

Dust if you must, but there's not much time,
With rivers to swim and mountains to climb!
Music to hear and books to read,
Friends to cherish and life to lead.

Dust if you must, but the world's out there
With the sun in your eyes, the wind in your hair,
A flutter of snow, a shower of rain.
This day will not come around again.

Dust if you must, but bear in mind,
Old age will come and it's not kind.
And when you go and go you must,
You, yourself, will make more dust.

Remember, a house becomes a home when you can
write "I love you" on the furniture. . . .
—Anonymous

Eventually, reporters get it. Then I proceed to tell them some of the ways our chapters have found to make their own fun and celebrate just being together.

LET'S DO LUNCH . . . AND MUCH MORE!

Aileen Fields (Rowdy Red Hatters, Palm Springs, California) offers some good advice as to a general game plan: "Try to choose fun, different things—not necessarily something you do every day. And be mindful of budgets. Some activities involve dinner out and others are in someone's home and are free. Some of the events chosen involve a lot of noise and hustle and bustle, and others are sit-down, quiet conversation-type things, so that members can get better acquainted. Nobody should do the all 'work' of planning by herself. Encourage every member to throw her hat into the ring!"

Many chapters choose to get together for a lunch or a tea for their first gathering. Merely venturing out in their red and purple usually provides a sufficient initiation into the fun of Red Hatting. Some chapters continue doing this sort of thing, enjoying food and one another, and don't branch out to other activities, at least for a while. But eventually, many chapters get pretty adventurous! Here are some outings Red Hatters have done. Perhaps they'll help inspire you as you plan your own:

The Scarlet Hussies of Roane County (Tennessee) had a rather traditional lunch meeting as their premier event, but they were inspired to go from the restaurant to the courthouse, where they visited the election commissioner to see about throwing the upcoming election to their queen mother. They then repaired to the assessor's office to lobby for property-tax relief and to offer to form an impromptu jury. Spontaneity exemplified.

"Miss Eulaylee," aka Sharon Simmons (the Pensacola Sassies, Pensacola, Florida) declares that her chapter often has swap-offs. (No, not *that* kind.) Their second annual Swap-Off was held at Faye Hess's beach house. "Each Sassie goes through her closets and drawers and wherever else she keeps her stuff and drags out anything she doesn't wear or use anymore (and gifts from mothers-in-law). The items are bagged and taken to the Swap-Off, where each Sassie holds up and describes each item to the other members, until some-one yells, 'I want it!' If more than one person wants an item, a dice roll-off is held to determine the winner. The items not claimed are donated to a charity thrift shop. We have had everything from pasties to computer printers show up. Everyone goes away with something." Now this is one of the best reasons to clean out closets I have ever heard of. And I bet some of the gals don't even realize that they did some productive closet cleaning in the pursuit of hav-ing great stuff to take to the next swap-off.

Queen Arlene Mickley (the Red Hat Mamas, Moorhead, Min-nesota) and her group are touring their local ethnic restaurants, one at a time. So far, they have had Chinese, Italian, and Mexican food. Future plans include French and Norwegian fare, and they will con-clude their tour by visiting the American Legion. Obviously, they are a bunch of ladies willing to venture into uncharted taste territory. I'll bet none of *them* always orders the same old thing! When they get finished with restaurants, they may want to pick other categories of places to visit. Kind of kicks my brain into high gear just thinking about the possibilities.

Suzanne Birdenflight (Soaring Sistas, Downey, California) made arrangements to take her entire chapter to a photo studio so that each one could have a glamour shot taken in her fanciest red-and-purple ensemble. They took advantage of the professional hairstylists and makeup artists there, so each could look absolutely fabulous in her new portrait. Now how many of us have had our portrait made—ever? Don't you think it is time that all of us got a glamour shot? Our loved ones would assuredly get a kick out of something like this, don't you think? I think I will have one taken of myself and frame it somewhere where I will see it often, maybe in my bedroom. I will then get into the habit of looking at the picture rather than in the mirror. I'll bet it will do wonders for my self-esteem—or at least my sense of humor.

I keep emphasizing that the most fun we have usually occurs when we venture en masse to public events. People are just not used to seeing women our age drawing attention to themselves—and lov-ing it. The larger the audience, the better. Joanne Barbera's Redwood Rubies (San Francisco, California) rented an old fire engine to take them on a tour of their city, over the Golden Gate Bridge and into Sausalito, blowing bubbles all the way. They got a big kick out of the honks and waves that emanated from other vehicles on the road, and they enjoyed being photographed by tourists, too. If any of the Redwood Rubies was ever shy, I imagine she's gotten over that by now. Talk about taking your show on the road!

Members of the Red Hat Society often enjoy attending movies together, agreeing that the average "chick flick" is best enjoyed in the company of one's sister chicks. Robin Francini, queen mum (Crooked River Rubies, Cayahoga Falls, Ohio) writes that her chapter enjoyed an opening night at an old landmark theater, that has recently been restored, taking in an old movie, *Roman Holiday.* In their first six months, they also went out to dinner, made hatboxes, took a road trip to a tearoom and their favorite candle store, went to a holiday program entitled "Tuba Christmas," and had a pajama party. She and her sister made each member a nightcap in either pink or red, so they could be coordinated even while sleeping! Boy, once we get going with ideas, we just pick up speed, don't we?

Some of our chapters have favored celebrities with their presence. Shirley Cash's group, the Ravishing Red of Roanoke (Roanoke, Virginia), went to the Roanoke Symphony's Picnic at the Pops to see guest star Ben E. King. They took picnic food, purple napkins and tablecloths, and red napkins and dinnerware. And they wore their red and purple, naturally. During the intermission, they paraded up to the stage and presented the conductor, David Wiley, and the guest star, Ben E. himself, with honorary red hats. They stopped the show, and received a standing ovation from the audience. I am sure they dropped demure curtsies. All the attention we Red Hatters get prepares us well for the gracious acknowledgment of wild applause.

Attending sports events is very popular with our ladies. The Baltimore Red Hat Hons spent a day at the famous Pimlico Racetrack, home of the Preakness. The track named a race after them and they were delighted to be invited to the winner's circle to have their picture taken with the horse and jockey that won. The jockey even wore a red hat for the photo. The Lynden Ladies with Lids (Lynden, Washington) rode an Amtrak train from Bellingham to Seattle, where they attended a Mariners baseball game. They were all attired in red baseball caps and matching purple T-shirts with big red hats on them. Of course, they also carried signs that read MARINERS MATTER TO RED HATTERS. They hooted and hollered their best when they saw themselves up on the big screen at the field—in ladylike fashion, I am sure.

Terry Santore, queen mother of the Order of the Crimson Sage (Wallace, North Carolina), tells of her chapter's first annual card party, held at a local Holiday Inn Express. They invited a few other local chapters to join them, which resulted in even more fun than they expected. She says that laughter and conversation could be heard all up and down the halls, and many members asked if they really had to wait a whole year to do it again. Well, of course they didn't. If they wanted to, they were perfectly free to do it again the next time they got together. Unless, of course, it interfered with something even more fun.

The Harbor Hills Hubba Hubba Ding Dings (Lady Lake, Florida) splurged on high tea at the famous Grand Floridian hotel. They rented five white limousines to transport all fifty of them in style! I think they booked the tea just to have an excuse to rent the limos. It isn't easy to come up with a good reason to hire a veritable fleet of limousines, but I am happy to report that they managed to find one. Is there no end to our resourcefulness? (Does anyone know if there is such a thing as a red or purple limousine?)

Sally Munson (Matson Red Hat Society, Princeton, Illinois) helped her chapter plan a Thrift Shop Scavenger Hunt. The members gathered together in a downtown area that was home to several thrift shops. They declared a dollar amount that each was allowed to spend, then scattered to shop for Red Hat Society outfits. At the end of their allotted time, they met for a meal and merriment, each sharing what she had found. (I wonder if the stuff they found actually had to fit them. That would certainly make it even more challenging, wouldn't it?) I would suggest that this activity is even a little altruistic, considering that most of the loot was donated right back to the thrift shops from whence it came. Come to think of it, they could have had an impromptu fashion show, as well. Ideas often build upon one another. This notion could be made even more fun if all red and purple items were taken back to a central place (maybe someone's home) and everybody tried things on to see what fit which member.

While we Red Hatters love going out and all the attention we get, an occasional evening at someone's home can bring enormous pleasure. Whether a chapter is just forming or has existed for quite a while, events held in more intimate settings can provide an opportunity for taking friendships to a deeper level. Mickie Lenz (Les Chapeux Rouges, Newington, Connecticut) says that the chapter's first gathering was an evening potluck, to which each new member brought an appetizer. The hostess provided wonderful wines and a scrumptious dessert, and they had a super time getting to know one another so much better than they had before. The chapter later repeated the experience, throwing an Italian potluck, with each woman bringing a homemade Italian dish. As they became closer, they scheduled unbirthday parties to make up for all of the birthdays they had missed during the years before they knew one another. They had become such good friends that it was hard to imagine that they had each experienced so much of life before their friendships began. They enjoy exchanging keepsakes to commemorate those parties. Just imagine how many unbirthdays we have among us. None of us ever lacks an excuse to help someone celebrate or surprise her with a special gift from the heart.

EVERYONE LOVES A PARADE

It was probably inevitable that Red Hatters would eventually discover the perfect excuse for dressing up, behaving royally, and garnering extravagant amounts of attention all at the same time—they could participate, as a group, in a parade! Let's face it, even though we are hard to ignore in the first place, we are *extremely* difficult to miss when we form an entire parade unit and march (or ride) right down the center of the street, perhaps sandwiched between a high school marching band and an equestrian group! No matter where you live, there is always a parade in the works somewhere nearby to celebrate a national or local holiday. Oftentimes, the only requirement for joining one of these processions is a simple sign-up. And the possibilities for play are endless.

Queen Sandra Robinson (the Bastrop Belles, Bastrop, Texas) says that she and her Red Hat sisters decided to design a float for their chapter and have everyone wear costumes with a southern belle theme. They immediately began to scour the local thrift and resale shops for long dresses and other such finery fit for a royal court. They had a banner made to fly from their float, and they persuaded Grand Dame Dolly Gregg, aged eighty-six, to ride on it in a rocking chair, accompanying Queen Sandra. The chapter went to work. In Sandra's words: "The day before the parade, several ladies gathered at the queen's palace to turn the flatbed trailer into a float. . . . 'Lady M' got her grandson's boom box to play the Red Hat theme song for the background music while they worked. First, the hay bales were covered with sheets that had been dyed purple by Princess Jo, and red carpet and red throw pillows were placed on the trailer bed. Large wooden scroll cutouts adorned with luminous curly purple plastic donated by Princess Pinky Pettit were attached to the four corners of the trailer. Next, a lawn chair was covered with a gold satin sheet and brocade fabric for the queen's throne. . . . Finally, a large patio umbrella was covered with a red sheet. Lace curtains were added to the brim, along with a tulle train and large bunches of flowers, to create a giant red hat to stand in the center of the float."

But, alas, all did not go smoothly. According to Sandra, "Queen Sandy was up at 5:30 the next morning to survey the situation. The temperature was around thirty degrees, with winds gusting up to forty miles an hour. As soon as dawn broke, Queen Sandy went outside to attempt to add the purple-beaded garlands she had forgotten the day before, and she found that one end of the tarp had blown up and the sheets were now wet! She scurried back to her palace and retrieved several plastic shower curtains from the royal linen closet. It would not do for the royal court to have wet backsides, especially frozen ones. So she covered her throne with a zebra-patterned curtain."

Although the weather did not improve, the Bastrop Belles persevered, and despite the loss of hats and decorations to the roaring wind, they not only completed the parade but made plans before the day was out to march in the next parade they could find. Why waste such a wonderful float on only one outing? Ah, such spirit!

At the other end of the weather spectrum, the Crimson Glorys (Sioux City, Iowa) demonstrated extraordinary fortitude when they cruised (also in a loaned car) and marched in the Rivercade Parade in ninety-seven-degree heat. Queen Renee Beacom says that they survived mainly by eating ice and frequently reapplying their makeup. After all, one must keep up one's standards.

Red Hatters have thus demonstrated the willingness to freeze or melt for the cause!

The Scarlet Foxes (Oswego, New York) had much better luck when they entered Oswego's annual Prairie Fest parade. The weather was unseasonably sunny, warm, and breezy. Their local Chevrolet dealer loaned them a shiny red pickup truck, and some of them piled into that, with more riding in two members' convertibles. Those who could not fit—twenty-two of them—marched alongside. Queen Julie Clinton's words provide a vivid visual description of their delegation: "I ordered a fabulous three-by-six-foot banner with a gorgeous female fox head wearing a beautiful big red hat with purple and red feathers, and the fox's tail was wrapped around her neck like a boa and painted purple. . . . We had a Red Hatter and a Pink Hatter carrying the banner with such pride." The queen and three others followed in the pickup. "We had white shorts on, purple tops or sundresses, our red hats, plus red leis, giant purple and red silk flowers, boas, American flags, and red and purple balloons everywhere, chapter poster boards, purple and red crepe paper, et cetera. We were decorated to the hilt. Behind us were the two convertibles, and the two riders in the backseats sat up high on the back of the car, just like homecoming queens (the ladies were in their sixties and seventies), positively glowing and beaming!"

Julie says, "I've decided that sitting in the back of a red pickup truck with a ridiculously huge bouquet of red silk roses and feeling like Miss America, smiling and waving, wearing my red and purple, beaming as only a new and proud queen can do, is indescribably too much fun! . . . My face still hurts from smiling so much, and I swear my left hand is still waving in my sleep!" I guess this proves the truth of the adage that it *is* hard to be queen. But ah, the glory.

The Serendipity chapter (McKinleyville, California) entered a float in the Rhododendron Parade in Eureka, California, and won a trophy for special merit. They made a seven-foot-wide red hat out of a beach umbrella, and Queen Carollyne Banner made a band of rhododendrons to embellish it. They used an old red velvet bedspread to make the banners announcing their kazoo band and trimmed the banner with fringe. They were joined on the float by a few members of the chapter When Pigs Fly (Arcata, California), who helped them, appropriately enough, ham it up! Is it any wonder they won a trophy?

Red Hat Society chapters have come together as groups to decorate cars, flatbed trucks, and all manner of other vehicles in order to participate in parades. The Crazy Daisys (Tustin, California) arranged to have an antique red farm tractor pull a trailer loaded with hay bales and draped with banners, and it traveled along the parade route of Tustin Tiller Days. PrinSis Jane and I were invited to ride with them that day, seated royally on bales of hay. Isn't it interesting what can be used to make a throne? (I must tell you, though, those hay bales are prickly. Next time, I am wearing some padding. Yet another example of suffering for one's public.)

Convertibles and pickup trucks—especially red and purple ones—have been pressed into service by chapters galore. Floats have been created out of pickup trucks, flatbeds, and anything else that has wheels. Figuring out what to do to jazz up the basic vehicle can be challenging, but there are a lot of women with great ingenuity who are more than up to that task. Ann Hoffer (Ladies with Hattitude, Wytheville, Virginia) says one of their members suggested making a red hat out of a satellite dish. The problem was locating an old one. She posted her name and phone number on several Dumpsters around town, asking for discarded satellite dishes, and she found *two* in short order. The husband of another member, an engineer, helped them fashion a hat out of the two of them, covered it in purple and red, put it on a lowboy, and the Ladies with Hattitude proudly marched beside it in their hometown festival parade. In my opinion, that is a group of highly resourceful women.

The dozens of chapters in the Villages, Florida, did not wait to be part of a scheduled parade; they scheduled their own. The first annual Red Hat Society Golf Cart Parade was held in October 2002. The Villages is a retirement community, and golf carts are used by many to zip around town. Seventy-six of the carts, all lavishly and uniquely decorated, composed the lineup for their first outing. Red and purple could be seen everywhere; only queens were allowed to add gold embellishments. Their parade was such an enormous hit, they decided to make it an annual event. In 2003 this event was repeated, with twice as many golf carts as before. Vice Mother Linda Murphy and I had the privilege of being the grand marshals! Most likely, the ante will go up next year. Any chance that someday it will rival the Rose Parade?

REACTIONS

Although I frequently recommend Red Hatting in public, it should be emphasized that drawing notice has not been our primary goal. Our goal is to enjoy one another and life, and to grant one another the freedom to play. We have no bitter, sarcastic agenda, as some women's groups seem to do. We are not angry or resentful women. We are not burdened with regret or bitterness. We may be trying to make up for "the sobriety of our youth," but our spirit is one of unmitigated joy! And joy is both attractive and contagious. Therefore, the reactions that we provoke from our audiences are almost overwhelmingly positive.

The first reactions we all noticed were those from other women.

Everywhere we went, we were approached by soon-to-be sisters, who saw how much fun we were having and clamored to join our fun. Innumerable stories have poured in about this phenomenon. Carolyn Kaye (Downriver Red Hat Divas, Allen Park, Michigan) writes that she even had a woman grab her arm in a restaurant and ask if she could *please* join them. As word has spread among our friends and acquaintances, most of us have had problems keeping our chapters from exploding in size. Believe me, membership in the Red Hat Society is a soft sell! I usually tell women that they should never have to urge another woman to join them. If she doesn't get that light in her eye and practically beg to join, the Red Hat Society may not be for her. We have found high-pressure salesmanship to be totally unnecessary. Red Hatting is highly contagious!

Barbara Merfeld, the queen of the Mad Hatters of Goldendale (Goldendale, Washington), sent this summary of the reaction received by her chapter on their premier outing to a fancy restaurant: "As I and my car-pool ladies approached the main door, a trio of other guests gaped at us. I waved my red-gloved hand in friendly fashion and said, 'The Red Hat Society!' and sailed through. . . . When all seventeen of us gathered in the lobby, we were the center of attention. Busy greeting the ladies, I was suddenly aware that one of the hotel staff was taking photos of us. The vice mother was not included in the photo op, as she had been approached by one of the staff, who wanted to join us! The interesting thing is that we received most of our attention from the men. One gentleman came to us at our two tables and said, 'Next time, you ladies should really spread out at other tables. It is too much to have all you beautiful ladies in one place.' Another gentleman came over to ask about us. When we explained that we were a society in which the members have to be fifty years of age, he said, 'Some of you are cheating.' As we were waiting to be escorted into the dining room, three young fellows in their early twenties passed us and smiled. A man hunched down beside our table to ask about the society for his mother. Even as we left the hotel, an elderly gentleman with his walker spoke to us and then wished us well."

Barbara Cavanagh (High Tide Hatters, Northport, New York) shares the story of her chapter's train expedition to Manhattan to see *Menopause, the Musical!* She says they had a "belly-laughing time. . . . Many, many people asked about our wonderful hats, took pictures of us, and cheered as we walked about fourteen blocks to the theater." As anyone who has ever been to New York City can tell you, it takes a lot to get noticed in that town!

Not long after I received Barbara's E-mail, I received one from another Red Hatter, whose chapter members also went to see that show. They were invited up onto the stage after the play to do a little Rockette chorus-line dance with the cast!

Red Hats saved Barbara Hammer (Rubies with HATtitude, Morris County, New Jersey) from getting a speeding ticket. A state trooper pulled a speeding carload of Red Hatters over and asked, "Do you know why I stopped you?" Barbara said with a smile, "Sure, you're curious about our red hats." She explained who they were and told him that they were on their way to see an exhibition of hats at a museum. She handed him a Red Hat Society flyer. He said, "Well, now I have to decide whether to give you a ticket or a warning." With quick wit, Barbara said she had a warning for him, and she whipped out a copy of Jenny Joseph's poem, "Warning." He walked back to the patrol car and started writing. He came back to her window, gave her a huge smile, and handed her a warning, saying, "Never in my twenty-two years on the force have I ever come across anything like this!"

Media attention is focused on us wherever we go. When a group of Red Hatters took the train from Boston, Massachusetts, to Portland, Maine, for lunch, they were taped by a TV film crew. Angel Burke (the Improper Bostonians, Boston, Massachusetts) says, "Even the train conductors heard of our trip and decorated their caps with red boa feathers, joking with us and dancing!"

It isn't just the American media that has been sitting up and taking notice. The Redcliffe Red Hatters (Brisbane, Australia) went on a cruise of beautiful Moreton Bay and wound up being featured on a television program later that week. They were also featured on the official Web site of Redcliffe as a part of a tourist promotion. Aussie Rose's comments were typical of Red Hatters: "We had a wonderful day and met lots of new people."

The Red Hat Tamales of Niles (Niles, Michigan) attended a Dyngus Day celebration (a Polish political holiday) in South Bend, Indiana. "It was absolutely amazing how they treated us!" said Carole Mobus. "One young man quickly cleared two tables and set up chairs. We could see people looking at us and clearly wondering what we were. Slowly, they came over and asked questions. Some asked us to dance. One man sat by a recently widowed member and talked to her. I haven't seen her smile so much in months! One young lady took information to give her mother."

Apparently our fame frequently precedes us. Charlotte Snyder (Lighthouse Bay Chapter 3, Bonita Springs, Florida) writes that several chapters in her area were invited to attend a football game featuring the Florida Firecats. They were to wear their purple and red, as those are the Firecats' colors, and they were to function as mascots for the day. Each of their nine queens was driven around the playing field in a separate convertible, waving and smiling. They even got to go out on the field to flip a coin to determine the opening play. During halftime, they were mobbed! After the game, they were invited to the team party to meet the players and the owners. And they are invited back for opening day next season. The team is even making them a banner! I guess it's true what they say: It *is* good to be queen! It is also good to be several queens, along with their minions, in the same place at the same time.

HUMOR KNOWS NO AGE

Young people and children love us, too! Judy Swope wrote to say that one of her newest members, Darlena Wise, got into her group due to the efforts of Darlena's grandson. He was having his hair cut in the same salon as Jody and heard her talking about the Red Hat Society. He asked for information on behalf of his grandmother, saying that she had seen something about the Red Hat Society on TV and expressed a desire to join. Darlena not only joined their chapter (the Passionate Plums, Barberton, Ohio) but she drives their official float, a pickup truck, in the parades that they participate in!

Janclay Britton, the "Contact Hat" for the Glad Hatters of Richmond (Richmond, Kentucky), says that her chapter members especially enjoyed the reactions of the little girls along the parade route when they were in the Apple Festival parade in Paintsville, Kentucky. (They won the hundred-dollar first prize for their glorious float.) She says, "Little girls don't see wrinkles and rolls if they're surrounded by glitter, feathers, and hats!" Next, their group will ride in their local Christmas parade!

Nancy Veits (Lady Hatterley's Cover, Palos Verdes, California) visited a local classroom, having been invited to make a presentation to kids in an English as a Second Language class. She tells how she explained the Red Hat Society to children, ages thirteen to seventeen, from Iran, Japan, China, Taiwan, Russia, Korea, Mexico, and Guatemala. She says they smiled when she was introduced as a queen, and she shared the Red Hat Society values and silliness with them. She read the poem "Warning" to them and they clapped and made her feel welcome, sharing experiences that they had had with their grandmothers and other older women. Nancy promised to join them again soon, and she says it was one of the most enjoyable experiences she has ever had.

I have also been fascinated to discover how much our own children and grandchildren egg us on!

Edithe Loetzer (the Lewes Red Hatters, Lewes, Delaware) was riding in one of two decorated vehicles in a Christmas parade with her chaptermates when they were temporarily stopped as they approached the viewing stand. Her eyes filled with tears as her grandson, James, who is fifteen, ran up to the car and presented her with a long-stemmed red rose wrapped in a purple ribbon! He was obviously proud of his grandmother.

Mary Andollina (Chapeaux Rouges d'Orleans, New Orleans, Louisiana) was interested to hear how her daughter views her Red

Hat Society membership. She explained to Mary's grandson that they were going shopping to find Grandma a red hat because Grandma was in a gang now, and their colors were purple and red. Oh well, we have been accused of being a gang before. It might even be true.

Elizabeth Wilson's six grown children liked the premise of the Red Hat Society so much, they arranged for their mother to be a part of it without even consulting her. Even though the kids were scattered all over the country, they each called or sent an E-mail to their mother the night before her seventieth birthday and advised her to be sure to wear slacks the next day. The next morning, she woke up to fresh-cut flowers and a cup of coffee, provided by her husband. The accompanying card contained the "Warning" poem and instructions to dress comfortably, put on makeup, and be ready for a visitor at 11:00 A.M. In the birthday package, she found silky purple drawstring pants and a purple plaid top, which she obediently put on. A male friend she had worked with on various volunteer projects soon pulled up on his motorcycle and invited her to hop on the back. Her children tell me that she had never been on a motorcycle, but she is known for being a very good sport about these types of things. The children had provided her chauffeur with an itinerary, and he took her on a grand tour around town, stopping at various places so that she could gather birthday wishes from her friends, all of whom met her wearing birthday hats and blowing on noisemakers. Says her daughter, Braxton Malan, "At each stop, an item from the poem was presented to her—an outrageous red straw hat at the first stop and an invitation to join the Red Hat Society, a bottle of brandy, summer gloves, decorated flip-flops with straps covered in satin ribbon, and a stick with a bow on it" (for running along railings, I presume). The tour culminated at a restaurant, where two of her best friends and one of her daughters were waiting. They had a four-hour lunch, which was filled with laughter.

Lady Mary Conner (the Blooming Red Lotus Flowers, Monroe, Michigan) says her group had an experience with a little boy who appeared to be about five years old: "He came over to our table and just stood there, shifting from one foot to the other. We finally asked him if we could help him. He looked at all of us, one by one, and said, 'You ladies look so beautiful in those hats. I never saw anything like this before!'"

Sometimes a child's reaction offers a bright spot of humor. Amber Vansantford (Medicine Hat, Port Orchard, Washington) says her grandson was visiting the day her new red hat, covered with feathers, arrived by UPS. When she removed it from the box and tried it on, he blurted, "Grandma, you look just like a chicken!" She says that the hat will henceforth be known by all as "the chicken hat." Well, that may be, but everyone knows that Red Hatters are anything *but*!

BEWARE OF DOG (AND CATS)

I think a word of caution is in order here. Although our garb is met with enthusiasm by the general public and by our families, there is one group whose reactions, while enthusiastic, may or may not be entirely predictable—our pets.

Suzie Wood (Mad Hatters, Costa Mesa, California) visited the Red Hat Society Imperium (our retail store) and purchased a whole bunch of items, including two boas, one purple, one red. Her three orange tabby cats ("the boys") met her at the door when she got home and followed her to the bedroom, where she unpacked her treasures. When she turned her back to put something in the closet, the first boa was snatched and went trailing down the hall, followed by three sets of galloping feet. Suzie says, "I could hear the glee in their voices. Over the sofa, across the chair, and out the cat door! After several minutes of negotiation and bribes, I was able to retrieve the boa. I now have it hidden on a top shelf deep in the closet. They keep looking up, trying to think of ways to ascend." Maybe she needs to remind "the boys" that the Red Hat Society is for girls only.

Nancy McKinney (the Victorian Roses, Wilmington, North Carolina) crocheted her first red hat and wore it to her first luncheon, to great acclaim. A few days later, she was showing it to her neighbors, and when they all went out to dinner, she left it on the sun porch. When she returned, the hat was half-eaten and pieces of loose string were scattered all over the floor. Nancy thinks it was the sugar starch that she had used to block the hat that appealed to her dog Dixie Belle's taste buds. She says that she laughed and cried at the same time as she cleaned up the hat mess. (We don't even want to ask about any other messes that may have ensued.) She laboriously made another hat, which she keeps out of Dixie Belle's reach.

As you can see, we women over fifty have gotten accustomed to not being seen—whether it be by Madison Avenue salesclerks or by construction workers who used to whistle our way. So it's nice, for a change, to be able to put on a red hat and purple clothes and have people notice us not for our legs or for our pocketbooks, but for our spirit and fun!

So, to sum up: We don't go out specifically to evoke reactions from anyone. But there's no reason we can't enjoy that, either.

10
Express Yourself!

I shall wear purple / With a red hat . . ."

—Jenny Joseph

Clothes make the woman. Wearing red and purple dress-up clothes makes the woman fun!

—Sue Ellen Cooper

*A*long with a newfound freedom to play, comes another opportunity: the chance to let other people see you as you really are, the chance to let that playful child out of the closet that she has been living in for far too long. We reveal our true selves in so many ways, and the aesthetic choices each one of us makes reveal her personality.

> "Anyone who keeps the ability to see beauty never grows old."
>
> —*Franz Kafka*

Some years ago, Kenny Rogers recorded a song entitled "You Decorated My Life," in which he paid tribute to a woman who had filled his life with color and joy. The lyrics spoke of the ways in which his special woman enhanced his life with her personality and her love. I believe that each of us has a unique opportunity and capacity to beautify our surroundings in order to provide pleasure for ourselves and for others whom we love. According to *The Random House Dictionary of the English Language,* "to decorate" means "to embellish, to enhance by beautifying." Let's all take the responsibility for embellishing and beautifying our lives and, by extension, the lives of others by whatever means we can find. I suggest that we start by decorating ourselves and our surroundings. What better way to express ourselves and demonstrate who we have become? In this way, we will decorate the lives of those around us, as well. Our bright colors and the smiles that we wear are a visual encouragement to others; I have the E-mail to prove it!

Like nearly every woman I have ever met, I *love* clothes. The vast majority of women I have known have spent some of their most enjoyable hours browsing through stores, fingering fabrics, oohing and aahing over the cut, color, and design of all types of garments, perusing price tags and then adjusting their expectations accordingly. We have experienced wonderful moments of satisfaction when we have found the occasional perfect garment, one that fits, flatters, accommodates our budget, and makes us look good in our own eyes and feel better about ourselves all at the same time. It tells the world who we are! Unfortunately, as we grow older, those moments occur further and further apart. We may (or may not) be able to afford more expensive clothes, but, as we have already discussed, the body which we cover with them has changed quite a bit.

So now we are faced with another reality check. This one doesn't appear suddenly; it creeps up on us gradually over the years. We can no longer shop in stores that cater to the hip. (And I don't mean a part of the anatomy!) We probably get that through our heads by the time we start crowding middle age, although it isn't an easy attitude adjustment. Then, as our encounters with dressing room mirrors grow increasingly unpleasant, we begin to grow more selective about the clothing we try on. We start weeding out things that we know will reveal more than we want others to see. This stuff doesn't even make it *into* the dressing room. We pass over the sleeveless blouses, the deep necklines, the thigh-high skirts and short shorts. When I first started doing this, I told myself that I was going to have to drop some weight and get more exercise before I allowed myself to consider wearing some of those things again. It took a fairly substantial amount of time before I was able to face the fact that the time for wearing clothes like that again was *never.* I want to look my best, and I don't look my best in those things. Alas! Barring a miracle—or massive amounts of plastic surgery (with all of its attendant discomfort, health risks, and horrendous price tag)—my current physical state is permanent.

And here lies exposed another untruth I used to try to tell myself. For my body's *current* condition is not permanent, either. Further adjustments in my attitude about my physical self and appropriate clothing will, inevitably, be required as I continue to age. Oh well! I shall be adaptable. I shall rethink the issue of clothing in my life, along with so many others. (And I shall remain cheerful, I promise.)

Anyone who has ever so much as been introduced to a man knows that men and women see clothing in entirely different ways. Although there certainly are some exceptions, the average man acquiesces to the need for buying clothes on practical terms. He knows that he needs to have a few, if only to satisfy basic requirements for modesty and warmth. He buys some. End of story.

The average woman sees clothing as necessary for much, much more than the fulfillment of basic needs. Clothing needs to be beautiful. It needs to flatter the wearer's body and express the wearer's personality. The search for just the right articles of clothing appeals to our sense of adventure and satisfies our need for treasure hunting. To the average woman, shopping is a participation sport, an end in itself. A day spent shopping is a balm to the spirit, a treat for the senses. Sometimes the contents carried home in shopping bags are almost beside the point.

It is nearly impossible to have too much clothing. After all, there are so many types of occasions to dress for! One needs dress-up clothes, casual clothes, kick-back clothes, and clothes for all sorts of in-between occasions. Then there are bathrobes, pajamas, underwear to locate—each important in its own way. A lot of us also deal with size fluctuations, necessitating even more clothes. And every outfit dictates the type of accessories needed. What type of undergarment (will my straps show?)? Is this slip too long to wear with that dress with the slits? What heel height for which pants? What belt for which outfit? And, when all of these questions are answered, we still have the problem of jewelry to deal with—glittery earrings for evening, plainer ones for day, depending on the outfit, of course. And let's not even go *near* the issue of gold versus silver, shiny finish versus brushed metal, et cetera. Oh, such problems!

So now, as I have said, I have to rethink shopping in light of age and body issues. For the sake of propriety (and for those who have to look at me), I will buy whatever size I actually need these days, rather than try to squeeze into the size I once wore. I will waste as little time as possible agonizing over the things I really should not wear and try to buy clothing that is age-appropriate, without being too out of it (if I can find it). I will accept that shopping for clothes is going to be a little less fun than it once was, at least for clothes that I wear in my everyday life. In this area, as in many others, I will accept the current state of affairs.

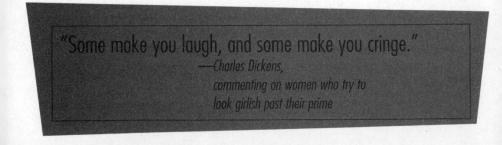

"Some make you laugh, and some make you cringe."
—Charles Dickens,
commenting on women who try to
look girlish past their prime

Donna Dowdy (the Desert Divas, Green Valley, Arizona) reports that her mother wanted to encourage her participation in the Red Hat Society, so she sent her a lovely dress and hat from her home in Missouri. Upon receipt of the package, Donna called her mother to remind her that she was no longer a size four, nor did she wear a small-size hat. Her mother's response: "Nonsense!" Donna didn't want to hurt her mother's feelings, so she dutifully tried them on, took a ridiculous photo for posterity, and then quietly donated them to her local thrift shop.

THE RED HAT SOLUTION TO WOMEN'S WEAR

The central character from the "Warning" poem is, basically, wearing any old thing she feels like wearing—and if it looks awful and others don't like it, so much the better. She honestly doesn't care what impression she conveys to others. Red Hat Society members aren't dressing to please others, either, though I think most of us still do care how we appear to other people. But we *are* dressing to make ourselves happy. We are showing our colors to declare our exuberance for life and our solidarity with like-minded women. Although we didn't set out to perform for anyone else, we have discovered that most people who see us out and about in our finery are amused and uplifted. These clothes actually help us connect with other people, which we consider an unexpected bonus.

Robin Crowley says that shopping for Red Hat regalia has brought her and her mother closer than they have ever been. "Not only do we enjoy the meetings themselves but we also have grand fun browsing secondhand stores for delightfully tasteless frocks,

"The beauty of a woman is not in the clothes she wears, the figure that she carries, or the way she combs her hair. The beauty of a woman must be seen in her eyes, because that is the doorway to her heart, the place where love resides."
—*Audrey Hepburn*

accoutrements, and accessories. At a recent tea, my mother was quite a sensation in her red satin fingerless gloves! While the gloves were a tacky touch, to me they represented an entire day's worth of shopping, lunch, and bonding with my mother. Pretty nifty for a five-dollar pair of gloves!"

We have adopted the colors mentioned in the poem, but only because we *like* red and purple together. We have discovered that they positively *sing* in their combined vibrancy and chutzpah! Now I ask you, who can be a shrinking violet or any other kind of wallflower when she is so adorned? Do purple and red clash? In our opinion, absolutely not!

So here is another area in which the Red Hat Society rides to our rescue! Remember our little friend Ruby's delight in playing dress-up? Remember your own? I sure do! Most of us probably have lost a lot of the fun we used to get out of shopping for pretty clothes, and we have resigned ourselves to finding something that is just suitable.

But dress-up clothes are another realm entirely, are they not? When one is playing dress-up, some rules of good taste and decorum may be safely discarded (*except* for the one about showing too much skin). In the Red Hat Society realm, tacky is okay and gaudy is positively good! Remember all the sparkly over-the-top clothing that you were attracted to when you were little? Now you not only *get* to wear it; you are *required* to wear it! The fun has automatically been restored to shopping! Not only do we give ourselves permission to buy items ordinarily considered too glitzy or too fancy but we actually get to *wear* them, whenever and wherever we want to! If we can't give ourselves permission, we can get it from our Red Hat sisters, who can be counted on to respond enthusiastically to our latest find, no matter how over-the-top it may be. There may even be envious cries of "Where did you *get* that?"

I was meditating on these thoughts recently while walking my dog, Frosty. (I got a dog partly because I knew that a dog would need frequent walks, and I was aware that I would, too, if I wanted to fight the constant battle of the bulge. It turns out that these walks are often when I do my best thinking, away from the phone and the doorbell. As with many other things, one good thing may lead to other, unforeseen good things. Ah, but I digress!) While walking, thinking about aesthetics, I was evaluating every house and yard I passed, playing mental games as far as changes I would make to each home's exterior if it were mine. That led me to wonder about the interiors of each house. Was the home with the crisp new paint job and gracefully landscaped yard as perfect on the inside as it was on the outside? Was it furnished with beautifully proportioned objects covered in beautiful fabrics? Was the wood polished and gleaming? Was the house next to it—the one with the ravaged roof, peeling paint, and weed-choked yard—as slovenly inside as outside? I assumed that the outside of each home probably represented the condition of the inside as well, and this may have been a valid assumption. There is only so much upkeep that we can do on *our* exteriors, as well. Yes, we can keep ourselves neat and clean. Yes, we can wear the most flattering of colors and fabrics. But we are unlikely to fool anyone about our age. But do we have to be dowdy? Does our clothing have to be boring? Why should a middle-aged woman in brilliant plumage be so surprising?

The red and purple we have adopted from the poem express our state of mind perfectly. All of us in our red and purple are guaranteed to stand out in crowds of conservatively attired people, which is undoubtedly one of the reasons we like to mingle with the masses. As an artist, I have always had a fascination with color. In the study of artistic principles, I learned that one way to make a color appear more vivid in a painting is to place it next to a dull one. In this way, the brighter color is made to pop in a way that it wouldn't otherwise. I learned also that there are whole books on the science of color theory and incredibly complicated classifications of color that address such issues as hue, intensity, contrast, et cetera. (Personally, I operate on instinct, so whenever science intruded on my art studies, my brain just went on hiatus.)

The field of psychology offers some fascinating studies on color and our reactions to it. Although not scientifically proven, many studies have suggested that the preference for certain colors can be an indication of one's personality traits. It seems to be common sense to suspect that a person whose favorite color is red is probably extroverted and enthusiastic. Red speaks of life, excitement, vigor, and celebration. It is the color of passion, roses, juicy apples, and lifeblood.

To the Chinese, the color red symbolizes happiness.

I have read that the psychological reaction to purple noted in many studies indicates that it is a bit calming, perhaps melancholy, and subdued. I am no psychologist or scientist, but I suspect that this may be true. Sociologically, rich, deep purple has long been associated with royalty. This connection was established hundreds of years ago when purple dye was so expensive that it could be used only on fabric for the clothing of kings and (how appropriate) queens!

Another interesting note: In the theater, red is associated with comedy, and purple with tragedy. Most of us have had plenty of both in our lives, often intertwined. So why not wear them together? We've earned the right! And, since our clothing features colors from both extremes, it follows that we must be extremely well-balanced women!

The woman in the "Warning" poem also feels that her red hat doesn't "suit" (flatter) her, and it doesn't "go" (coordinate with her purple outfit). Now, I must take serious exception to her opinion. I think there is a warm or cool red to suit every face, particularly since red casts a rosy glow over the skin. And purple and red certainly *do* go! They make a jazzy, upbeat combination! So there!

What constitutes true red and true purple? As an artist, I have always been very sensitive to color, and I can testify that there are as many shades of purple and red as there are personalities. Colors can be brilliant and pure or grayed and subdued. I think we should grant one another wide latitude when it comes to specificity of color. Close enough is just that. Color is the foundation of our attire, but there remains a lot of room for individuality. Anyone who has the opportunity to view a large gathering of Red Hatters will notice that the inevitable array of shades and tints before them is a fabulous sight, a virtual Mardi Gras for the senses! Hooray for glorious color, in all its variations!

HATS

I suppose that hats were first worn purely as a protection from the elements. I would guess that the first hat was probably nothing more than a big leaf or a small animal skin. For centuries, hats were worn primarily by men, often as an indication of rank. I have learned that hats were not a staple of women's wardrobes until the mid-1800s. At that time, they were worn primarily by women of upper-class status, and each hat was designed exclusively to flatter the features of the individual wearer's face. This is probably not going to be an option for most of us. Each of us will have to locate the hat that is right for her, and we will have to do it the hard way—by hunting for it—high and low, if necessary.

Some women swear that they cannot wear hats, claiming that their heads are too small or too big, or too . . . something. Florence Bergstrom, a milliner friend of mine, firmly believes that there is a hat shape to flatter every woman's face. She has sold beautiful, hand-crafted hats for years and has proven her point over and over, making converts of many previously hatless women.

When the Red Hat Society women began to wear hats, there were those who loved our premise but did not want to wear the requisite hat. Our reply to such ladies is, "Hats on!" We ask that each new member follow the advice of my milliner friend, Florence, and spend a little time finding the right hat to suit her face. But finding *a* red hat is not the same thing as finding *the* red hat. If the search for the perfect hat gets too prolonged, we suggest just slapping something red on her head until she finds the right one.

It seems that there is a logical progression that each Red Hatter goes through. Her first step is to find a red hat, any red hat. The second step is embellishing the hat, perhaps with a veil or a flower. Before long, the wearer may decide she needs a hat with a bit more flamboyance, a bigger brim, so that she can make a more definitive statement. She purchases a second red hat. After that, it usually isn't too long before hat mania sets in and the collection stage begins. It is very interesting to listen to the average group of Red Hatters compare the size and variety of their individual collections. I must warn you: Collecting red hats can become an addiction! Why? As you progress in the Red Hat Society, you become happier with yourself and more full of fun. You gradually let go of some of the sober attitudes that might have been holding you back from the playful attitude that you feel yourself developing. And one of the best ways to project a playful attitude to others is to wear fun, attention-grabbing clothing. After that, some women's competitive natures rise to the forefront (in good humor, of course) and the desire to have the biggest, most incredible hat looms large.

To make a large hat fit a small head, merely apply a length or two of self-adhesive weather stripping from the hardware store around the inside of the hat's crown!

The founding chapter members found their hats, as I have said, in thrift and antique stores for very reasonable prices. If you remember, the very first red hat I purchased cost eight dollars, which was on the high side, considering its thrift shop origins. Rose Ellen (Scarlett O'Hatters, Minneapolis, Minnesota) found her red wool fedora in a thrift shop for the grand sum of seventy-five cents! Quite a bargain compared with mine!

> The best way to store an expensive hat is upside down in an enclosed hatbox.

Looking for something beyond the obvious, Lori Schoneveld (Lynden Ladies with Lids, Washington) considered her basic needs met when she located a bright red bathing cap! She felt that it was so grand, it just *had* to have been worn by Esther Williams, so it certainly would do for her. And I'll bet that when she wears it, everything goes swimmingly, too.

As vintage red hats have grown harder and harder to find, due, no doubt, to the burgeoning population of Red Hat Society members, some of us have literally had to dig deep to find one. Nancy Sparks Morrison (Ravishing Reds, Roanoke, Virginia) was sorting through a box of thrift shop hats, finding red only on baseball caps, which, in her opinion, just didn't fill the bill. She was about to settle for one of those, when she uncovered a bright red graduation mortar with its tassel still attached! She realized that this was the perfect hat for a Red Hat Society member, as membership in our group constitutes a graduation itself. Life has been our school and experience has been our teacher! Perfect!

Should one actually be required to spend money on a red hat? Some women have managed to avoid any expenditure at all, even minimal outlay for thrift shop fare. Jean Simpson (Jazzi-Belles, the Villages, Florida) used the empty plastic flowerpot she had left after transplanting an Easter lily to make her hat. She spray-painted it and embellished it with a ribbon rose that, penny-pincher that she is, she had saved from a box of Valentine candy. In case this demonstration of her resourcefulness wasn't adequate, she added some purple netting from a table decoration saved, appropriately enough, from a church event. Here is a woman who knows how to make do.

Spray paint and glue guns have come in handy to some of our Red Hat sisters, and many have managed to fashion silk purses out of sow's ears. Some who have chosen to start with a basic bargain-basement red hat have taken embellishment to new heights. Pat Latreille (Amarillo's Audacious Adorables, Amarillo, Texas) writes that she and her vice mummy challenged each other to craft hats, then trade them, so that each could wear the other's creation. Pat writes, "Vice Mummy was presented with a red adornment, complete with grapes, Christmas bows, spangly stars, dangling pom-poms, feathers and flowers, a hummingbird, and silver jingle bells." The queen mum was crowned with "a tall, red velvety crown adorned with gold, huge pearls, diamonds, and rubies and trimmed in white ermine." (Undoubtedly, these jewels were all genuine.) Some may call this sort of thing overkill. Pat and her vice mum call it great fun.

Sandy Robinson (Bodacious Bastrop Belles, Bastrop, Texas) obviously takes great pride in her hat, which she created especially to wear to a parade whose theme was "Hats Off to Seguin" (Seguin, Texas).

Judy Lewis, a well-known artist (the Red Rascals, Prescott, Arizona) spotted the perfect purple netting to adorn her red hat at the grocery store—a purple-netted sack of onions! She added it to her hat, with lovely results. The only problem, according to her queen, Cindy Craig, was that "it kept the rest of us in tears."

Perhaps warnings are in order in regard to using both spray paint and glue guns. Witness the following:

Barb Manderville (Barb's Buddies, Des Moines, Washington) tells of wearing her freshly painted straw hat to church and then out to breakfast. When she took her hat off at the table, everyone burst out laughing. Her forehead bore a broad red stripe of red paint. Next time, she will allow more drying time!

Elke Lagace (Red Hot Chili Peppers, Sarasota, Florida) wrote to describe the first hat she created, which involved spray-painting a white straw hat and gluing on some feathers and flowers. She thought it was quite lovely, and she spent a few minutes in front of a mirror, strategically viewing it from all sides and adjusting its tilt. She says it looked wonderful, but unfortunately, the hot glue had not quite dried and the hat had become adhered firmly to her head! She says that her hair was considerably shorter the next day, even thinning in spots. The moral of the story? Beware of the glue gun.

If all else fails in one's quest for a red hat, there is always the department store or the Internet. There is a red hat out there for anyone who is ready to wear one. One is not enough for most of us for very long, however. After all, where can a hat be found that will complement all of our fashion statements and all of our events? Perhaps a bigger hat next time, one with a wider brim? Perhaps one with a brim that dips provocatively below one eye? Maybe a veil to add mystery?

Hats are great fun to wear. The different styles available allow each person to express a particular attitude rather easily. A demure salad plate–size red straw hat perched squarely on top of the head is charmingly sedate and dignified, and it may complement a blouse with a Peter Pan collar, for example. The wearer will probably stand up straight and wear spotless gloves with it. A huge-brimmed hat with leopard-skin trim will not be worn by a shrinking violet, but probably by a lady who has quite a bit of self-confidence and perhaps a bit of an attitude to go with it. The Red Hat Society has plenty of room for both of these women, and all of those in between.

A few innovative women have even opted for bright purple or pink hair to wear under (or instead of) their hats. I have seen two Pink Hatters who passed on the hats and went straight to hot-pink wigs. When I found out that the store right next door to the Imperium sold purple wigs in several lengths, I was a goner. (Of course, wigs and hats worn together are rather toasty. This combination might be better saved for a cold day.) A wig is the ultimate answer to a bad hair day.

As the red-hat fever has begun to spread, it has run afoul of cultural considerations in at least one country—England! Unbeknownst to some of us, in years past a woman wearing a red hat in that country was sending a signal that she was, shall we say, "a lady of the evening," who was not wearing underpants! Some stories and poems on that subject have persisted in that part of the world, giving women there good reason for being wary of wearing red hats.

Linda Geramina (Ruby Teazers, Raleigh, North Carolina) sends this story about her chaptermate Donna Shields's visit to England: "Having had a difficult time finding a suitable red hat that fit comfortably, she decided to have one specially made for her during her stop in London. She went into a millinery shop and told the young salesgirl that she wanted to purchase a red hat. The girl stepped back, a shocked expression on her face." Thank goodness Donna was able to explain herself satisfactorily. But beware, ladies!

What do you do if you *have* found a hat but you rush out the door on your way to a gathering and forget to take it with you? (This can happen, ladies! I suggest you wear your hat out of the house, instead of carrying it.) However, if you *do* forget your hat, there is always a way to work around it without remaining seriously out of uniform. Miriam Storey (the Red Hatted Ladies of Tranquility, Pensacola, Florida) tells us that one of her ladies did forget her red hat. The answer was, quite literally, at hand. They pinned one of her red gloves to her head with a hat pin. Emergency averted. Queen Miriam plans to keep a small fold-up red hat in her bag as a form of crisis management for the future. I have always heard that it was the *Boy* Scouts whose motto was Be Prepared. They have nothing on Miriam.

Because of what they mean to us, we must have the courage to wear our red hats wherever we go, regardless of the reaction. Nancy Coey (the Daunting Divas, Raleigh, North Carolina), a professional speaker who has addressed both of our first two conventions, has suggested that since our red hats symbolize so many things for us (confidence, self-acceptance, joy, pride), we should wear one at all times. Of course, she acknowledges that this can be impractical to do in the literal sense. But Nancy advises us all to put on our individual red hats (at least mentally, if not literally) before leaving the house each day. Sounds good to me!

Express Yourself! 171

May I share something with all of you? When I was very small, I had a friend, Mrs. Silkins, who wore a red straw hat with shiny cherries on it. She was just my size, and we spent a lot of time together. I remember very clearly her bright blue eyes and the way the skin around them crinkled when she smiled. She was a lot of fun to be with—much more adventurous than I was. Over time, I noticed that she wasn't around anymore. I brought her up in a conversation with my mother a year or two after Mrs. Silkins and I had lost touch. My mother raised her eyebrows and explained to me that Mrs. Silkins had been an imaginary playmate—not real or visible to anyone but me. The shock and confusion I felt at that moment is still with me today. I'm not assigning any particular meaning to this story; make of it what you will. I just feel a sense of wonder and amazement when I remember her. Her spirit has returned—and is personified in Ruby RedHat!

PURPLE CLOTHING

Now that we have discussed hats, what is to be worn on the body? Purple clothes! Should you wear a purple dress, a purple pantsuit, purple jeans with a purple T-shirt, purple palazzo pants, a purple ball gown? Yes. Wear whatever you have or want to buy, as long as it's some shade of purple. The main considerations are:

1. Do I like it?
2. Is it comfortable?

Most of us have passed the stage where we will wear almost anything, no matter how much it pinches or binds, in order to look fashionable. To quote the late Gilda Radner, "I base most of my fashion taste on what doesn't itch."

Ruby Valencia (Red Hot Roses, St. Paul, Minnesota) shares her thoughts about clothing: "All through my middle and later years, I complained about having to dress in suits and heels and grumbled that one of these days I would wear sneakers, T-shirts, and jeans all the time. I would be comfortable, by golly!" That says it rather well, don't you think? I hope that Ruby is now fulfilling her dream.

Perhaps a word is in order about the rigidity of our purple clothing requirement. Queen Rita Saulsbury (Harrington Red Hatters, Harrington, Delaware) says that one of her members whispered confidentially to her that she had a problem: She had had no trouble finding a purple dress, but she wasn't having any luck in her search for purple underwear! The lady said that in order to be sure she didn't break any society rules, she had solved the problem for that first gathering by attending without *any* underwear! Oh dear, some of us really have a terrible time believing that the Red Hat Society doesn't have any rules! Now, if some of us *want* to extend our self-expression (if only for our own benefit) to our underwear, that's okay, too. The wonderful author Judith Viorst dealt with that issue very well:

> *Despite the advent of Medicare,*
> *I will still buy bikini underwear*
> *And scorn the notion that seniorhood*
> *Means it's too late to be up to no good.*

Purple bikini panties and purple teddies? Purple negligees and purple bras? Hey, if it feels good, wear it.

Queen Beverly Druckrey (Belle's Bubbles, Mission Viejo, California) couldn't find anything purple that she liked, so she went shopping in the back of her own closet. She found the lovely purple-beaded dress which she had worn to her son's wedding ten years before, along with matching shoes and clutch. Her hair is gray now, but the dress still fits. With her long rope of pearls, she looks just lovely in it.

Margaret Webb (the Selected Few, Lubbock, Texas) went to the lengths of hiring a dressmaker to fabricate her floor-length purple velvet sheath and gold-trimmed cape.

To date, I haven't heard from anyone who just couldn't find anything purple to wear. If purple is not always a popular color, it has been at one time or another, and the thrift shops are probably full of discarded purple ensembles. I don't know if we have had the slightest influence, but purple is currently popular again.

There is always good old dye, and your washing machine. Kay Foster, a member of the Red Hat Beaded Babes (Fullerton, California), has earned the title of "Lady Dye," because of her expertise in the art of transforming clothing from its original state to the desired purple. She writes that quite often when she can't find what she wants, she reaches for the dye bottle. One Saturday morning, her chapter met at her home for a dye party. Each lady brought clothing—stockings, trims, lace, gloves, et cetera—to dye purple or red. She says that by the end of the day, they had not only transformed a lot of clothing; they'd had a great time sharing their lives—a party to "dye" for!

SHOES: IMELDA MARCOS'S GOT NOTHING ON US

Yes, an outfit extends to our feet, as well (at least, if we want it to, and some of us assuredly do). Henrika Prescott (Panama's Red Hats and Purple Parasols, Panama City, Florida) takes great pride in her high-heeled red tennis shoes, which she bought in 1984, purely because she loved them. Because they bore the label of a big-name designer, they were quite an extravagance, and she is thrilled to have an excuse to get them out and wear them again.

At the other end of the expense spectrum, one Red Hatter named Lucy, who says that she has a problem finding shoes that fit, simply spray-painted an old pair of shoes bright red. She says that she has to touch them up after each wearing because the paint tends to crack with use, but then, what price fashion?

Lucy can't find shoes to fit her. But Janice Austerman (Divine Divot Divas, Naples, Florida) says that she and her friend Flo are looking for people to fit their shoes. At the end of last summer, Flo popped into Janice's with a great thrift shop find—six pairs of red shoes, all size seven. Now all they need to do is find six women to fill them.

DYEING TIPS:

1. If it's valuable or important to you, do not dye it. If it's something such as a thrift store dress, though, go ahead and try.
2. Fabrics that dye well:
   a. Lace has different threads, and some will dye lighter or darker. Makes a pretty effect.
   b. Cotton: Dye in hottest water.
   c. Nylon: Most of the time, it dyes well. It's hard to get dark colors to take, though. Sometimes dyeing nylon causes a crinkling of the fabric.
   d. Satin: Do not dye. It loses its bounce.
   e. Polyester doesn't absorb dye. (Sometimes a garment may be of one fabric, but the thread may be polyester. You could wind up with white stitching on a purple garment. Be prepared.)
3. Make sure used clothing is clean and rinsed thoroughly before dyeing. Even new clothing should be washed before dyeing.
4. To mix fabric dye, follow directions on the dye bottle or package.
   a. Use vinegar to set dark colors.
   b. Use two bottles or boxes of dye for dark colors (purple or red).
   c. Liquid dye is easier on fragile fabrics, such as lace.
   d. If worried about garment shrinkage, you can dye in warm water. Mix dye in hot water, according to directions. Let cool. Add wet garment. Stir until it is the color you want.
5. Hang the garment and let it drip-dry.
6. The washing machine is an easy way to dye. After use, run the empty machine with detergent and bleach to remove dye.

The Summer Shoe Pledge

Please raise your big toes and repeat after me:

I promise to always wear sandals that fit. My toes will not touch the ground, nor will my heels spill over the backs. And the sides and tops of my feet will not pudge out between the straps.

I will go polish-free or vow to keep the polish fresh, intact, and chip-free.

I will not cheat and just touch up my big toe.

I will sand down any mounds of skin before they turn hard and yellow.

I will shave the hairs off my big toe.

I won't wear panty hose even if my misinformed girlfriend, coworker, mother, or sister tells me the toe seam really will stay under my toes if I tuck it there.

If a strap breaks, I won't duct-tape, pin, glue, or tuck it back into place, hoping that by some miracle it will stay put. I will get my shoe fixed or toss it.

I will not live in corn denial; rather, I will lean on my good friend Dr. Scholl's, if my feet need him.

I will resist the urge to buy jelly shoes at Payless for the low, low price of $4.99, even if my feet are small enough to fit into the kids' sizes. This is out of concern for my safety and the safety of others. No one can walk properly when standing in a pool of sweat, and I would hate to take someone down with me as I fall and break my ankle.

I will take my toe ring off toward the end of the day if my toe swells and begins to look like a Vienna sausage.

I will be brutally honest with my girlfriend/sister/coworker when she asks me if her feet are too ugly to wear sandals. Someone has to tell her that her toes are as long as my fingers and no sandal makes creepy feet look good.

This pledge was on the Internet (author unknown) and passed along by Marcy LaSalle (the FUN-Key Flint Red Hat Society,

Flushing, Michigan). Since the Red Hat Society has no rules, the pledge is purely voluntary.

ACCESSORIZE, ACCESSORIZE, ACCESSORIZE!

Red hats, purple clothing, and red or purple shoes. These are pretty sassy combinations, aren't they? But a lot of us are not content to stop there. Once we get rolling, we just pick up speed! Why should we confine ourselves to these items of finery only, especially when there are so many other possibilities for self-adornment? As time has gone by, Red Hatters have tracked down red and purple gloves, feathered boas, lavish "jewels," parasols, and more. The treasure/bargain hunt goes on, showing no signs of stopping.

There is plenty of room for ingenuity, too. Some products, such as nail polish, come in many shades of red and purple. It wasn't long before the ingenious Jan Lumley (Vaguely Vogue Vamps, Holiday Island, Arkansas) found some unique uses for it. She says she loves the new sparkly polishes and has painted the rims of her sunglasses purple and her earrings red and purple, as well as buttons, hat-pin beads, and the little hat ornament on her car antenna. And she says, "Of course, we *all* paint our toenails." We do, don't we? Especially those of us who are willing to take "The Summer Shoe Pledge."

"Bodacious Barb" (the Red Hat Snowbirds, Sarasota, Florida) and her friend Gail decided to visit every used-clothing shop on U.S. 41 from Port Charlotte north to Sarasota, in an effort to find things they could wear to their Red Hat Society meetings. They bought a lot of items in purple and red. Gail even purchased a red lace teddy, even though she had no idea of what she might do with it. She later hot-glued that two-dollar teddy around the crown of a one-dollar hat, purchased at the Dollar Store. It looks like a million bucks!

There is another "accessory" that I believe is sported every-where by our wonderful ladies—a Red Hattitude! I was so gratified to receive an E-mail from a twenty-four-year-old woman who works in a fabric and craft store in Bay City, Michigan. She just wanted me to know that their store had experienced a run on all of their red and purple fabrics and trims, and she had begun to ask questions about why those two colors were suddenly so popular. To quote Susanne: "Well, I must say the local Red Hatters are some of the most wonderful guests we have had in our store. They don't get annoyed when someone twenty-four years old is asking them so many questions, and they appreciate any suggestions we give them to make their red hats the most unique and most personal for them. I just thought I would let you know that the women who are representing you in Bay City and Essexville, Michigan, are doing an excellent job, and one day I hope maybe I can be the lady explaining what I am going to do with a hat with sequins and feathers." These Red Hatters were great goodwill ambassadors.

That same hattitude was displayed by Joyce Hall (Keystone Red Hats, Beaver, Pennsylvania). For her appointment for a colonoscopy (*not* fun) she dressed for success in a red-and-purple-flowered satin gown, her purple boa, and red hat. Her female gastroenterologist had a good laugh, and she declared Joyce the highlight of her day!

THE HUNT

As interesting as our clothing is, what is even more interesting is the places some of us find our items of finery. One Red Hatter passed along the tale of her Red Hat sister's experience: "My sister, who lives in Virginia, had gone to the dentist and noticed his purple latex gloves. She casually asked where she could get some." The dentist asked her reason for wanting them and she explained that her Red Hat Society chapter would get a kick out of them. He sent her home with a box containing five hundred pairs!

Sue Davis, a member of my own chapter, is our reigning champion. She has an absolute gift for ferreting out the most amazing finds wherever she shops—often thrift shops and rummage sales. She has earned her self-bestowed title of "Thrift Store Goddess." Her most dazzling acquisition to date is an elegant vintage Norma Kamali dress—purple satin, and to die for—in exactly her size. The price tag? Six dollars! I try to give her a run for her money, but it is not easy. My proudest possession is my fake-fur purple coat with huge shoulder pads, located in a vintage clothing store. It was no bargain, though, at forty dollars! But, I ask you, how often do you come across a prize like that? And not to mention the purple sequined sunglasses found in the same store! Heavenly! (While Sue admired my fur coat, I could tell she did not consider her title to be the least bit threatened.)

Driving home from their first Red Hat function, two members of the Red Hat Rascals (Prescott, Arizona) took a shortcut through an alley and found their attention drawn to a large Dumpster that appeared to contain entire wardrobes of discarded clothing. Mary Jo Castigliano and Ruth Ann Bragg just could not pass up the chance to root around to see whether there might possibly be anything red or purple in there. Mary Jo leaned over too far and fell in, necessitating rescue by a passing truck driver. Since he was pulled over anyway, they enlisted him to help them yank out some more stuff. I guess the purple-and-white skirt rescued from the bottom recesses of the bin made the whole effort worthwhile. (That, and the fun of retelling the story in the months to come!) I wonder what the truck driver's story sounds like?

Volumes could be filled with tales of our searches for hats, clothing, purses, shoes, gloves, and the like. So many of the stories are highly entertaining, and someday they may warrant a book all their own. Suffice it to say that we Red Hatters are capable of infinite variety in almost every area. One chapter (Godiva Girls, Lutz, Florida) makes its home in a nudist colony. The ladies only have to find purple clothing for their forays off "the reservation," so to speak. Otherwise, they need little more than a red hat and perhaps a purple belt. (They assure us that they do fully dress the part when they hit the town.)

HOMES

> "We shape our dwellings and then our dwellings shape us."
> —*Winston Churchill*

When women hear the word *decoration,* it usually isn't long before their thoughts turn to the interior decoration of their homes. This is proved by the proliferation of magazines, books, and entire TV networks that deal exclusively with the hundreds of ways in which we can manipulate our surroundings, and instructions for ways to do it.

> "I have written my life in small sketches, a little today, a little yesterday. I look back on my life like a good day's work. It was done and I feel satisfied with it. I was happy and contented. I knew nothing better and made the best out of what life offered. And life is what we make it, always has been, always will be."
> —*Grandma Moses, in her autobiography.*

I love art of all kinds. I love color, good design, beautiful things. I love decorating! One of my favorite pastimes has always been leafing through home-decorating magazines and books. I would guess that the majority of women share this interest. The enhancement of our surroundings is very important to us, both for the enrichment of our own lives and the nourishment of our families. I have always taken great pleasure in finding just the right pot for a particular plant, or just the right fabric to make just the right pillow for a certain chair in my home. I am also a devotee of "junking" expeditions to flea markets or garage sales. I consider it infinitely more exciting to find some little oddity that can be painted, or perhaps used as is in my home to add warmth and/or personality, than to just go to a furniture store and buy something. One of my favorite finds was an old dresser with curved legs. It was painted a sickly green, but I paid my nephew to sand it down and paint it a warm cream color. Then I spent hour upon hour painting flowers and patterns on the drawer fronts, knobs, and legs. The dresser sits in my guest room, and it still gives me pleasure to look at it. It is interesting to reflect that it was this very passion that led, at least indirectly, to the beginning of the Red Hat Society. Who knows, maybe what I was subconsciously trying to do was find new motives for prowling the thrift shops and antique stores.

When I bought the vintage hat and the poem for Linda, my first idea was that she could hang them next to each other on the wall of her room, just to remind her of the attitude they expressed. The stimulus for this was the concept, frequently demonstrated in home-decoration resources, of creating vignettes for one's home. I have often found inspiration for creating vignettes in my own home. They don't serve any functional purpose; they just nourish my soul. (It took me a very long time to explain this to my husband, "Mr. Practical.") I derive immense pleasure from my little grouping of old toy chairs and my display of colorful kitchen crockery. It feels good to have the things that I love out where I can see them, and I do my best to arrange them artfully.

I suggest that it might be fun for some of us Red Hatters to create our own vignettes within the confines of our homes to remind ourselves of the special joy and friendships the Red Hat Society had brought to our lives—perhaps a framed photo or two of our chapter or our special friends in their outfits, perhaps a few of our favorite red hats on hooks, maybe a special quotation or other memento, maybe an old greeting card that contributes to the sentiment. We are free to decorate our personal spaces in any way that we choose to do. Our homes are one of the few places that we should be able to grant ourselves complete freedom to display who we are and what we are about.

The Red Hat Society is not the only place where rules are no longer ironclad. The days of home-decorating rules have been declared officially over, not only by us but by all of the professional home-decor gurus, too. We are now encouraged to mix and match styles, colors, and accessories to suit ourselves. A little Red Hat Society vignette might be a good place to start!

Could it be that there is a connection between decorating your home and decorating your life? I believe there is. As I mentioned, for a period of six years I was a co-owner, with two other artist friends, of a mural-painting and faux-finish business. We worked in businesses and public places, but most of our work was done in private homes, under the auspices of interior designers. Often, we would be called in to add finishing touches to a lovely home that was beautifully and expensively furnished. We would look at the space, take note of the colors, fabrics, and patterns we saw, and discuss the home owner's interests and preferences. Then we would submit watercolor sketches of various ideas for decorative painting, usually a hand-painted border or a full mural. We would then meet with the designer and home owner to present our sketches.

There were countless times when we would observe the home owner's eyes light up at the sight of the little paintings—perhaps a brick wall with ivy and flowers massed in front of it, or a view of a distant gazebo viewed across a lake. But so often, that same client's eyes would immediately dart to the designer, an obvious questioning look on her face, which seemed to ask, Do we like this? Sadly, the designer's opinion often carried far more weight than the client's own. Most often, the designer did recommend going ahead with one or the other of our ideas, which was great for business. But I was dismayed to see how often these women were afraid to trust their own instincts. I realized that I had often demonstrated much of the same hesitancy in trusting my own judgment and taste.

After all, the homes I visited belonged to these women! They were the ones who would be living with these works of art for a long time. And many times, their initial reaction conveyed an immediate delight at that prospect, followed almost instantly by the need for the designer's approval. And, after receiving that, they would sometimes ask the designer whether she thought her friends would "get it." In other words, would they be seen as too extravagant or too bold if they had a beautiful mural up their stairway or across one wall of their home? This observation led me to wonder, At what point do we stop catering to everyone else's taste and opinions and allow ourselves to follow our own hearts (as freely as our budgets allow anyway)? Was this yet another of those great "as soon as" situations, or were we to spend our entire lives squelching the expression of any impulse that someone else might frown upon? Most of us admire individuality in others but are afraid to express any ourselves, for fear of incurring judgment.

I am happy to say that Kathy Roland (Virginia Peninsula Scarlett Belles, which draws its membership from several towns) doesn't share that fear. She recently finished painting her bedroom "Grape Soufflé," which she describes as a medium lavender, and her dining room "Opera House," a true red. The finishing touch was glossy white woodwork. The result? Kathy says, "They look great and make me feel wonderful!"

I have already mentioned many ways in which Red Hatters have experienced newfound connections. Donna McElroy (Rosebud Hues, Venice, Florida) sends a story about how an object used to decorate one woman's home brought about a warm connection with another. While Donna was working as a volunteer at the local Hospice House, she became acquainted with Shirley Schmid, a nurse at the facility. After Donna shared the story of the Red Hat Society with Shirley, Shirley told her the story of her first exposure to the "Warning" poem. She had created a cross-stitch of the words to the poem, a project that had involved many hours of work. Since it had been such a huge effort, she'd splurged on a lavish frame for it when it was done. It had hung on her wall for years, occupying a place of honor, but eventually it crashed to the floor and was badly damaged. After Shirley became a member of Donna's chapter, she took it to a meeting at Donna's home to share the story, then left it behind, a token of her and Donna's newfound friendship. Decorative objects may seem frivolous, but they can be invested with deep meaning when they serve as reminders of friendship.

It has become apparent that the Red Hat Society has many members who are quilting enthusiasts. Some of them have expressed their allegiance to our disorganization by crafting quilts featuring all manner of red-and-purple designs, some featuring appliquéd red hats.

Another way that some women express their artistic side is in the decoration of their homes and tables when they decide to hostess a Red Hat event. I'd like to give you just a couple of examples of the lengths to which some enjoy going. (They must enjoy it, because there certainly aren't any rules!) Peggy West (Sassy Sisters, Dunn, North Carolina) played hostess for a luncheon and viewing of a video of the first annual Red Hat Society convention. With the help of two of her members, Lorctta Warren and Sally Wood, she began her decorating by wrapping the lantern poles in her front yard in red and lining the walkway with purple candles with bows. Inside of the house were purple and red flowers, red hats and purses, and purple and red candles. Miniature lights were strung through greenery. There were displays of dolls, which were dressed in red, purple, pink, and lavender, and flower arrangements featuring miniature hats. Peggy created a virtual fairyland for her first Red Hat event, and I am sure that her chapterettes were grateful.

Lea Louwerse (the Canterbury Belles, Vinton, Virginia) takes pleasure in devising elaborate table decorations for their gatherings, whether they meet in homes or restaurants. One of her members sent us a description of one of Lea's decorations for a chapter event: "Everything was done in purple and red. Umbrellas were purple; every flower was purple or red. She made two chocolate cakes decorated as hats, of course, with bows and flowers in purple. We brought our teacups and saucers in red or purple bags and the ladies exchanged teacups and saucers. If you came with red, you got purple, and if you came with purple, you got red." Red-and-purple tablecloths stamped with red hat designs added charm to the backdrop for the event.

The celebration of Christmas and other such holidays gives us a further opportunity to decorate our homes in Red Hat spirit. Elaine Kloepful (the Mad Red Hatters, Madison, Wisconsin) sent us photos of her tree, which was covered with purple bulbs and red hat ornaments and topped by a doll who looked suspiciously like Ruby RedHat. Red ornaments are easy to find, of course. Purple might be a little harder, but we have discovered we are up to the challenge. And the tree itself provides the greenery. At our store, the Imperium, in Fullerton, California, we like to wrap our tree in red and purple boas and hang the dozens of wonderful handmade ornaments that Red Hatters have sent us—everything from a tiny hand-knit purple sweater to a pair of hand-painted seashells.

VEHICLES

What else is left to decorate? Why, vehicles, of course. Red Hat Society chapters have come together as groups to decorate cars, flatbed trucks, and all manner of vehicles in order to participate in parades. And Red Hatters who are in the market for new cars report a strong preference for purple and red. They go so nicely with our bumper stickers and decals. Such instances as decorating for parades, however, are only temporary. Those vehicles may be spiffed up or borrowed for special occasions only. But there are Red Hatters who have seen fit to embellish their personal vehicles in ways absolutely guaranteed to astound the rest of us.

One enthused Red Hatter, Alyce Cornyn-Selby (City of Roses Our, Portland, Oregon) painted her reproduction of an antique Bugatti bright purple, then finished it off with red-painted wire wheels. She proceeded to drive it on a cross-country journey, with a stop-off in Chicago to give the keynote speech at our first convention. She later completed a book about her trip.

Ronnie Warren, husband of Red Hatter Loretta Warren (Sassy Sisters, Dunn, North Carolina), has a totally restored 1937 Teraplane. (Yes, this is a car.) When Loretta's chapterettes saw its snazzy new purple paint job, they knew they just had to declare it the official vehicle for their chapter. They all gathered around it and had their picture taken to verify its status.

Some women have had their more traditional cars painted red or purple. I have always had a red car, since that is my favorite color. As a matter of fact, my current car is painted an ever-so-appropriate hue, "Inferno Red," with a personalized license plate that reads RED-HATS. And I was pleased to find a vendor at the local mall who whipped up a custom license-plate holder that reads EXALTED QUEEN MOTHER. The perfect car for not calling attention to myself, wouldn't you agree?

Sue Green (the Lone Star Red Hat Society, Nederland, Texas) has begun to need a mobility scooter in order to get around better. What color do you suppose she selected? Why, candy apple red, of course.

Sylvia Portaro (Rowdy Red Hatters, Palm Springs, California) wins the award for transformation of the largest vehicle. She purchased a thirty-four-foot-long RV. With the help of her daughter and son-in-law, Tia and Mark, she transformed it into a Red Hatter Salon, complete with red and purple seating cushions, paint, and accessories. The RV has a purple stripe running horizontally along its exterior.

Sharon Johnson (the Purple Madam Seniors, or P.M.S., Huffman, Texas) also has an art car. Interestingly enough, she created the car as a sixtieth-birthday treat for herself. I know that some cars "go like sixty"; is there a connection between one's sixtieth birthday and wild cars? Perhaps we should make that a Red Hat ritual. Should we all begin decorating our cars when we reach *that* milestone? (Hmm . . . something to contemplate. My little red PT Cruiser is already cute, but maybe some airbrushed purple flames on the front fenders? . . . Okay, back to Sharon's story.) Her car was designed to honor all women of the world and what we have contributed to it. "Photos were laminated and glued all over the body of the sedan. The glove on top lights up for night parades and I play 'I Am Woman' by Helen Reddy on the tape. The inside and trunk are decorated with dolls and other female artifacts."

Not long ago, Sharon and her chapter joined the Texas Ramblers (Houston), the S.O.B.s (Sexy Old Broads), and the Ladies with Hattitude to form a contingent of the Kemah, Texas, Christmas parade. Their lineup included Sharon's car, now embellished with red hats, *and* another art car, "Harmony, the Hippo," owned by Sue Shefman, also a Red Hatter. Several other red and purple cars and thirty marching ladies completed the delegation. After the parade, the ladies were surrounded by admirers, who asked questions and took pictures. Ah, the price of fame!

THE GRASS IS ALWAYS GREENER . . . WITH PURPLE AND RED

Louann Darcy (Red Hats R Us, the Villages, Florida) expressed her allegiance to all things purple and red by planting a red crepe myrtle bush on one side of her driveway and a purple one on the other. She says that they are beautiful when they bloom!

I am happy to report that the street that I live on is lined with well-established jacaranda trees. They bloom prolifically every spring, producing gorgeous drifts of purple. They were there a long time before my husband and I moved in, and we certainly claim no credit for them, but we do enjoy the serendipity of living on a street that appears to pay homage to the Red Hat Society once a year. The red flowers in my window boxes? Those were my idea. At the Red Hat Society office, we are taking a page out of Louann Darcy's book. We are filling window boxes and outdoor planting areas with purple and red flowering plants and bushes. We must set a good example for the rest of the world.

What else can we decorate? It is obvious from my mail that a lot of us have been moved to share our renewed joy in playing dress-up with our pets, most of whom seem to accept their adornment with equanimity. I have received plenty of photos of dogs and cats adorned in hats, boas, and the like.

Jenny Housley (Red Riding Hoods, Lexington, Kentucky) won the Red Hat Class segment of the Ride Aside2002 in Lexington, Kentucky, riding her friend Sue Duncan's horse. The horse, Janie Nite Tracker, wore a red bridle and visor to coordinate with Jenny's outfit. Jenny's miniature donkey made an appearance in her red-and-purple garb, as well.

My dog, Frosty, has red sunglasses and a purple-and-red bandanna for his neck—embellished with red ball fringe. He also sports a tag on his collar with a crown on it, a gift from Lady Bug at the office. He is okay with the bandanna, but the glasses, not a hit, have been retired to the closet shelf. Oh well, he's a boy anyway. . . .

AND IF THAT WASN'T ENOUGH . . .

The Young and the Wreckless chapter (Brandon, Florida) made the ultimate commitment to Red Hatting. Four of their bravest members had red hats permanently tattooed on their very bodies—two on the upper thigh, one on the lower leg, and one on the chest. Jackie Durocher, age seventy-one, says her husband just loves it. Oh my!

11
Rituals

Any serious attempt to try to do something worthwhile is ritualistic.

—Derek Walcott

e women do love the sense of continuity and warmth that is provided by the observance of traditions, both with our own families and with others close to us. Who is it that lovingly packs away the tattered construction-paper Christmas ornaments made by the chubby hands of their preschoolers, then gets them out again year after year to hang on the family Christmas tree in all their faded glory? Who is it that takes the time and trouble to prepare the family's favorite turkey dinner with all the trimmings on Thanksgiving?

For many years, my family took an annual ski trip with another family. And for twenty-five years now, all the members of my extended family have participated in a pre-Christmas progressive dinner. We eat one course of our meal at each of several houses, thereby getting a chance to admire one another's holiday decorations and stuff ourselves with goodies. As the years have passed, we have lost some dear ones because of death or divorce, but we have also gained new members due to marriages and births. The makeup of the family may change, but the family itself goes on.

The Red Hat Society is becoming a cultural gathering place, a family of sorts, for women in our age group, and it is my fond hope that the group will grow and endure in much the same way that families do. The observation of rituals binds people together and validates their importance to one another. I have said that a large number of women have reported making new friends through the Red Hat Society. While many of these connections began as casual friendships, a lot of them have become much deeper over time. In a way, friendships are a ritual. They need regular nourishment and attention. One of the best benefits of the Red Hat Society is what it has done to help friendships blossom and grow. We all know that an acquaintance can grow into an intimate friend if the relationship is nurtured by constant association. Our regular gatherings, both large and small, provide effortless opportunity for women to spend enough time together to form deeper ties and enjoy regular connection with special people.

Since Red Hatters are women, and women love rituals and traditions, it was not long before individual members and whole chapters began to come up with all manner of ceremonies and observances of their own to add spice to our basic premise. The creation of new rituals adds pizzazz to developing friendships and draws women closer together in shared humor and amusement. Because the Red Hat Society has great connections and communications among its various chapters, one chapter's idea is often picked up and adapted or elaborated upon by another one. And so the mythology grows! (And so does the fun quotient!)

The most obvious crossover between the Red Hat Society and the normal rituals of society has been manifested in the embellishments of funerals and weddings—two types of occasions that are, fortunately and unfortunately, integral parts of all of our lives at one time or another.

FUNERALS

Red-hatted women have supported families of lost loved ones many times, and I am sure they will continue to do so. Funerals are painful for all, but the attendance of respectful and loving "sisters" is a great comfort to families. I am sure it is no small thing to know that the wife or mother you have lost was loved and will be missed by others as well, and that her passage through life made a difference to the world. Phyllis Mosher (D.A.M.S.E.L., the Villages, Florida) says that one bereaved husband in her area issued a blanket invitation to all Red Hat Society chapters in his area (and there were many) to attend his wife's funeral in their regalia. A large number of them showed up, including many who had not even known her, as a demonstration of sisterhood. Since this husband and wife had retired to an area far from most family and friends, he was comforted to see masses of his wife's sisters in their purple and red, demonstrating that she had been a part of something wonderful. Their presence provided the opportunity for close family members to share how the Red Hat Society had been a great help to this woman in her battle with illness.

HERE COMES THE BRIDE

Red Hat weddings? Helene Barker requested that her chapter mates attend her wedding in their full regalia, which they were happy to do. Helene's niece, Debbie, wrote that they brought such joy, happiness, laughter, and love to a special occasion. The world is a beautiful place for those who choose to see and share the beauty. *Choosing* and *sharing* are the operative words, I think. Where there are many lovely women, garbed in brilliant hues, there is beauty, as well.

Tracy Simon Higgins, a Pink Hatter, wrote to tell us about her recent second wedding, which took place exactly one week after Helene's. At that time, she was the activity director at Sheldon Park, a retirement facility for seniors in Eugene, Oregon. She was very attached to her people and wanted to include them in her wedding—all two hundred of them. The only way that she could find to do that was to have the wedding at the center itself. Since she had always loved the poem "Warning" and was extremely fond of purple, the theme for the wedding was obvious. The maid of honor and the soloist were both over fifty. The woman attending her guest book was ninety-five! Tracy wore a white gown and carried a purple parasol, and her two adult attendants and four girl attendants wore purple. The reception table was decorated with hatboxes, purple gloves, fresh purple tulips, and photographs of the residents. Each honorary mom at the wedding was presented with a red hat. Tracy plans to dye her wedding gown purple when she turns fifty (in eight years) and wear a red hat with it when she and her husband renew their wedding vows, which they hope to do on a cruise ship. That girl really knows how to make her own fun, doesn't she?

Here is a fascinating coincidence. The second Red Hat wedding I heard about, this time a *Red* Hatter's, occurred on the very same day in August as Tracy's, just a state away, in California. Sue Amidei, the widowed queen mum of the Renoir Red Hats (Orange County, California), was fortunate enough to meet a very nice man in the course of her volunteer activities. On one of her early visits to him in Arizona, Sue disembarked from an airliner in her red-and-purple regalia. She had been to a chapter gathering earlier that day and had not found time to change. But she also thought it wise to test the reaction of this "charming, proper, reserved, retired accountant," as she describes him. She wanted to be sure he understood the kind of person she was. He was surprised, although obviously proud of her, and a romance quickly developed. Eventually, Sue agreed to become his wife. The wedding plans were soon under way, and in true Red Hat fashion, they had a "nonrehearsal" dinner the night before they married. I asked Sue what colors were used in the wedding. Her answer: "What do *you* think?" In Sue's words: "The Red Hat Society has a very special meaning for us, and I'm so glad Herman tells everyone how he thinks of me coming down the escalator to the baggage claim area in my 'official Red Hat uniform,' rather than visualizing me as a grandmotherly casserole queen in a snood." Yes, we Red Hatters can be quite glamorous, as well as romantic!

HAPPY BIRTHDAY TO US!

Birthdays are another milestone that often call for rituals of some kind. Stories have literally poured in from women who have seized on the Red Hat premise as a theme for fiftieth (and other important) birthdays. Some have even thrown Red Hat–themed birthday parties for themselves. These ladies have launched their chapters by giving themselves birthday parties in which the surprise was actually for their guests. The chapter founder had invited several of her friends to come to her birthday party, requiring each guest to wear something purple. During the course of the party each guest is presented with a red hat and make a member of a brand-new chapter of the Red Hat Society. Of course, the party girl usually declares herself queen of the chapter, since it's *her* birthday!

"AU CONTRAIRE"

It took the Sasscee Gals (Tucson, Arizona) to come up with a uniquely Red Hat birthday idea, which they refer to as "Au Contraire." At each monthly gathering, those who have birthdays falling within that month must wear their colors backward (actually upside down) to call attention to that distinction. A Red Hatter must wear red clothing with a purple hat; a Pink Hatter must wear pink clothing with a lavender hat. To add extra zest to the event, the birthday girl (or girls) must notify her chapter that her birthday is coming up the following month, so it will not take the other members by surprise. And said birthday girl will be required to address the chapter in some special way during that gathering (recite a poem, sing a song, perform a bit of shtick). After all, she will be standing out like a sore thumb anyway. While they were instituting their own rituals, the members of this chapter also decided that they would dress *entirely* in red for Valentine's Day observances.

As I often do, I borrowed this wonderful idea they had come up with and suggested it as something any and all interested chapters might want to do. This is just another way that we all benefit from the creative and innovative thoughts of our sisters. We all get to add another witty ritual to our repertoire.

For a group hungry for a celebration, a year can be too long to wait. The WannaBees of the Coachella Valley (California) also came up with a unique ritual, which was described to me by Queen Diane McDowell. To celebrate their six-month anniversary as a chapter, they held a "half birthday" party for themselves. Refreshments consisted of half a cake, half cookies, and half-and-half in their tea. The party began, in British fashion, at "half two." Apparently, there is just no end to Red Hat bright ideas!

CORONATIONS

Given our stage in life, the chance of huge numbers of Red Hat weddings or other such occasions for celebration are probably pretty low. That is not a terrible tragedy in itself, but what other ritual is there to be found that can rival a wedding for pomp and circumstance? Royalty that we are (even if self-proclaimed), we have come up with a way to indulge our hunger for the big event so many of us love to put on—the coronation! Some coronations are relatively modest and fairly short. My own surprise crowning, arranged by my vice mother, Linda Murphy, took place at the Chicago convention. Loudly announcing, "By the authority no one has vested in me," Linda declared me "Exalted Queen Mother of the Red Hat Society." She then saw to it that I received a glittery crown, a purple velvet robe with faux leopard spots on its white collar (applied with a black felt-tip marker), and a scepter. The ceremony was great fun—short and sweet.

In contrast, there was the coronation of Queen Nancy Veits (Lady Hattersley's Cover, Palos Verdes, California). The husband of one of their members, "The Richard," dressed in leggings and sporting a wig, presided, and the consort of Queen Nancy herself, "The Earl," served as bartender, wearing a red cap and sequined tie. Queen Nancy shares a description of the day: "The entrance gates were guarded by a gallant in his medieval mail suit (or is that 'male' suit?). The garden tables were swathed in miles of purple and red netting, baubles, bows, beads, sparkles, and flowers. . . . We had purple and red plates, nappies, and the most delightfully gaudy purple throne ever seen. . . . On its seat was a pillow with the embroidered message 'Too much cleaning makes you croak.'" The red hats and purple dresses swayed in the afternoon breeze in the beautifully decorated backyard.

After appropriate refreshments, including champagne, the royal procession began: "A flower-strewer led the way, followed by the elegant sword-bearers, the scepter-bearer, the crown-bearer, the gift-bearer, the bouquet-bearer. . . ." Finally, the queen herself entered, followed by her train-bearer. Unfortunately, she had no train, so the bearer carried a miniature engine and coal car on a silver tray. The queen was greeted with bows, waves, and blown kisses as she approached her adoring throng. The party lasted two hours longer than scheduled, and, as the last guests straggled out, "The Richard" was heard to remark that he hoped that Queen Nancy would now be queen "for life." He had worked very hard to get his and his wife

Arlina's garden ready for the party, and he didn't want to repeat that experience anytime soon.

The Red Hat Flashes of Greenville (North Carolina) decided to take turns being queen of the chapter. Their first queen, Dianne Batson, writes that they "had a ton of capable leaders," so she saw no reason to insist on being queen year after year. (Please don't put this notion in the heads of the founding chapter's members, okay? I am not ready to abdicate.) At the dinner, to celebrate the passing of the queenship to Sharon Autrey, the members surprised Dianne with a retirement ceremony they had cleverly concocted. At the end of dinner, all the ladies stood and formed a line, each holding a rose in her hand. One by one, they approached Dianne's chair, handed her a rose, and expressed appreciation for the great start she had given them during their first year. Dianne reports that there was lots of hugging, with lots of hats getting knocked to the floor in the process, and "sweet words of appreciation and expressions of friendships were exchanged." The new queen, Sharon, was heard to quip, "Isn't that wonderful? Having sixty-two roses, and none of them on your casket!"

PLEDGES AND VOWS

Whether they ever get around to coronating their queen or not, some chapters have instituted vows for the swearing-in of each member. Perhaps the queen will circulate around the room with her scepter and formally bestow each member's title. For example: "I dub thee Lady Lounge-About"; "I dub thee Countess Can't Be Bothered," et cetera.

Some queens have lifted sections of the original "Red Hat Society Statement of Purpose" and fashioned vows from it, as follows:

"I (underlined) do solemnly swear on my red hat that I will do my best to uphold the spirit of the Red Hat Society."

"I will greet middle age with verve, humor, and elan."

"I will take my silliness seriously, knowing that it is the comedy relief of life."

"I agree to join red-gloved hands with my red-hatted sisters and go for the gusto together."

"I will strive to help create new bonds and strengthen existing bonds among my sisters as we move forward to wherever life takes us next."

Obviously, there are endless possibilities for silly ceremoniousness. The imagination and adventurousness of the group are the only limits.

REDUATIONS

Remember when we were Brownies and reached the age where we could leave our little brown dresses and beanies behind and begin to wear the infinitely more grown-up uniform of a Girl Scout? The ceremony that saw a girl through this transition was called "flying up."

A woman's progression from Pink Hatter to Red Hatter also needs to be solemnly observed (well, observed anyway). Lady Di (Dianne Davis, queen of the MZ-Tea-rious Ladies, Long Beach, California) coined the term *reduation* for such an occasion, then introduced it to the rest of us on the Queen Mother Board on our Web site. (This is our bulletin board, where our members post messages to one another.) In true Red Hat fashion, she gave no particulars, leaving it to individual chapters to express their own creativity in developing their ceremonies. In very short order, chapters began to dream up some rituals.

Vicky Cohen (Sin-Tex Scarlet Women, Waco, Texas) had started her chapter as a Pink Hatter, giving herself the title of "Grand Scarlet Madam." But soon it was time for her to move up to full status. Her group invited another chapter, the Brazos Belles of Central Texas, to participate in the ceremony, since the Sin-Tex chapter had spun off from that chapter in the first place. The assembled ladies of two chapters bestowed upon Vicky a regal cape of royal purple, a feather boa, and a crown. Then the entire chapter stood and played "Hail to the Queen" on their kazoos. She is now properly installed!

When the VIVAS (the Villages, Florida) threw a party for their first reduate, they celebrated with an evening dessert and champagne affair. The members gathered around her and waved wands over her head, each offering a wish for her using words that began with the first letter of the well-wisher's name. Given my first name, if I had been there, I would have suggested that she *savor* every moment of her life.

Queen Mother Deena Valdez (Red Hat Mommas of Pinellas Park, Florida) uses a ceremony written by their "barristress." The candidate has to agree to join the Red Hat Society and to follow all the rules (if there are any). Deena writes, "She holds a red candle and stands in front of the rest of us. I, the queen mother of our group, administer the oath. I also make some kind of goofy red hat for her to wear during the whole get-together. I have used plastic top hats and paper crowns from the party store. The last ones I made, I glued purple metallic funky hair inside the hat." Everyone in the group brings red, pink, or purple carnations for the birthday girl to take home. They held their last reduation at the John Ringling House in Sarasota, Florida. Appropriately enough, John Ringling was the founder of the circus!

The West Orange Red Hat Society (Winter Garden, Florida) has come up with a charming added touch for their reduations. When one of their members reduates, they allow her to invite a new Pink Hatter into the group and pass her abandoned pink hat along to the new member. What a beautiful way to invigorate a chapter and emphasize the aspect of handing down wisdom. It also ensures that their chapter will be continually enlivened by new blood.

Although some reduations are quite simple, Queen Mother Purple Pansy's (Akron Red Hat Flashes, Akron, Ohio) puts on a Reduation Investiture Ceremony that is "nothing short of a stage production"—with a script, throne, reduation robe, and a pink sash to step over ceremoniously. She mailed me the script, and I am *impressed*! Among the vows taken by the reduate is the renunciation of the pink and lavender of her youth! The ceremony is a compilation of snippets taken from the following life events: graduations, baptisms, birthday parties, weddings, church services, sorority inductions, coronations, debutante balls, beauty contests, and college homecomings. They videotape the whole production and vow that they just may take their show on the road! In a caravan of red and purple buses, I would assume.

The Sasscee Gals (Tucson, Arizona) decree that their reduate wear black to her ceremony, as it is such a solemn occasion, and they are "soooooo serious" about reaching this pivotal birthday. Members are encouraged to present the new Red Hatter with items to wear, such as a gray wig, glasses, a cane, support hose, Depends, boxes of laxatives, watermelon seeds to spit, and a red hat and purple scarf. They will take tons of pictures for their scrapbook and the reduate will have the option of either making a speech or turning a somersault!

Queen Judith Hughes (the Grateful Red, Homer, Alaska) describes her chapter's first reduation ceremony as "quite the occasion," and this is not an exaggeration! Mary, their reduate, was chauffeured to the party. Although she wore her lavender and pink, she carried her birthday suit of red and purple with her in a bag. When she arrived, she was handed a pink rope and instructed to follow the line, which was draped over trees and shrubs, and meditate on the items that she came across that were tied to it. She found a baby pacifier, a diaper, a child's toy, birth-control pills, a breast pump, cards with notations about carpooling and PTA meetings, a miniskirt, a pink boa, false eyelashes, and high heels. The rope led her to the door of the house, on which was posted a sign reading LEAVE THE ITEMS YOU HAVE COLLECTED HERE. THEY REPRESENT A PAST THAT IS BEHIND YOU. Inside the house, she read a note by the fireplace that instructed her to burn her pink hat on the prepared fire.

After doing this, she was instructed to go upstairs and put on her birthday suit of red and purple. Then there was a *red* rope to follow through the house. Attached to this one were eyeglasses, estrogen pills, a hot-water bottle, a red pair of gloves, a purple wig, and "power pellets" (M & M's), among other things. When she arrived downstairs again, her chapterettes were waiting, each with a pink balloon and a pin, and they proceeded to pop Mary's "pink bubble."

Judith says, "As queen mum, I gave a speech summarizing the many accomplishments of our reduate over the preceding fifty years. One of our members created a bulletin board of photos of Mary through the decades: Mary as a child, Mary as a youngster, Mary as a young nurse, Mary as a mother, Mary and her husband. Luckily, I had a hot flash in the middle of my speech and was able to demonstrate the power of aging. And, of course, I 'hatted' our reduate with a homemade creation complete with red bird and nest."

The group then presented Mary with a walking stick for the journey ahead. It was wrapped in purple and red yarn and adorned with charms with various meanings. There were also many gifts of purple and red conferred by her sisters, followed by a huge potluck feast and a cake ablaze with candles. "Happy Birthday" was, of course, rendered on kazoos.

Mary had not been thrilled about reaching her fiftieth birthday, but she later announced that she had never felt "so honored or empowered by any previous birthday."

It is a rare Red Hat Society event that doesn't involve food. Sandy Treptow (Red Hatted Chickadees, Maple Grove, Minnesota), reports that they had a potluck for their first reduation. Everyone had to bring a red-and-purple dish to share. They had apples, lasagna with purple cheese, a couple of red-and-purple salads, and a purple cake decorated with red frosting. Sandy says: "It was a fun-filled evening and it almost makes one wish we weren't old enough to wear red and purple so we could do this again!" They will obviously be on the lookout for their next Pink Hatter, then.

Not every establishment of a tradition necessarily involves a ceremony. Some traditions develop slowly, over time, and others are the brainchildren of individuals. Whenever and wherever a new tradition is begun, it is usually put out there on our Web site for other chapters to adopt—or not!

RED HAT SOCIETY DAY

The very first get-together the founding chapter had was on April 25. It might never have occurred to me to mark that date in any particular way, but I began to get E-mails from Red Hatters suggesting that we proclaim a Red Hat Day. What an excellent idea! The logical thing was to commemorate the first-ever tea. How did we get that date declared official? The same way we do everything else: We just proclaimed it ourselves.

How do we celebrate it? However we want to. Many chapters wrote to tell me that they arranged large group mall crawls, lunches, et cetera. Many women wore their regalia to work, which met with highly varied reactions. It is my hope that we will continue to come up with new and improved ways to celebrate our own special day as the years go by.

Debbie Thorpe's Wild, Wacky Women of Winding River (Bolivia, North Carolina) decided to bury a time capsule in Debbie's yard to commemorate the occasion. They filled six glass bottles with such items as the official announcement of the holiday, a small red hat, a wine cork, and numerous other trinkets.

With Red Hatters like these, I don't feel any particular pressure to think up innovations. If I don't get at least one bright idea a day, I know that someone else will.

THE RED HAT SOCIETY THEME SONG

Mike Harline is the husband of one of my chapter members. Back in the sixties when folk music was king, he sang in the Fabulous Landsmen, a local group that met with some success. Although he went on to a different career, he still enjoys playing his guitar and singing at coffeehouses in the area. As he watched our little founding chapter grow into this huge disorganization, he was amazed and amused and became one of our biggest boosters. One day, he surprised me with an extraordinarily special gift—a song he had written just for us! I remember being moved almost to tears, for I realized that even though he is a man, he really got it. The words spoke of us women spending all of our lives doing for others and stated that it was now time to do for ourselves a little. And it had a catchy, funky beat—it didn't sound like a song for the elderly! In the ensuing years, Mike has recorded that song, as well as several others he created in the Red Hat vein. Many chapters have played his CD on their parade floats and made up dance routines to its beat. He is, now and forevermore, the "Official Red Hat Society Troubadour."

Here are the song lyrics:

Well I heard that they were coming,
I heard that they were on the move
I heard that they were stunning
With nothing left to prove
And when I asked about them
and how they came to be
They all laughed and they all smiled
and said these words to me!

Chorus:

Red Hat, Red Hat, Red Hat Society
All my life I've done for you,
Now it's my turn to do for me
Red Hat, Red Hat, I'm just as proud as I can be
With my purple dress and my red, red hat
The Red Hat Society

Sue Ellen's little whimsy suddenly caught fire
Now the purple dress and the red,
red hat are a national attire
You'll see them in the work place,
you'll find them at the mall
But you better believe all around the world,
they have heard the call!

Repeat Chorus

Red Hat, Red Hat, Red Hat Society
All my life I've done for you,
      Now it's my turn to do for me
Red Hat, Red Hat, I'm just as proud as I can be
With my purple dress and my red, red hat
      The Red Hat Society

Now the way I understand it,
      they don't want to change the world
They just like getting together, they just like being
      girls
They like good conversation they just like havin' fun
with a purple dress and a red,
      red hat for each and every one!

Repeat Chorus

Red Hat, Red Hat, Red Hat Society
All my life I've done for you,
      Now it's my turn to do for me
Red Hat, Red Hat, I'm just as proud as I can be
With my purple dress and my red, red hat
      The Red Hat Society

Spoken:

Yes the Red Hats are a-comin'
And they cannot be ignored
And there's a bond between them
That wasn't there before
I've seen them come together

With a smile on every face
I've heard the sound of laughter
Fillin' up the place
They've found an understanding
They've found a brighter day
And wouldn't the world be a better place
If we all felt that way?

Sue Ellen is an artist, Marsha teaches school
There's doctors and there's lawyers,
and all of them are cool
But whatever the occupation,
or wherever they may be
They've got one thing in common,
as you can plainly see!

Repeat Chorus

Red Hat, Red Hat, Red Hat Society
All my life I've done for you,
Now it's my turn to do for me
Red Hat, Red Hat, I'm just as proud as I can be
With my purple dress and my red, red hat
The Red Hat Society
—Reprinted with permission of Mike Harline

MASCOTS

Red Hat Society chapters function very much in the manner of a team, practicing mutual aid and teamwork all the time. Sports teams are well known for having mascots. Red Hatters are well known for playing games, which are our form of sports. So it was a natural development that some chapters (teams) would want to adopt mascots. The Red Hat Society as a whole had led the way, I guess, with our adoption of Ruby RedHat. Stories and photos began to trickle in early on, and the trickle has increased now to a steady stream.

There are plenty of chapters that do not have mascots, but plenty do.

Quite a number of these mascots are dolls of various types, dressed in red and purple. Some are homemade; some are purchased. Each is endowed with a personality and an attitude by its chapter. The Vermillion Vixens (Butler, Pennsylvania) have Rosie, the Red Hat Mama. The Akron Red Hat Flashes (Akron, Ohio) have Dame Purple Paparazza, who even has her own bodyguard, a police officer who is a member of her chapter. The Decadent Dames (Phoenix, Arizona) take their mascot, Rubee Dame, Ladee of Great Fame (who cannot be tamed) everywhere.

The Ruby Teazers (Raleigh, North Carolina) take their mascot, also named Rubee, everywhere, too. Apparently her name is a derivative of *rube*, because she is "just a tad rough around the edges." Apparently, she has been known to stick out her foot to trip waiters, or to tap her cigarette ashes into people's tea. When they go to restaurants, they put her in a high chair at the table. If she misbehaves, they move her high chair into a corner, facing the wall, until she settles down.

Dolls do not have a corner on the market, however. The Floozies with Panache (Riverside, California) have adopted a little white bear named Edith Elaine and a lop-eared white rabbit named Ruby Rabbit. Although both are stuffed, they are lavishly outfitted in small velvet dresses, red turbans with feathers, and jeweled accessories. It would be lovely if Ruby Rabbit could establish a relationship with the mascot of Wine and Roses (Ontario, Ohio), Rose Rabbit. A photo shows Rose standing out in her yard, among the flowers, wearing an adorable purple sundress and an enormous red hat made of netting—a bit more casual look than Ruby seems to favor. But if the country mouse can visit the city mouse, I would think the city rabbit could at least be a pen pal with the country rabbit. They could compare notes about their chapters.

A purple bear functions as mascot for Fairway's Fair Ladies (Orlando, Florida). She attends all their events, but she brings along her own chair to sit in—a white wooden Adirondack chair with CHICKS RULE painted on it—in red.

The Water Lilies (Middleburg Heights, Ohio) knew one another from a water-exercise group before they formed a Red Hat Society chapter. Their mascot is a resin frog named Miss Lily. Miss Lily has been given the full glamour treatment. Besides her red hat and purple rickracked-trimmed skirt, she sports bright red lipstick *and* toenails. The chapter does not limit her to sitting poolside. Wherever they go, she goes.

A stuffed frog named Fergie functions as mascot for the Red Hat Clog-Hoppers (the Villages, Florida). The chapter is made up of dancers who regularly perform their country clogging routines in various venues. She wears her regalia, including her own tiny clogging shoes, and sits in a chair at the side of the stage whenever they perform.

Sandra Robinson (the Bodacious Bastrop Belles, Bastrop, Texas) originally chose a Miss Piggy doll, a gift from her daughter, for a chapter mascot. Who better to exemplify the Red Hat attitude? But later on, when she acquired a handmade doll, fully outfitted in Red Hat regalia, she faced the problem of how to discreetly dethrone Miss Piggy. Fortunately, she was struck with the realization that Miss Piggy is undoubtedly far too young to wear a red hat, and Miss Piggy herself would be the first one to tell you so. A simple change from red to pink and purple to lavender for Miss P. made it possible for the two mascots to coexist amicably. (Knowing Miss Piggy, as we all do, we see that there could have been big problems if she suspected that she was being upstaged or replaced by another mascot.) Sandra has provided both of them with a tiny tea table and chairs and a tea set just their size. They spend a lot of their time sitting there. Don't tell Miss Piggy, but Ole Queenie accompanies Sandra on her travels to Red Hat functions, riding in a purple hatbox, snuggled in a boa and Sandra's red hat.

OFFICIAL INSTRUMENT

Musical talent is undoubtedly possessed by a great many Red Hatters, but it is certainly not universal. The beauty of the kazoo is that it is an equal-opportunity musical instrument, thereby making it just perfect for us. The playing of one requires no innate musical talent (well, it helps to be able to carry a tune) and no practicing. A kazoo can be carried in a purse and pulled out and played anywhere at any time. In a pinch, a makeshift kazoo can be improvised by using a comb with a piece of tissue folded over it. What better instrument for impromptu musical celebration? Not long after we had christened the kazoo our official instrument, "Hillbillie Belle" (Austintacious, Austin, Texas) sent me an E-mail describing one of their luncheons, which was held at a very proper restaurant. She says that she and her pals abruptly stood up, took out their kazoos, and played a lively tune while spontaneously marching around their table. Then, musical presentation complete, they sat down and resumed eating in ladylike silence, no doubt leaving other diners to draw their own conclusions.

THE WAVE

I guess I can take credit (or blame) for the Red Hat wave. (Just don't tell Queen Elizabeth I borrowed it.) It is a gesture that we all use for various occasions, such as waving to our adoring public when we are parade participants, or acknowledging gawkers as we stroll en masse to public events. One simply cups one's hand, fingers held tightly together, and swivels one's wrist side to side ever so subtly. It is a gesture of great grace and elegance, as befits a group such as ours, don't you agree? This is a gesture we use to wave good-bye, to say hello, and to acknowledge the crowds anywhere we go. It occurs to me that a discreet wave, accompanied by a questioning look, may be a good way to inquire silently whether a stranger is one of us.

Another way of identifying other Red Hatters when we are not in costume is to quietly say our slogan, "Red Hatters Matter." Queen Sharron deMontigny (Red Hot Red Hats, Corvallis, Oregon) says she tried that. She saw a women in a red hat, so she approached her and recited our slogan. "Well, I really surprised her," Sharron says, "but she immediately gave me a hug and said, 'We sure do!'"

Gloria J. Mansfield (Glorious Gals in Red Hats, Silver Spring, Maryland) has taken the time to describe various types of waves for us. According to Gloria, there are:

the little kid wave
the kid in class who is frantic to go to the bathroom wave
the soldier wave (salute)
the Granny (Beverly Hillbillies wave)
the Queen of England wave

But, as she says, "the saddest of all is the Red Glove wave—the one that says good-bye to a member who is moving away for good." My sentiments exactly. The truth of this sentiment was illustrated when one of Gloria's chapter members was returning to live in her home country of Australia. Each of the Glorious Gals opened a nicely packaged pair of red gloves, put them on, and did the Red Glove wave. Gloria says it was a lovely way to say good-bye to one of their dear friends.

GIFT EXCHANGES

Many chapters have instituted gift exchanges for special occasions. The Crimson Glorys (Sioux City, Iowa) have an annual Christmas gift exchange. The gift must be purchased at a rummage or garage sale, a thrift shop, or a secondhand shop, and it cannot cost more than two dollars. They tell their members to let their imaginations run wild. E-mail Queen Renee Beacom says: "Well, let me tell you, we found everything from red and purple jewelry to red and purple gloves, fingernail polish, and purses. . . . But the clincher was a pair of purple high heels, and they fit one of our ladies to a tee." The Glorys also plan to institute a system of secret sisters, so that they can exchange occasional surprise gifts. After all, fun is our whole purpose!

Some of us search for unique opportunities for joyful gift giving. Jan Berry, "Queen of Diamonds" (the Berry Best of Oxnard, California) enjoys presenting gifts to the planners of each monthly event. She keeps a fancy "Queen's Treasure Box" with a hinged lid and has the hostess of the month select a gift in front of the membership. Some of the items she stocks in the box are purple-and-red Mardi Gras beads and berry-scented air fresheners. Now she has an excuse to keep her eyes open for absolutely any little thing that is purple and red.

The members of some chapters have chosen to give one another small tokens to show that they are valued and understood. Debbi Thorpe, queen of the Wild, Wacky Women of Winding River (Bolivia, North Carolina) shares her innovative idea for trademark necklaces, which have become a tradition for them. Each woman's necklace starts with a plain gold or silver-tone chain, although some have used ribbon or rickrack. Various embellishments are given to the wearer by other chapter members. Debbie explains: "The charms are attached with safety pins, ribbons, wire, or pinned directly into the links of the necklace. As far as the trinkets, anything goes. We do try to give something that fits that particular Red Hatter's personality." One member is a master gardener, so her friends give her things such as pins or charms with flower themes. Another works as a volunteer for the preservation of sea turtles and is an excellent golfer, so she is apt to receive a plastic turtle or a miniature golf tee. The contribution can be something old or something new. Debbie says the best ones often come out of a kitchen junk drawer, but may come elaborately wrapped nonetheless. The wrapping is probably worth more than the charm, but that's okay.

I was thrilled to receive a necklace from the Wild, Wacky Women myself! Each of their members graciously contributed a charm from her own necklace, which is very special to me. Some of the items on this necklace are a tiny lavender plastic shoe, a frog bejeweled with imitation pearls and rubies, a clip earring, a sewing machine bobbin, a pop-top, a whistle, a ring (with the two-dollar price tag still attached), and a badge bearing the words DISCOVER THE JOY OF COLLECTING. What fun it must be to hunt down the perfect charm for that certain person!

MEMORY BOOKS

An idea was sparked, appropriately enough, by Sparky Bartlett at our first convention in Chicago. She came all the way from Canada, bringing with her a little purple bound book to pass around to everyone she met. They could write their greetings, phone numbers, E-mail addresses, or whatever else they wanted to jot down. The next year, in Nashville, she brought a different little bound book, which resembled a purse, handle and all. Doesn't that bring back the tradition of yearbook signing that we had in high school? Memory books are a wonderful way to capture information that you will want to refer to later. After all, any Red Hat Society regional meeting or convention can lead to new friends with whom you will want to keep in touch!

BRIM BRUSHING

Because hugging one another is something we love to do, and because that activity often results in hats being knocked askew or off our heads completely, we have instituted another ritual, this one called "brim brushing." When we greet one another affectionately, we are careful to hug gently, in genteel fashion, allowing our hat brims merely to touch lightly, thus replacing the all-out hug with something less dangerous to one's appearance. This not only keeps our hats off the floor; it spares our hair and our makeup. Even though we are getting older, we still insist on maintaining all of our glamour, don't you know! By the way, air kissing is a perfect accompaniment to brim brushing. And we are oh so genteel when doing that, as well.

TOASTS

Pat Latreille (Amarillo's Audacious Adorables, Amarillo, Texas) has instituted a toast to be made at the end of every one of her chapter's get-togethers. Each lady hoists a drinking vessel, whether or not there is anything in it, and recites this toast along with her sisters: "To Amarillo's Audacious Adorables: Long may we live and long may we enjoy gathering together in RED HATS!"

Since Red Hat Society members are famous for embroidering on one another's good ideas, may I propose a toast of my own? "To each and every Red Hatter, may you continue to seek and find all the joy, fun, and sisterhood that life has to offer!"

12
Join Us!

Where there is no joy there can be no courage.
—Edward Abbey

Live your life and forget your age.
—Norman Vincent Peale

*R*emember how the old-fashioned telephone cords used to get bent in funny configurations because they were stretched in the wrong directions too many times? The only way to get them back to normal was to bend them in the opposite way for a while to restore their equilibrium. Sometimes we have to use that technique with ourselves in order to change bad habits we may have developed. The following permission coupons may be torn out and used to help you as you embrace this new phase of life, a phase where the focus is on you!

🐛 *Permission* 🐛

To fly a kite, even if you can't find a child to do it with.

✂ -

🐛 *Permission* 🐛

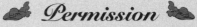

To browse and window-shop for hours
(without looking at your watch).

✂ -

🐛 *Permission* 🐛

To wear blue nail polish (or lime green, or purple).

✂ -

🐛 *Permission* 🐛

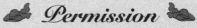

To take a nap just because you want to.

✂ -

🐛 *Permission* 🐛

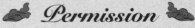

To let the dishes sit in the sink until tomorrow—
or next week.

✂ -

🐛 *Permission* 🐛

To draw a hopscotch pattern with chalk on the
sidewalk—and play—with or without a companion.

✂ -

🐛 *Permission* 🐛

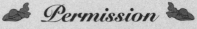

To run through the sprinklers in your bathing suit, or . . .

✂ -

Permission

To try a new hair color or style without consulting anyone.

Permission

To ride a carousel.

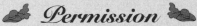

Permission

To say no to something you don't want to do. Permission not to feel guilty included.

Permission

To sign up for a class in painting, or fencing, or Russian, or whatever else it is you always wanted to do.

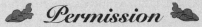

Permission

To eat pizza for breakfast.

Permission

To experiment with a new way of doing something—anything!

Permission

Just to be yourself, without apology.

The Red Hat Society is an idea whose time has come! If you are still reading this, I assume that the time has also come for you to be a part of it. At least I hope so.

We have all been told that one should warm up before beginning any vigorous physical exercise. We need to flex our muscles and get the blood flowing so that we don't pull a muscle, stress a tendon, or some such disastrous thing. If you are ready to adopt the Red Hat spirit, you will also need to prepare properly by flexing and loosening up your attitudes, opening your mind to new possibilities, and exercising the facial muscles used in smiling.

I hope that you are now sufficiently warmed up to begin. It would not be very much fun to belong to a Red Hat Society chapter of one. In order to kick up a ruckus and have a lot of fun, you need some cohorts. If you do something by yourself (like the lady in the "Warning" poem), you will be labeled an eccentric. But if you participate in the same activity with a group, especially a good-size group, onlookers will assume that there is a method to your madness. In our case, they would be wrong, but that doesn't matter when you are with your Red Hat sisters. Any pleasurable experience is enhanced when you can share it with people you care about.

So by now I hope I've made my case why it is important to gather several women together and establish your own chapter of the Red Hat Society. That may sound daunting. So many of us have been part of large charities, interest groups, and the like and we remember what a chore they were to organize. I have heard from an awful lot of women who said, "I really want to join a chapter, but I wouldn't want to start one." Ladies, ladies! There are probably as many *ways* to start a chapter as there are chapters! None of these methods involves what most of us would consider work.

So, how did some of them get going?

ALL IN THE FAMILY

My own chapter picked up speed quickly when I added my sisters, Jane and Robin, and my cousin, Vicki. We all know that mighty oaks begin with tiny acorns! Each of them immediately thought of a friend or two (or more) who would enjoy this. The instant bonding that we did with one another's friends showed the proof of the old adage, Anyone who is a friend of my friend is a friend of mine.

But for sheer family numbers, we have all been bested by the Sassy Scarlets (Amanda, Ohio). The eight members of this chapter are all sisters!

GET TOGETHER WITH A FEW OLD FRIENDS

The nine members who started the Golden Girls (Ocala, Florida) have been friends for over thirty years. They now range in age from sixty-nine to eighty-two. They have gone to the beach every summer and played cards together every week. The Red Hat Society is just one more way they have found to promote togetherness. They didn't have to do much to start a chapter, as they were actually a chapter in search of a name.

High school reunions have provided the impetus for a bunch of new chapters. The resourceful women who now comprise the Red Hat Belles of Bethel (Bethel, North Carolina) decided to form a chapter after reconnecting at their high school reunion, when they realized that they still enjoyed one another's company. They knew that the formation of a Red Hat Society chapter would provide them with an impetus to keep in touch more regularly. Those who now live some distance away will be able to attend gatherings only when they revisit their home-town, but at least, in this way, they have guaranteed more minireunions for those who live within a certain distance of the old hometown.

Queen Diane Kephart (Scarlett O'Hatters, Palmdale, California) told everyone at her fortieth high school reunion about the Red Hat Society, and she says that everyone she told vowed to go back to their home states and either find a chapter to join or start one. Diane says, "We all now have a link that spans time and distance and keeps us close in heart."

SHARED INTERESTS

I suppose that anyone who loves dancing, especially tap dancing, is probably an extrovert. I mean, all that loud clack-clacking and all! The Wise Women of Webster (Webster, New Hampshire) had already been dancing together for years, but they had never gone out in purple and red before they formed their chapter. They all had red derbies left over from a former recital, so they found a wonderfully economical source for their red hats.

The core of the Ladies of the Purple Sage (Yakima, Washington) consists of seven women, friends for over twenty years, who share the unique pastime of making "egg art." Every Tuesday, they get together to bejewel, bead, cut, and glue fabrics and insert music boxes or tiny scenes inside of blown eggs. The highlight of their year is their annual trip to the Northwest Egg Show. They say that when they don their red hats and head out, their personalities really change. Isn't that eggsciting? (Sorry, I just couldn't resist.)

There are Red Hatters of many faiths, and in Stow, Ohio, a chapter has been formed that is made up of women from the various churches in town. Because they meet once each season of the year, they call themselves the Duchesses of Summer-Fall-Winter-Spring, a name inspired by the Indian princess in the *Howdy Doody Show* from the 1950s. Their greeting for one another is along the same lines: "Howdy Doody!" Their chapter's motto is K.I.S.S. (Keep it simple, stupid.) I guess they have our policy about working down pat.

SHARED HERITAGE

Nubia Pizano Ascher's chapter (Uy, Uy, Uy Latin Prima Donnas, Los Angeles, California) is made up of women originally from Latin American countries—Argentina, Columbia, Chile, and Uruguay. Some of her members emigrated originally to South America from such places as Austria, Armenia, Spain, Italy, and Greece. Technically, however, they fill Nubia's bill. She says, "We emigrated here for different reasons, and each of us has her own story to tell. . . . We are the product of a combination of many influences that make us unique, colorful, warm, and a little out of the ordinary." (As are we all, I might add.)

BORROW SOMEONE ELSE'S IDEA

Debbie Thorpe's chapter ultimately arose from an article about a men's (yes, I said men's) club that she read about. She says, "There had been an interesting article in our local newspaper about several men who started a unique club. The club was based on their overcrowded backyard sheds, their ability to accumulate more than lawn mowers, and their love of 'junk' purchased at flea markets and yard sales. Each gentleman seemed to have developed a theme as to how he wanted his particular shed to look. Members of this club meet once a month at one of the respective sheds and they have what is known as a 'Shed Sittin'.' Food and drinks are provided by the host, along with gifts for the other members. The gifts must be appropriate for their sheds. . . . Being an old 'junker,' I thought this was terrific, right up my alley. . . . Behold, a woman's version of a 'Sittin', was born."

Debbie put mismatched old chairs under a tree in her garden and then added pink yard flamingos, plastic chickens, baskets, old plastic tables, coffeepots turned into wind chimes, and purple-and-red pinwheels. She edged the tree with old ceramic plates, partially buried in the ground. The tree has become a "shoe tree"—yes, a real tree full of old shoes hanging from the branches. A purple umbrella helps to shade a Boston fern, and old boots work as planters for many different types of ivy. When Debbie received an article about the Red Hat Society in the mail from a friend up north, she knew she had the extra ingredient to make her "sittin's" really special. Last we heard, twenty-five women in red and purple were enjoying the sittin' area on a regular basis, sometimes playing croquet, laughing, and eating together. When their chapter (the Wild, Wacky Women of Winding River, Bolivia, North Carolina) became official, they held a small ceremony under the tree, with each member receiving her pin and membership card. Those of us at Hatquarters (our office) were very honored to receive a couple of red shoes in the mail for us to autograph. We sent the shoes back, and Debbie sent us photos of them being formally installed on their shoe tree.

A LITTLE EXTRA HELP?

There are large numbers of older women in assisted-living facilities. Many of them have lost their husbands and given up their homes, and some of them are restricted in their mobility. Queen Mum Cindy Craig got the Red Rascalettes started in the Aldersgate Village Assisted Living Home in Topeka, Kansas, originally for the benefit of her mother, a resident. Cindy knew that these women were unable to get out and shop for their outfits, so she made the rounds of the local thrift shops and then took her finds to the home. Here is her story:

Boxes big enough to hold a stove were filled with every size and style of purple outfits the thrift stores had available. Twenty straw hats were spray-painted red and loaded into another big box. These would all be shipped from Arizona to Kansas. Imagine the faces of the nursing staff when the boxes arrived. The outfits were set out and each lady was told to take one hat and one outfit. Suddenly, the staff became intrigued with what was happening. Everyone wanted a red hat. When people heard that more red hats were needed, they started showing up with them. The residents had heard that if you belonged to the Red Hat Society, it meant that once in a while you had the opportunity to go out to eat. This had not happened for them in a while, and now it became an expectation. The activity director decided to organize an outing. A revolt was in the planning stages otherwise. For one night, the Red Rascalettes became a little spunky and enjoyed a night on the town.

It might have taken a concerted effort for these ladies to get their night on the town, but they got it, thanks to a few very caring people.

JUST DO IT

In my opinion, it is a mistake to wait for opportunities for enjoyable new experiences to happen to us. Sometimes we have to stir up a little something on our own initiative, instead of sitting around daydreaming or wishing something would happen.

Just because you have never had the get-up-and-go to do something like start a chapter on your own doesn't mean that you can't do it now. You might surprise yourself. Julie Clinton (the Scarlet Foxes of the Fox Valley, Oswego, Illinois) discovered our Web site shortly before her fiftieth birthday and went on-line to look for a chapter in her area to join. Dismayed that she couldn't find one, she mustered her courage and placed an ad in the local paper:

> I am starting a new Fox Valley area chapter of the Red Hat Society. You've read about them. Now let's join in the fun. If you are a woman 50 years old or older (ladies in their 40's are welcome too), and you love to have fun, dress up, and be silly, come join me. . . .

To Julie's amazement, she received sixty phone calls! The local library allowed her to use their largest meeting room, and fifty-six women showed up at the first gathering. To break the large group into several smaller ones, Julie passed around a basket with slips of paper containing the names of several animal groups. Each person drew a slip from the basket and found her sister animals by circulating around the room, making the requisite animal noise of her group ("moo," "meow," and so on). Bedlam ensued until they were separated into six groups. (Obviously, this ice-breaker works as well with mature women as it does with six-year-olds!) Julie asked them if they would like to break up into several chapters or just remain "one big happy band of merry women." They opted for the latter choice. Julie has some advice for those who think they are too shy to do something like this: "I am delighted to make so many new (and crazy) friends. If you get any inquiries or E-mails regarding starting new chapters, tell them that I am so proud I did this. I didn't know I had it in me. . . . Life is indeed filled with fabulous surprises."

Peggy Brown (Midnight Lace & Royal Roses, Lawrenceville, Georgia) attended a two-day conference on the subject "Management Skills for Executive Assistants." During one of the sessions, a discussion developed about the kinds of things women do and what kinds of qualities they require. Peggy writes, "Although I cannot remember the context, the Red Hat Society came up. I made the comment that there were no chapters in my area. The instructor looked directly at me and said, 'Then why don't you start one?' To me, it was almost a dare. I could do that. I went on the Internet and found that there were chapters here, but they were all closed to new members. So I clicked on 'Start Your Own Chapter.' I found out what to do and then called my best friend. We scheduled our first event at a beautiful little tearoom and began to invite friends. . . . I am now up to about thirty members. We have had the most sensational year, and my ladies have so many plans for the future. It has been one of the most freeing things I have ever done. I cannot imagine not having the Red Hat Society as part of my life. I have made new friends and done things I would not do on my own. I encourage my ladies to remember that life is a gift to be celebrated every day."

Waiting for someone else to take the initiative is often a mistake. Liz Thayer (the Red Riding Hoods, Fair Oaks, California) knew that her friend was toying with the idea of starting a chapter of the Red Hat Society, but a year went by and the friend just didn't get around to it. Liz dubbed herself "Lady Not Waiting" and made folders (on red paper, of course) entitled "The Red Hat Society of Fair Oaks Birthing Manual." She called a group of prospective members together and got the chapter going herself! No, she didn't crown herself queen; she apparently preferred to keep her original title.

QUEEN'S "DUTIES"

I need to emphasize that the person who takes the necessary steps to get a group started may certainly become queen of that chapter. After all, first come, first served. However, the queen is by no means in charge of planning everything from that point on. Most groups simply agree that each member will plan one event, another the second, and so on. The person who plans an event is responsible for setting the place, the date and time, and letting everyone know the details. One member may be inspired to make reservations at an elegant restaurant, provide table decorations, et cetera. Another may simply find out when a movie starts and suggest everyone meet at the theater. There is just no way that a chapter of the Red Hat Society should be too much work for anyone. If it starts to feel like work, you're not doing it right!

AGE REQUIREMENT

If you are a female, you can be a Hatter of one type or another. If you are fifty or over, you qualify to be a Red Hatter. If you are under fifty, you may become a Pink Hatter. Once in a while, I am asked whether one can be too old to join us. That question is just plain dismaying. Of course you can't be too old.

I have already made it clear that we make a big deal out of fiftieth birthdays. Actually, we make a big deal out of anything we can find to make a big deal out of. But it is not often that we get to make a celebration out of a Red Hatter's 106th birthday. After all, that is a fiftieth birthday multiplied by two, with six added for good measure. I had the privilege of joining Queen Linda Richards (Lincoln Hills Red Hat Society, Lincoln, California) when a member, Olive Ruby (that name again) Title celebrated that birthday in the company of over two hundred other local Red Hatters, all in full regalia. Olive herself looked absolutely lovely in her flowing purple dress and gorgeous red hat, wrapped in yards of red tulle flowing down her back. She was born in 1896, so she has lived in three centuries, including all of the twentieth. She has seen twenty presidents of the United States come and go and has buried four husbands. (Ruby announced to the birthday throng that she didn't kill any of them. Obviously, there's no age limit on that famed Red Hat sense of humor.) Olive's daughter, who is seventy-three, told us that her mother maintains a positive outlook on life. She has never been heard to speak ill of anyone in her entire life. That should give us all food for thought.

CHAPTER SIZE

As in the case of just about everything else, each chapter is free to choose the size they would like to be. The founding chapter started out with a scant five members and grew rapidly to over twenty. Red Hat Society chapters all sprout from the same tiny seed of an idea, but each one blooms in its own way into something unique. The concept spreads primarily by word of mouth and incites enthusiasm in most women who hear about it. I have often remarked that I would never have had the energy to cheerlead women into joining us. And I always advise others not to pursue any woman who has to be coaxed into membership. This does not mean she is not a wonderful person; it may just mean that she is not currently at a point in her life that allows her to respond to our brand of lightheartedness. Give her space and time, love her anyway, and leave the door open.

Recruitment is rarely a problem. I have talked to many current queens who started a chapter with only themselves and one or two others. They have managed to gather as many members as they can handle (maybe more) just by going out and attracting attention. As we become better known, we find large numbers of women are actively looking for chapters to join. A simple posting on our Web site about a new chapter starting up in a given area will result in enough responses to get going.

Getting a chapter off the ground is rarely a problem, either. I have heard from far more women who have had the opposite problem. How do you get it to stop growing? We try to be inclusive, but many groups opt to close their chapters to new members when they reach a specified number. This is done purely because it is much more difficult to schedule activities for a large group than a small group, and many venues lend themselves more easily to a small group. It is usually not difficult to reserve a table for ten; it is a major undertaking to reserve a room for two hundred. As Queen Vivian Trolan (Rivah Belles, Burgess, Virginia) says, "I have limited our club to ten so that we can all eat at the same table in a restaurant. We are all friends and do not want to sit at different tables. At church recently, a lady told me she understands that to get into the Rivah Belles, she would have to watch the obituaries! I have suggested to some ladies that they go to the Red Hat Web site and start their own club." The Red Hat Society does ask that any chapter that is not accepting new members offer information and encouragement to those who want to join them. We hope that these women will understand why certain chapters are closed and will realize this is not meant as a personal affront. We encourage them to start their own chapters. Most of them do just that.

Some groups that are full to the brim (for some reason, these hat images keep coming up) have taken names and put them on waiting lists, seeing that as their only solution to growing larger than they want to be. I would suggest that people on waiting lists be put in touch with one another. There is the kernel of a new chapter right there.

Another kind solution practiced by some is a guest event where interested women in the area can attend as a onetime guest. Jean Blomquist (Rosy Chapeaux of South Putnam County, Florida) writes that her chapter decided to have a guest day: ". . . and it was splendid! Eighteen of us met at a special place that can handle larger groups. It was so colorful and fun. We have decided to do this several times a year and encourage the starting of new chapters."

Some women have been loath to turn anyone away. Maggie Then (Sun City West Red Hatters, Sun City, Florida), in the spirit of inclusiveness, was reluctant to close her chapter to anyone in her retirement community who expressed interest. The last time I heard from her, her chapter had grown to over five hundred women! Maggie says that she has lots of enthusiastic help planning huge events, chartering buses, et cetera, and has no regrets. But she doesn't necessarily recommend this for anyone who doesn't have a ton of time on her hands and a flair for organization.

Maggie's chapter makes Susie Stoddard's appear modest in number. The Santa Barbara Hattitudes (Santa Barbara, California) has over one hundred members. Susie writes, "I am dealing with a group that prefers to be large! I have 130 women on the roster and they are still inviting their friends! Being part of something big is very appealing. I am retired and have time to spend with the project, so I am just going ahead with it, planning probably three events a month so everyone that wants to attend can do so."

Of the three chapters I have mentioned, which is doing the right thing? All of them!

As I see it, two rather distinct philosophies have emerged among Red Hat chapters. One group is probably comprised mainly of a few longtime friends with a few friends of friends included. The women in this group may have known one another for a long time, possibly from school or work. They use the Red Hat Society as a means to help them make sure they get together regularly and to give them permission to have some scheduled fun. They usually expect fairly regular attendance. Over time, they will probably find that their relationships with other chapter members have deepened, due to their making the time to see one another regularly at Red Hat Society events and sharing their lives. This is surely a positive thing.

Another type of chapter may be composed of a seminal group that then grows, perhaps quickly and haphazardly, perhaps deliberately, into a large conglomeration of women. Each one tells another, who tells another. Some of these groups may take a casual attitude toward attendance, asking only that each member show up once in a while, when a particular scheduled event strikes her fancy. The roster may list one hundred members, but the average attendance at a given event may average twenty-five. These women have the opportunity to make the acquaintance of a lot of people they would not otherwise have known. They will probably begin to number women from very different walks of life as their friends. This is also a very positive thing.

Our policy of "no rules" continues to set the standard.

FREQUENCY OF MEETINGS

We are often asked how often a chapter should meet. How often does your chapter feel like getting together? There's your answer.

Once you have enough people to get a chapter established, it is a good idea to take stock of the preferences of the members. The queen, or whoever is heading up the group, needs to have an idea of how her members feel about the direction that they want the group to take. After all, there are so many possibilities!

Susie Stoddard (Santa Barbara Hattitudes) made up a questionnaire and handed it out at her chapter's inception. She has managed to come up with a way to assess her group's preferences and have fun doing it:

1. ***Do you prefer:***
   ☐ Small group—around 15 to 20 maximum per event so you can get to know each person.
   ☐ Larger group—anything from 20 to 60 is fine with me.
   ☐ Either one is okay with me. Just call my name and I will be anywhere anytime!

2. ***Are you available to attend:***
   ☐ Friday events, mostly.
   ☐ Saturday events.
   ☐ Evening events—just not in the middle of the night!

3. **Do you prefer to attend:**
   ☐ Once a month *only*.
   ☐ Would like to attend more than once a month.
   ☐ I am ready and willing to go anywhere anytime! Did you call?

4. **Prefer to pay:**
   ☐ $10.00 or under for an event.
   ☐ $15.00 or under for an event.
   ☐ $20.00 to $25.00 for an event.
   ☐ No cost is too much for this much fun!
   ☐ Vary the costs.
   ☐ I might hit the lottery and pay for everyone!

5. **Do you prefer:**
   ☐ Veggie meals.
   ☐ Desserts with the meals.
   ☐ No desserts with the meals.
   ☐ Have dietary restrictions or preferences, which are:

   _____

   ☐ I will eat almost anything that is not bleedin', bawlin', or crawlin'!

6. **Are you interested in taking trips or cruises, etc.?**
   ☐ Yes, would love to go on a trip or cruise with other Red Hat ladies. Here are my suggestions: _____
   ☐ No. I prefer a group with lots of *men*.
   ☐ Not interested in going out of the area.
   ☐ Don't bother me. I have enough trouble remembering when the next event is.
   ☐ Other: _____

7. **Do you sing, dance, or play a musical instrument?**
   ☐ Sing—prefer group singing.
   ☐ Sing—will do solos.

- [ ] Mostly sing in the shower.
- [ ] I can read music.
- [ ] No, I cannot read music.
- [ ] "Shore" I can read. I'm reading this, ain't I?
- [ ] Play a musical instrument: _____
- [ ] I play mostly CDs, cassettes, and the stereo.
- [ ] Yes, I can dance. Type/style _____
- [ ] Nope. Ain't doin' no dancin'—no way, nohow!

8. **Would you be interested in seeing our own Web site on the Net? It would tell about our group and our events, have pictures of all of us, and a page for our interests, businesses, hobbies, etc.**
   - [ ] Yes.
   - [ ] No. What's a Web site?
   - [ ] Yes, and I would love to help set it up.
   - [ ] Yes, and I would like to help maintain it.
   - [ ] *Noooo!* I can barely get my E-mail to work!
   - [ ] *No.* I just found out yesterday where my browser window was. I thought it was some kind of Peeping Tom!
   - [ ] Would someone tell me where "any key" is?

9. **Would you be okay with adding $.50 to each luncheon for the kitty?**
   - [ ] *No.* You're robbing us blind as it is!
   - [ ] Just how hungry is that cat anyhow?
   - [ ] Other suggestions: _____

10. **Would you like to start a smaller group?**
    - [ ] Yes, I would love to.
    - [ ] *No,* not interested.
    - [ ] How much smaller is "smaller"?
    - [ ] I would like to help out with this group. I would be willing to
    _____

11. *Anything else you would like to say?*

_____

_____

_____

BIOGRAPHIES

In many cases a chapter grows in such a way that many members are unfamiliar to some of the others. This can be a very good thing, as it opens doors to new connections. But how can the ice be broken? How can a life thus far be effectively summarized? Queen Terry Santore (the Crimson Sages, Wallace, North Carolina) wrote out thirty questions, designed to help her members get to know one another better. She meets with each new member and has her draw fifteen cards at random and answer the questions. Terry also takes a digital photo. Then she works the answers into a written biography of that woman and posts a page about her on the Web site of the Crimson Sages. Here is a sample of the questions a new member might be asked:

• Where were you born? What was your childhood like?
• Who makes up your immediate family?
• Is there something you always wanted to do? Is it within your reach?
• What are your hobbies? What gives you the most joy?
• What is the one thing everyone would be surprised to know about you?
• What do you feel is your greatest talent or attribute?
• What cause are you most passionate about?
• What is your most prized possession?
• How would you describe the perfect day?

Intriguing questions, aren't they? Can you see how interesting it could be to read the answers provided by all your friends, new and old alike? This idea can be used in various ways to help us get to know one another and to open interesting discussions. Terry's summarized results are posted on her chapter's Web site for her chapter members and others to read. When you think about it, this kind of thing makes interesting reading for members of other chapters. Who knows what kind of connections they could provoke?

MMMS

One more way we are connecting with other women who are not in our usual circle is by becoming MMMs (Missionaries to the Matriarchal Masses). This is the term we use for all Red Hatters who help spread the word to other women. The word can be spread simply by sharing the concept or by passing out our MMM cards—cards that we make available with our logo and our Web site on them. It sometimes saves a few hundred words which might otherwise be necessary to explain the whole concept. Of course, now that I think of it, most of us love to talk, so saving words may not be that important!

A lot of our members are happy to pass out the cards wherever they go, just to spread our message to other women who are in our age range. We joke that we are eventually going to take over the world, but are we really joking? We are not missionaries in any strong-armed sense, as we don't even hang around to follow up with these women; we just want to make others aware of the fun we are having and let them know how easy it can be for them to join us. A lot of them have been so immediately charmed that they have thanked the MMMs for giving them this gift.

Barbara Rowe's chapter (the Red Fedoras, Chesterfield, Virginia) came up with an extremely inventive method of getting out our message. Barbara says, "I am in the process of making a shirt with a woman wearing a red hat on the front and the wording ASK ME ABOUT THE RED HATS on the back. I have the license plate stating that I'm a member of the Red Hat Society, and I'm constantly being asked about it. I figure I will attract more attention with the shirt."

Annette Geoffrion, or "Marguerite the Magnificent" (Forget-Me-Nots, Chicopee, Massachusetts), visited her cousins in a small town in the hills of northern Italy and took her red hat with her. Her attitude was contagious and her cousins got busy making red hats and flaunting attitudes of their own to the rest of the villagers. When she returns in two years, she expects to have a welcoming committee—a sea of red hats! Because of travelers like Annette, and also the Internet, the Red Hat Society has already spread, as of this writing, to seventeen countries. Although most of the chapters are being started by Americans living abroad, we are making inroads with the natives here and there, notably in Australia and New Zealand.

Speaking of MMMs makes me think of M&M's. A while back, there was a nationwide contest to choose one new color of M&M's. The choices were purple, aqua, and pink. An alert went out to all Red Hatters on our Web site: "Vote for purple!" It wasn't long before the contest ended. The winning color? Purple!

GATHERINGS ON A GRANDER SCALE

Every chapter of the Red Hat Society comes up with its own events, and every chapter has unique experiences in the course of those events. Well, if we were having this much fun in our smallish groups, some of us began to wonder whether there might be even more fun to be had in larger ones. Only a few months after the founding chapter's preliminary publicity and the subsequent formation of dozens of other chapters in Southern California, we decided to see what would happen if we invited women of surrounding areas for tea and gab. We reserved a banquet room and invited ladies from around the area to join us. To liven up our event, we contacted Barbara Kincaid, who owns a huge collection of vintage hats, and asked her to bring a bunch of them to our tea and teach us a little about their history. She kept us rapt with enjoyment as she explained the various types of hats that have been worn through the centuries, modeling some of them herself.

What fun it was to converge by the dozens in a large venue! As we streamed into the tearoom, we were saluted by honks and waves from passing cars, and we quickly realized that "the more, the merrier" is a valid concept. A large number of purple-and-red-clad women is quite a sight to see. We discovered that this occasion had given us the chance to meet more people and spread the fun even further than before. Thus was born the concept of a regional get-together. In the usual spirit of disorganization, we spread the word to all chapters that they might want to try a joint event with two, three, or more chapters. Obviously, it would serve to broaden their horizons and provide multiple opportunities for the formation of new friendships for those interested in expanding their social lives.

The first Red Hat Hoot (group train trip) was our trip to San Juan Capistrano, during which we were taped for a segment of the *Today* show. (I talked about this event in chapter 1.) At that time, I merely put out a notice on my weekly broadcast, saying that the founding chapter was going to take a train trip on a certain Saturday in June. I issued a blanket invitation to any and all Red Hatters (or potential Red Hatters) to join us, getting on the train at any station along the way that they wished. The goal was simply to hit the town in force, meeting and greeting in disorganized fashion. I didn't take reservations, or count heads; we just showed up! And it worked just fine. Every time the train pulled into a station, there were cries of excitement from those already on the train as they saw a sea of red hats on women waiting to get on! When the train disgorged us in San Juan, over 250 women alighted, to the cheers of about 150 more who were on hand to greet us, waving signs and balloons! We congregated briefly as a group, then scattered all over the little antique district to do some bargain hunting and meet new friends. Every group found a place for lunch when they got hungry. No muss, no fuss! Amtrak accommodated us on the return trip by adding a couple of extra cars. They suggested that we might want to forewarn them of our next area-wide train trip so they could be ready for us.

The following year, we did a similar thing, this time traveling north to Ventura, another charming little seaside town with a lot of quaint shops. The second Red Hat Hoot was even more successful than the first, and this time we suggested that those interested make a whole weekend of it! In our typical way, some did and some didn't.

Many of the chapters in Iowa got together for the First Iowa Red Hat Christmas Tour. They converged on Kansas City for a tour of the Toy and Miniature Museum, carriage rides, window-shopping, dinner, and a fantastic light display. This sounds like a particularly fun way to get some Christmas shopping done while hanging out with your friends.

Sometimes a get-together will consist of a date made by only two or three chapters. The joint attendance of the New York City Ballet's production of *Cinderella* by the Rapid Free Radicals, the Red Hat Honeys, and the Spirit of Red and Purple (all of Rapid City, South Dakota) is a good example of such a gathering.

Two queens in North Carolina, Terry Santore (the Crimson Sages) and Elizabeth Costanzo (the Victorian Roses, Wilmington), got together and laid the groundwork for a Saturday-afternoon luncheon cruise. They invited chapters from their surrounding areas and were rewarded for their efforts when 241 women from fourteen different chapters accepted the invitation to sail down the Cumberland River with them. Queen Terry described the scene:

> We gathered outside the boat for about a half hour and giggled at one another's outfits, hats, etc. . . . While cruising, there was narration from the captain, but no one paid any attention. You can imagine 241 women all talking. Who could hear him? We had a great lunch, and then on the sound system came some ragtime songs. And next thing you know, there were ladies up doing the Charleston! Boy, could they move!

Soon the whole area was covered with purple and red and they danced away. Before it was over, someone started a conga line, and at least 150 ladies joined in! When the boat docked an hour and a half later, no one even knew it. We were having so much fun! When we got off, we had the afternoon to shop. Elizabeth and I had arranged for over forty stores to give us discounts from 10 to 25 percent, so the ladies had a great time and improved the economy of Wilmington! After that, some even stayed on for dinner. All in all, it was a great day. I love getting the different chapters together. You get to meet such interesting ladies!

> "The atmosphere was warm and the feelings were comfortable. . . . I know that we are not a group to do anything, but I can imagine in generations to come that our daughters and granddaughters will carry this on and they will speak out as one. Perhaps we will have a president who is a Red Hatter."
> —Jan Isenberg
> (Red Hat Momas, Sun Lakes, Arizona),
> commenting on a large gathering she had attended

It wasn't long before enterprising women took the initiative to plan cruises and tours. You name it; they've done it. Actually, I shouldn't say that; none of us knows what they'll think of next. (I just hope they keep inviting me.)

Since regional events were becoming so popular, a national convention was an obvious next step. As I have said, our first one was held in Chicago in the spring of 2002. Over four hundred red-hatted women showed up, and we found out just how much fun there was to be had in large numbers. Anyone watching the lobby of the Westin Hotel on the afternoon our ladies started arriving had quite a pageant to watch. Almost every time that revolving door spun, it disgorged yet another smattering of ladies, most clad in purple, some wearing red hats, some carrying them in huge bags. There was an air or excitement that surrounded each cluster of ladies, and a sense of building up toward something grand. And grand it certainly was! There were speakers, entertainment, group activities, city tours, teas, and a formal banquet. There was a pajama breakfast, a talent show, karaoke, and dancing (including the requisite conga line). After three days of nonstop activity, we met on Sunday morning for a gospel brunch, which brought down the rafters and sent us all on the way home on a high. The same lobby that had been the scene of excited arrivals just days before was now the setting for hugs, tears, and many cries of "See you next year!"

> "The convention was one of the most inspirational, moving experiences of my fifty-two years. Having that many women in one room happily engaged in learning from one another was soooo uplifting. The high from Chicago really fired me up in my everyday life as well as my professional life. And still inspires me to accomplish feats of wonder daily."
> —Sandi Narramore (Dallas Darling Dahlias, Dallas, Texas)

Our second annual convention was a foregone conclusion before the first one had even ended, so we took a poll to find out where our ladies wanted it to be. Nashville, Tennessee, was the winner. As soon as we got home, we started to plan. To our amazement, we soon had reservations for five times the number of women we had gathered for the first one.

Two thousand women joined us in Nashville in the spring of 2003! Among our activities were a riverboat dinner cruise, a golf tournament, a pajama breakfast, a talent show, a bluegrass brunch, a banquet, and "shoptions" (options for one of our favorite activities—shopping). One night, our ladies took over the famous Wild Horse Saloon for line dancing and a southern barbecue. Words fail me! All I can say is, "You had to be there!"

In 2004, we shall descend en masse upon Dallas! I would expect that there will be a run on red and purple cowboy boots and hats, not to mention anything fringed in red and purple.

WEB SITE (COMPUTERS REVISITED)

I often wonder if the Red Hat Society would ever have come into existence without the Internet to serve as our instant connection. I am sure the idea would have spread, albeit a lot slower. But it would have proved very difficult to build the type of connection we have built if we had had to share all the information by snail mail. Well, one thing is absolutely certain: Without the Internet, we would definitely *not* be where we are now. So, with further apologies to Dr. Seuss, I have added this verse to the poem about computers that I shared in chapter 1:

> *I know I said I wouldn't learn*
> *I said it in a manner stern*
> *Computers were not useful items*
> *I made the choice that I would fight 'em.*
>
> *But if I really had done that*
> *Refused to share about my hat*
> *And missed the chance to make connections*
> *With all of you, in all directions*
>
> *It would have been a loss for me*
> *Prevented Red Hat history*
> *Thank goodness old dogs learn new tricks*
> *We've found a world of fun in "clicks"!*

Our Web site address is www.redhatsociety.com.
Some of the basic features of the Web site are:

- An explanation of who we are and what we are about
- The ability to search for Red Hat Society chapters worldwide, with contact information

- On-line registration of new chapters
- Information on upcoming national and local large events
- Chat room—join a conversation as it happens
- Ruby's Ramblings (We try to keep track of her interesting life.)
- Our on-line store
- Queen Mother Board (This is our centerpiece for communication. All official members are encouraged to post messages to one another on any of the following suggested topics:

> Help me find a chapter in my area.
> Chapter news: What has your chapter done lately?
> Upcoming chapter events: What do you plan to do next?
> National convention connections: Roommates?
> Creative Pursuits: Painting? Quilting? Hobbies?
> Suggestions: What useful ideas can you share with us?
> Recommendations: Share a favorite book or movie with your
>   sisters.
> Travel: Where have you traveled? Where did you stay? Rec-
>   ommendations? Warnings?
> Spiritual issues.
> Technical support: Help, I hate computers!
> Personal news: New grandchild? Anything
>   to share?

The chatter that goes on can be absolutely fascinating! It is easy to log on, intending to spend only a few minutes, then later glance at the clock and realize that an hour has passed. Don't say I didn't warn you!

I know, starting your own chapter or going to a meeting room full of strangers can be intimidating, but believe me, you'll be so glad you did it. Sooner than you think, your life will be enriched, and fuller than you ever expected.

Afterword

Go! You might meet somebody!
> —the best advice my mother ever gave me

SO HERE WE ARE!

*T*he Red Hat Society still calls itself a disorganization, and we are proud of our lack of rules and bylaws. We are all helping to develop an enormous nurturing network of women over fifty by joining red-gloved hands and spreading the joy and companionship we are building around the world. We have also discovered a mission of sorts: to gain higher visibility for women in our age group and to reshape the way we are viewed by today's culture. We are all familiar with militant women's groups of the past, which stridently sought to achieve their agendas, political and otherwise. Well, we are decidedly *un*strident, but we do hope to advance *our* agenda with good humor and laughter. If we do not join together under our Red Hat Society banner, but remain isolated, unconnected groups, this will not happen. Therefore, we are continuing to work on building a dis-organization within which we can all connect—and eventually take over the world!

Margaret Meade said, "Never doubt that a small group of thoughtful, committed citizens can change the world." I agree with that, but I would insert three words of my own: "Never doubt that a small group of thoughtful citizens, who should be committed, can change the world."

This book begins with the poem that inspired the first chapter of the Red Hat Society. It ends with our new, very own poem:

The Red Hat Society

A poet put it very well. She said when she was older
She wouldn't be so meek and mild. She threatened
*   to get bolder.*
She'd put a red hat on her head, and purple on her
*   shoulder.*
She'd make her life a warmer place, her "golden
*   years" much golder.*

We read that poem, all of us, and grasp what she is
*   saying.*
We do not need to sit and knit, although we are all
*   graying.*
We think about what we can do. Our plans we have
*   been laying.*
Instead of working all the time, we'll be out some-
*   where playing.*

We take those colors to our hearts, and then we all
*   go shopping,*
For purple clothes and hats of red, with giant brims
*   a-flopping.*

We've stopped our slaving all the time, our staying
      home just mopping,
We order pies and chocolate fudge, and rich desserts
      with topping.

We crown ourselves as duchesses and countesses and
      queens.
We prove that playing dress-up isn't just for Hal-
      loween.
We drape ourselves in jewels, feathers, boas, and
      sateen.
We see ourselves on television and in magazines.

We laugh, we cry, we hug a lot. We keep each other
      strong.
When one of us goes out for fun, the rest all go
      along.
We gad about, we lunch and munch, in one big
      happy throng.
We've found the place where we fit in, the place we
      all belong.

                      —Sue Ellen Cooper

All people need a place to belong, a place where they feel that
they fit in without trying too hard. The Red Hat Society aspires to be
just such a place for the increasing number of women who are entering midlife determined to savor every minute of their existence. Will
we manage to change the world? Maybe. Maybe not. But we know
that we *will* manage to make some changes in our own lives.

We are *not* done!

Appendix: Would a Rose Smell So Sweet?

*I*f there were ever any doubts about the capacity for humor among our members, it would be quickly dispelled by reading samples of the names that many chapters have given themselves. Where do the ideas come from? Get a group of women intent on lightening up together and they will start to brainstorm. Before long, their biggest problem may be which clever name, among the many they have come up with, to settle on. Just choosing a name can get the merriment started.

The names of the Red Hat Society chapters have become famous in their own right. They express the personality, humor, and vitality of their members. Diane Jones (the Leading Ladies, San Antonio, Florida) writes, "The day before my friends' and my annual trip to the mountains of North Carolina last year, I had read about the Red Hat Society for the first time. During the drive up, we (three of us) talked about it, then said, 'We have *got* to do this!'" Diane and her friends are from a very small town, and many women there have known each other from childhood, so they knew they could get a chapter going in no time. While they vacationed in the cabin, they puzzled over a name for their group. As Diane thumbed through a catalog of ladies' wear, she spied an advertisement for Leading Ladies bras, and—voilà!—their group was named!

Debbie Miller (Mad Red Hatters of Covina, Covina, California) says that when her chapter began, they chose the name Mad Hatters. The initial eight members were four pairs of mothers and daughters. It was some time later that they realized how appropriate their chosen name was. Mad obviously should stand for "mothers and daughters"! Funny how names are sometimes chosen and the full realization of how serendipitous they are comes later.

It's interesting that choosing a name for one's chapter is one of the first steps in getting a group going. Sometimes a queen and her vice mother choose a name first and then gather members for their already-titled chapter. But often the group has a good number of potential members at their first meeting, and deciding upon the chapter's name is one of the entertainments they choose to get the fun started.

Most of us have had experience choosing names for our children, but we probably took that very seriously. We felt that the names we chose for those precious children must somehow express everything we felt about them and also communicate those feelings to others. Such a weighty responsibility. This was usually complicated by the fact that there was a second person, probably a husband, whose opinion had to be honored. It's certainly a good thing that we were not in our silly names phase back then—at least it is for our children!

But choosing names for Red Hat Society chapters is something else entirely. This name *needs* to be silly; in fact, it just cries out to be. But this time, there are probably quite a few opinions to be honored. Why not try on all kinds of names for size? Why not enjoy playing with words as a group? Or just challenge your funniest member to outdo herself?

Frankly, after hearing many of the designations that our chapters have come up with, I have wished that I could have been a fly on the wall while the group bandied ideas about. I swear, you can hear the echoes of their laughter in the names they chose. This is demonstrated especially well in the pun category of chapter names that follows. Don't blame me, blame them. Brace yourselves.

PUNS

The Grateful Red—Bonita Springs, Florida
The Bloody Merries—Beach Haven, New Jersey
Femmes Vitales—Little Rock, Arkansas
Red Hot Flashes—Greenville, South Carolina
Hats in the Belfry—Atwater, California
Grape Friends—Downey, California
The Grand Ol' Hags—Glendale, California
MZ-TEA-rious Ladies—Long Beach, California
Lady Hattersley's Cover—Palos Verdes, California
SerendipiTeas—Riverside, California
The Whooping Crones—Santa Ana, California
Better Red than Dead—Vernon, Connecticut
La Vie en Rosies—Brooksville, Florida
The Scarlet Purplenells—Clearwater, Florida
The Grapeful Red—Deerfield Beach, Florida
The Red Hot Senior-itas—Fort Myers, Florida
The Pertty Dozen—Lakeland, Florida
Curvettes—Palm Coast, Florida
Hat's Meow—Punta Gorda, Florida
Tropical Hat Waves—Wesley Chapel, Florida
Red Hat Mental Pausers—Griffin, Georgia
Indy Annas—Greenwood, Indiana
Damsels in Purple DisDress—Des Moines, Iowa

Caught Red-Handed—Le Claire, Iowa
Bluegrass ThoroughREDS—Lexington, Kentucky
Floosi Annas—Tallulah, Louisiana
Carpe Divas—Wooster, Ohio
Okie Dokies—Alva, Oklahoma
The Moore, the Merrier—Moore, Oklahoma
Above Bored—Springfield, Oregon
Rapid Free Radicals—Rapid City, South Dakota
TEAnnessee Red Hatters—Nashville, Tennessee
Austin-tacious—Austin, Texas
In-Texicated—Austin, Texas
Tea and Symphony—Powhatan, Virginia
Red Hat TeasHers—Germantown, Maryland
Grape Expectations—Owings Mills, Maryland
Behattitudes—Westminster, Maryland
Elle's Belles Red Hats—Randolph, Massachusetts
P-Earl Greys of Au Gres—Au Gres, Michigan
Mini Pearls—Cottage Grove, Minnesota
Well-Red Ladies—Minneapolis, Minnesota
Summer Sisters (Summer Not)—Norcross, Minnesota
Latte Dah—Wabasha, Minnesota
Antiq-Belle-Ums—Lexington, Kentucky
Family A'Flair—North Syracuse, New York
Vermillionaires—Pittsford, New York
Goodness Gray-cious—Waterford, Michigan

JUST FUNNY

These are not punny; they're just plain funny! Don't you just know that someone started with a basic idea, and then the shouted embellishments came thick and fast, until the winning name became obvious when it was greeted by the loudest laughter.

The Power Surges—Sun City West, Arizona
Red Crested Purple-Breasted Roadrunners—Apple Valley,
    California
Scones'n'Crones—Elk Grove, California
The Frankly My Dears—Mission Viejo, California
Slower Lower Red Hats—Lewes, Delaware
Royal Order of the Shrinking Violets—Olympia Fields,
    Illinois
Crones and Cronies—Pekin, Illinois
Is It Hot or Is It Just Me Red Hat Society—Peoria, Illinois
Laissez Les Bons Temps Rouler ("Let the Good Times Roll")—
    Baton Rouge, Louisiana
Boston Baked Beings—Boston, Massachusetts
Nantucket Basket Cases—Nantucket, Massachusetts
Chapter Eleven—Ann Arbor, Michigan
Wrinkles in Time—St. Louis, Missouri
Old Spice Girls—Havelock, North Carolina
Ministry of Silly Walks—Pevertville, Tasmania
The Late Bloomers—Rutland, Vermont
ElderBerries—Lynchburg, Virginia
Chapter of Vague Recollections—Richlands, Virginia
The Crepey Myrtles—Virginia Beach, Virginia
Elegant Dairyaires—Pewaukee, Wisconsin
Seaside Beach Bags—Seaside, Oregon
Ultra Violets—Wetumpka, Alabama
Varicose Vixens—Gainsville, Florida

FLOWERS

Most of us love flowers, so it makes perfect sense to sort through
the names of various blooms until we hit on one that works for us.
Some of our chapters have done just that. Do they stick to flowers
that are purple and red only? Well, of course not!

Yellow Roses of Texas—Howe, Texas
Spring Valley Violets—Huntington, West Virginia
Wilting Red Roses—Bakersfield, California
Fiery Fuschias—Farmington, Arkansas
Rosy Petals—Costa Mesa, California
Rebellious Rose Buds—Hemet, California
The Wild Roses—Huntington Beach, California
Orange Blossoms—Orange, California
The Vintage Roses—San Juan Capistrano, California
The Santa Clarita Posh Peonies—Santa Clarita, California
Hyacinth—Mansfield, Connecticut
The Scarlet Sisterhood of Pansies and Petunias—New
    Canaan, Connecticut
Rose Hips—Simsbury, Connecticut
American Beauty Roses—Bradenton, Florida
The Red Geraniums—Brooksville, Florida
Purple Rose Petals—Clermont, Florida
Ruby Begonias—Spring Hill, Florida
Hibiscus Honeys—the Villages, Florida
Red Hat Petunias—the Villages, Florida
Purple Posey Pals—Glen Ellyn, Illinois
Perennials—Lafayette, Indiana
Rose Potpourri—Burton, Michigan
Purple Iris—St. Louis, Missouri
Lilies of the Valley—Wyoming Valley, Pennsylvania

FOOD

Who among us doesn't love to eat? With food (and drink) on our minds most of the time, how could we avoid sifting through food until we settled on the most amusing food name for our chapter. Those ladies who came up with the puns have nothing on these creative divas.

The Tea Bags—Santa Ana, California
The Candied Apples—Anaheim, California
Red Hot Chili Peppers—Anaheim, California
The Cherry Tarts—Auberry, California
Fried Red Tomatoes—Auburn, California
Raisin Queens—Fresno, California
Mai Tai Girls—Huntington Beach, California
The Sweet Tarts—Irvine, California
The Loose Tea Ladies—Orange County, California
Red Hot Horseradish—Rohner Park, California
Cranberry Tarts of San Pedro—San Pedro, California
Razzberry Tarts—Clearwater, Florida
Cherries Jubilee of the Space Coast—Coca Beach, Florida
Precious Peaches—Inverness, Florida
Mixed Nuts of Mandarin—Jacksonville, Florida
Raspberry Reds—St. Paul, Minnesota
Macaroni—Augusta, Missouri
Concord Vintage Grapes—Concord, Ohio
Sun Dried Tomatoes—Oregon, Ohio
The Cherry Pits—Ottawa, Ontario, Canada
The Peaches of Freestone County—Fairfield, Texas
Pecan Delites—Groves, Texas
Stewed Prunes—Kingwood, Texas
The Merrishinos—Palestine, Texas
The Strawberry Preserves—Winfield, West Virginia
Hot Cakes—Richland Center, Wisconsin
Red Hat Tea Cozies—Unalaska, Alaska

Jolene Hall, a member of this last group, writes that Unalaska was hit by a typhoon one day while they were meeting for tea. The wind outside hit eighty-five to ninety miles per hour. She says, "We joked that the tempest was *not* in the teapot this time!"

JEWELS

Every single Red Hatter is thought of as a gem, by herself as well as by the rest of us. Since we are all jewels in the crown of the Red Hat Society, why not use the names of jewels in our chapter names?

Red Hat Rubies—Banning, California
Red Hot Diamonds—Diamond Bar, California
The Hemet Alexandrites—Hemet, California
The Garnet Girls—Milton, Florida
Diamonds in the Red—the Villages, Florida
Ravishing Rubies—Chicago, Illinois
Evening Pearls—Muscatine, Iowa
Pearls of Wisdom—Winnipeg, Manitoba, Canada
Gem Dandy—Franklin, North Carolina
Many Pearls and Rhinestones—Clarksville, Tennessee
Redondo Rubies—Redondo Beach, California

In this chapter, each member has also chosen a jewel name for herself!

ANIMALS AND INSECTS

Why? Why not? Most of us are probably animal lovers! And chapters with names like these have a head start if they should decide to choose a mascot.

Crimson Doves—Albert Lake, Minnesota
Dragonfly—Akron, Ohio
Purple Peacocks—Cheviot, Ohio
Ladybug Red Hat Society—Little Elm, Texas
Red Dragons—Nacogdoches, Texas
Cackling Crows—Woodbridge, Virginia
Red Foxes—Wisconsin Rapids, Wisconsin

Red Crested Double-Breasted Chickadees—Cape Coral, Florida
The Red Gators—Fort Myers, Florida
High Order of the Fabulous Flamingoes—Largo, Florida
Feathered Friends—Odessa, Florida
Manatee Red Hat Society—Palmetto, Florida
The Red-Capped Chickadees—Palmetto, Florida
The Purple Panthers—Sarasota, Florida
The Happy Hens—Fresno, California
Desert Foxes—Indian Wells, California
Crimson Butterflies—Lakewood, California
Red-Hatted Buffaloes—Pine Grove, California
Red Hat River Rats—Riverside, California
Silver Foxes—Estes Park, Colorado
Red Hat Society Kittens—Grand Junction, Colorado
The Purple Butterflies—Beverly Hills, Florida

REGIONAL NAMES

Sometimes, it's just common sense to let everybody know where you are by making your town part of your chapter name. Sometimes the mention of a local product or attribute can help provide an identity.

The Dixie Teacups—Athens, Alabama
Rhett's Red Roses—Foley, Alabama
The Arctic Roses—Valdez, Alaska
Rare Red Auroras—Palmer, Alaska
Red Hat Tamales—Prescott, Arizona
Phoenix Phoxes—Phoenix, Arizona
The Ozark Scarlett Women—Cherokee Village, Arkansas
The Purple Mountain Majesties—Cherokee Village, Arkansas
Island Girls—Merritt Island, Florida
Cape Cod Cuties—North Falmouth, Massachusetts
The Swanee Sisters—Goldsboro, North Carolina

Rushmore Red Hats—Rapid City, South Dakota
El Paso Red Hat Border Babes Society—El Paso, Texas
The Maple Sugar Babes—Essex Junction, Vermont
Waltzing Red Matildas—Upper Ferntree Gully, Victoria, Canada

ANAGRAMS

Why limit ourselves to regular words when we can indulge in
a little wordplay? Thinking up a chapter name like this is not for
the faint of heart or the time-challenged. But it can sure provide a
lot of fun.

D.E.W. (Do Everything Women)—Sparks, Maryland

P.O.O.P.S. (Pentwater Outlandish Outrageous Purple Society)
   —Pentwater, Michigan

W.I.N.G.S. Sisterhood (Women in Need of Gadding Someplace)—Bloomington, Minnesota

B.O.M.B. (Bodacious Ozark Mountain Babes)—Branson,
   Missouri

The W.H.I.M.S.E.Y.S (Wise, Hip, Independent, Mature,
   Sassy, Elegant/Eccentric Youngsters)—St. Louis, Missouri

T.U.L.I.P.S. (Truly Unique Ladies in Purple Society)
   —Marion, New York

R.O.A.R. (Royal Order of Awesome Redhats)—Rochester,
   New York

W.O.E. (Women Out of Estrogen)—Shelby, North Carolina

C.R.O.N.E.S (Carolina RedHat Order of the Newly-Enlight-
   ened Sisters)—Columbia, South Carolina

O.H.M.Y.! (Outrageous Hats, Misguided Youths)—Bryan, Texas

G.E.M.S (Graciously Entering Midlife Screaming)
   —Midland, Texas

R.E.A.P. (Red Hats Energize a Person)—Wilmauma, Florida

G.R.I.T.S (Girls Raised in the South)—Powhatan, Virginia

The Sassy R.E.D.S (Real Elegant Dames)—Peace River, Alberta, Canada

G.O.D.D.E.S.S.E.S of SW Florida (Glorious, Outrageous, Darling, Delightful, Enlightened, Spectacular, Sensual, Elegant, Special)—Bonita Springs, Florida

F.L.I.R.T.S (Feisty Ladies in Red Toppers)—Bonita Springs, Florida

Plantation G.A.L.S (Gregarious, Awesome Ladies) —Leesburg, Florida

H.A.T.S (Happy Attitudes Toward Seniors)—New Port Richey, Florida

L.A.D.I.E.S (Lovely, Ageless Dames in Excellent Shape) —Tampa, Florida

D.A.M.S.E.L. (Ditzy, Adorable, Mad, Sassy, Elegant Ladies)—the Villages, Florida

V.I.P. (Villagettes in Purple)—the Villages, Florida

W.O.W. (Wiser Older Women)—Topeka, Kansas

A.I.R. Heads (Adorned in Red)—Port Charlotte, Florida

"Each day, and the living of it, has to be a conscious creation in which discipline and order are relieved with some play and some pure foolishness."
—*May Sarton*

HOBBIES

Some chapters were originally formed by women who shared the same hobbies. Since the members already had a particular interest in common, they decided to make use of that interest to signal to others what they liked to do.

Fairway Fair Ladies—East Orlando, Florida
Sew and Sews—Homosassa, Florida
Classy Crimson Cloggers of Lady Lake—Lady Lake, Florida
Tee Bags—Lady Lake, Florida
Red Hatters Quilting Queen Bees—Lake City, Florida
Mah-Johngg Dragon Ladies—Spring Hills, Florida
Taptations—Summerfield, Florida
Bingo Babes—Nampa, Idaho
Crimson Crafters—Waterville, Maine
Belly Dancers with Hattitudes—Ogden, Utah

HATS

The varieties of red hats we have seen are as endless as the ideas for chapter names. When English words are exhausted, there are plenty of other languages and heritages to be mined.

Blushing Bonnets of Brea—Brea, California
Raspberry Berets of Root River—Greendale, Wisconsin
Crimson Crowns—Fullerton, California
Rojos Sombreros—San Diego, California
Fedoras and Fun—Centennial, Colorado
Les Chapeaux Rouges—Longmont, Colorado
Buddies in the Burgundy Beanies—Rocky Hill, Connecticut
Crimson Cloches—Fort Myers, Florida
Hat & Soul—Fort Pierce, Florida

Hata Dearg (Gaelic for "Red Hat")—McHenry, Illinois
Hatpin Has-Beens—Huntington, Indiana
Rouge Toques—Matawan, New Jersey
Scarlet Stetsons—Fort Worth, Texas
The Scarlet Toppers—Lubbock, Texas

COLORS

We are nothing if not colorful! We can express that quality in our names. Of course, references to shades and tints of red and purple make the most sense.

Purple Pension Spenders—Sun City, Arizona
Vermillion Vamps—Sun City, Arizona
Scarlet Sippers—Canyon Lake, California
Crimson Chaos—Costa Mesa, California
Red Flames of Fresno—Fresno, California
Scarlet Gems (Proverbs 31:25)—Reedley, California
Purple Playmates—Englewood, Colorado
Magnificent Magentas—the Villages, Florida
Magenta Magic—North Myrtle Beach, South Carolina
Barely Beyond Pink—Spearfish, South Dakota

ROYALTY

Though most Red Hatters claim to be royalty, some emphasize their positions in their chapter names.

Queens at King's Point—Sun City Center, Florida
Queen Anne Society of Venice—Venice, Florida
Queen's Ransom—West Columbia, Texas
The Duchesses of Bedford—Fairfax, Virginia
Royal-Tea Rose Queens—Fresno, California
Chandler Cactus Queens—Chandler, Arizona

Now, any newly formed chapter whose members have read these (very partial) lists of chapter names should have no trouble coming up with its own moniker. Surely there is creative fodder here. Just get a few women together and start playing with words. After all, it's just one more way to play! I can honestly tell you that just when we think that every possibility has been exhausted, someone comes up with something no one else has thought of yet.